D1741798

Young Children as
Intercultural Mediators

LANGUAGES FOR INTERCULTURAL COMMUNICATION AND EDUCATION

Series Editors: Michael Byram, *University of Durham, UK* and Alison Phipps, *University of Glasgow, UK*

The overall aim of this series is to publish books which will ultimately inform learning and teaching, but whose primary focus is on the analysis of intercultural relationships, whether in textual form or in people's experience. There will also be books which deal directly with pedagogy, with the relationships between language learning and cultural learning, between processes inside the classroom and beyond. They will all have in common a concern with the relationship between language and culture, and the development of intercultural communicative competence.

Full details of all the books in this series and of all our other publications can be found on http://www.multilingual-matters.com, or by writing to Multilingual Matters, St Nicholas House, 31-34 High Street, Bristol BS1 2AW, UK.

LANGUAGES FOR INTERCULTURAL COMMUNICATION
AND EDUCATION: 26

Young Children as Intercultural Mediators

Mandarin-speaking Chinese Families in Britain

Zhiyan Guo

MULTILINGUAL MATTERS
Bristol • Buffalo • Toronto

To children and parents migrating in the world

Library of Congress Cataloging in Publication Data
A catalog record for this book is available from the Library of Congress.
Guo, Zhiyan, 1971-
Young Children as Intercultural Mediators: Mandarin-speaking Chinese Families in Britain/Zhiyan Guo.
Languages for Intercultural Communication and Education: 26
Includes bibliographical references and index.
1. Bilingualism in children—Great Britain. 2. Intercultural communication—Great Britain. 3. Children of immigrants—Language—Great Britain. 4. Translating and interpreting—Great Britain. 5. Chinese—Great Britain—Languages. 6. Mandarin dialects—Great Britain. I. Title.
P115.5.G7G86 2014
305.7'951041–dc23 2014003588

British Library Cataloguing in Publication Data
A catalogue entry for this book is available from the British Library.

ISBN-13: 978-1-78309-213-0 (hbk)
ISBN-13: 978-1-78309-212-3 (pbk)

Multilingual Matters
UK: St Nicholas House, 31-34 High Street, Bristol BS1 2AW, UK.
USA: UTP, 2250 Military Road, Tonawanda, NY 14150, USA.
Canada: UTP, 5201 Dufferin Street, North York, Ontario M3H 5T8, Canada.

Website: www.multilingual-matters.com
Twitter: Multi_Ling_Mat
Facebook: https://www.facebook.com/multilingualmatters
Blog: www.channelviewpublications.wordpress.com

The policy of Multilingual Matters/Channel View Publications is to use papers that are natural, renewable and recyclable products, made from wood grown in sustainable forests. In the manufacturing process of our books, and to further support our policy, preference is given to printers that have FSC and PEFC Chain of Custody certification. The FSC and/or PEFC logos will appear on those books where full certification has been granted to the printer concerned.

Typeset by Deanta Global Publishing Services Limited.
Printed and bound in Great Britain by the CPI Group (UK Ltd), Croydon, CR0 4YY.

Contents

Acknowledgements

To complete this book, I have been very fortunate to receive support from a number of people. First of all, I must express my gratitude to Professor Mike Byram for his insightful and meticulous editing of the whole manuscript to transform it into a book, a process through which I have learned so much. I am very grateful to the reviewers at the different stages for their expertise, without which the book would not have its current shape. I also must thank Professor Helen Spencer-Oatey and Dr Annamarie Pinter for taking the time to share their experiences; without their encouragement, I would not have even crossed the first hurdle.

I am deeply indebted to Professor Nigel Hall and Professor Helen Colley who guided me through the adventure of my doctoral study, on which this book is based. Without their scholarship and academic rigour, the study would not have had its initial success. I was also very lucky to receive financial support from the Overseas Research Scholarship, which enabled the smooth completion of the study. I am so thankful to the eight children and the parents of the six families who allowed me to step into their family homes and permitted me to share their lives in the new world.

Finally, I am very grateful for my family, my husband Hua and my daughter Jintong (who has culturally mediated so much of my life in England) whose love and company have been indispensable during the whole process; and for my parents, my parents-in-law, my sister and brother in China, whom I see least in my migrant years, but whom I love most dearly.

Acknowledgements

Preface

I am a migrant with a 13-year-old daughter who goes to a local secondary school in the West Midlands in England. Having lived for nine years in a culture different from where I was born and brought up, I have been learning about it from my daughter. This constant, interesting learning experience was not only my original incentive for my doctoral study, completed several years ago and the basis for much of this book, but it also continued to drive me to share my experience and my studies with the wider world. Hence my desire to write this book.

My daughter was about four and a half years of age when she came to the UK. She did not know any English, but within a very short period of time, she had picked up English and spoke it with a Mancunian accent. She enjoyed her days at school and settled in very well. I came to the UK in pursuit of a doctoral degree. I had started learning English as a subject in secondary school, got my first degree in English education and have used English for my work ever since. Although I thought I had learned a lot about the language and culture during my stay in the UK, I found myself learning continuously from my daughter about British culture as well as the language. This learning started almost from her first day at school: from listening to her telling me about her day, reading storybooks with her and even supporting her participation in social activities. It happened so frequently in my everyday life and covered such a wide range of topics that I could not help but be intrigued and amazed.

My awareness of learning from my daughter became so strong that I shared this experience with my friends who are also (im)migrant parents. I was surprised to find that I was not the only parent with such an experience. They told me different anecdotes of learning from their children about various aspects of British society. Some of them had followed their children's advice, carrying out cultural practices that they had never done before in their home countries. All these personal experiences offered me food for thought about this social and cultural phenomenon in im/migrant families.

Almost at the same time, I attended an Educational and Social Research Council (ESRC) seminar series on child language brokering coordinated by Professor Nigel Hall. The discussions there equipped me with theoretical approaches developed in the new childhood studies that emphasise children's active and agentive roles in their social life. A number of studies on language brokering provided me with a valuable starting point for my literature search and review. Taking language brokering as an explicit form of child cultural mediation, I started exploring this cultural phenomenon in immigrant or refugee families. In order to see how parental learning from children occurs, I recognised that it would be ideal to observe the daily life of families, and ethnography appeared to be an appropriate methodological pathway. As a Mandarin speaker myself, it was also easier for me to focus on the Chinese community and with acquaintances who had similar experiences to my own, access to sites for fieldwork became manageable. I will place the discussion of the methodological issues in the Appendix for interested researchers and now tell the story of child cultural mediation.

Introduction

To help introduce the topic of this book, let us begin with two short texts taken from different sources. The first is from a local newspaper in Manchester, the *Metro News*, Friday 11 February 2005.

Extract I

At 11 years old, Madia Hussaini should be carefree and full of hope for the future. But instead, she is leading the fight to save her family from deportation and the threat of being killed in Afghanistan. The Hussaini family, who live in North Reddish, say a warlord in their native land is pursuing a murderous vendetta against them, but the Home Office has rejected their pleas for asylum in the UK.

The family has lodged a final appeal with the government and friends and neighbours in Stockport have launched a campaign, backed by local MP Andrew Bennett, to stop them from being deported. There has been an outpouring of sympathy from across the town, and 1500 people have signed a petition.

Madia, the Hussaini's eldest child, has been thrown into a position of vital responsibility because her parents speak no English. Madia has learnt English at school and so speaks for the family at countless public gatherings, and meetings with lawyers, politicians, community representatives and journalists, where an interpreter is not at hand. Madia told the Metro News: 'The first time I had to speak publicly I was really embarrassed. But now I enjoy helping my family, and speaking for them has helped me with my English and my schoolwork'. (*Metro News*, 2005)

This is a quite extraordinary example of a young child acting as a mediator for her parents. There can be few children of this age who find themselves dealing so publicly with issues of such great complexity, something well outside most children's experience. In this instance, Madia Hussaini is not just a general cultural mediator but more specifically she is a language broker, as much of her work involves translating between her parents and many agencies and individuals. It is all the more remarkable as Madia is using English skills that she has relatively recently acquired, yet she views as opportunities to extend her understanding of English the very things that must be so complex for her. While there would be some support from various agencies for her parents with their lack of English, it is clear that the main responsibility for the family's social, administrative and economic activities falls on Madia. She is actively involved in mediating, while understanding that she is intentionally mediating for her family, and may have to make decisions for her parents.

The second extract, which is in two parts, is taken from *Sour Sweet*, a novel written by Timothy Mo, which depicts a newly arrived Cantonese-speaking family running a restaurant in 1960s' London.

Extract II

   (Man Kee, a five-year-old boy of a Chinese restaurant owner in London, had just finished his first day in English school. His mother Lily and his auntie Mui try to ask him about what he did at school).

   They tried everything: coaxing, bribes of ice-cream, gentle threats (no TV for awkward boys). All they could extract from him was a cryptic: 'Ho Wan!', 'Good playing!' or perhaps: 'I enjoyed myself.'

   Ho Wan! Lily could hardly believe her ears.

   Mui placed a hand on her sleeve. 'Nephew, are you hungry? Would you like a biscuit?' He had already eaten.

   'Son, what did they give you?' Mince, jam tart, and custard, he told them in English.

   The girls (Lily and Mui) watched him leave the room and followed him with their eyes down the garden. Their mouths were very slightly open. They could think of nothing to say to each other. There was something new happening; something which Lily realised was beyond her experience and from which she was forever excluded; something she could give no name to; something which separated her from Son. (Mo, 1992: 171).

   (About two years later, Man Kee started helping with taking money from customers).

   The way to look at it, Lily told herself, was this: Number One priority – Son was learning the business; Number Two – under present circumstances any help she got was worth having. ... Clever Son had no difficulty working out the correct amounts. ...

'Now, Son, how much brown cash equals one green cash?'
'Twice ten shillings is one pound.'
'Son!'
'Ah Mar-Mar, we play buying things at school in play-shop with plastic meat and pretend-money'
'Clever boy.' Kiss. 'But bad to tell lies, Son'. (Mo, 1992: 194)

In this extract, the boy, Man Kee, is clearly not taking on the major responsibilities that Madia has, but he is nevertheless operating in a role that mediates British culture for his parent. Man Kee is not aware that he is doing this and indeed seems a reluctant participant in the process. His mother, on the other hand, is acutely aware from his behaviour that her son, even at the age of five, is presenting her with experiences and actions that do not fit her cultural assumptions about how children should behave towards their parents and what counts as appropriate and proper schooling. For her, the experience is rather confrontational and confusing. She knows that something is happening in the school day, but it is something 'beyond her experience and from which she was forever excluded'. Unintentionally and perhaps unwittingly, Man Kee's behaviour reveals to his mother previously hidden aspects of British culture. He is an unreflective mediator, but nevertheless for his mother the experience is powerful and disturbing.

The above examples offer the opportunity to explore a number of important and significant issues that form the basis for this book. The first point is that the extracts involve migrant[1] families with either permanent or temporary residence in the UK, who are faced with living in a culture that is very different from that of their homeland. This is not an uncommon experience as families across the world move from culture to culture, sometimes for economic reasons and sometimes to avoid conflict and oppression. These moves are complex and arriving in a new culture is a major upheaval, but the complexity increases significantly when it is not just the culture but also the language that changes. Some families may have access to existing cultural groups or friends in the new country, but for others, life can be very strange and frightening, generating high levels of dependency on agencies whose power to assist may be quite limited. While there might be a genuine desire to understand and live in the new culture, accessing the opportunities to do this may be quite restricted.

The second point is that the families in the above examples have children, who, in one way or another, can help their parents accommodate to or at least understand aspects of the new culture. It is possible to argue that all children are to some degree cultural mediators (e.g. with respect to popular culture) but for families who move to a new culture, with a new language, the role of children as cultural mediators may be of particular significance in the acculturation process. Young children appear to adapt easily and, on entering the UK, they are usually enrolled in full-time schooling. As a consequence, they have substantial opportunities to learn the new language, partly because language support is usually available in schools, but also because within classrooms these children are often surrounded by native English speakers. Through this educational and social contact, children develop competence in the new language and take on patterns of behaviour which are highly influenced by their new experiences. The beneficiaries of this developing knowledge are the children's parents, and thus to varying degrees, family life.

Thirdly, whether the cultural mediation is explicit, as with Madia, or more implicit, as with Man Kee, the role of children cannot be viewed entirely as one of subordination and dependency on their parents. Historically, childhood has usually been positioned as a period of dependency and of obedience, which is usually accompanied by an economic assessment of the costs of bringing up children. Even in the week in which this Introduction is being written, one newspaper headline asks, 'Can you afford £47,000?', because a recent survey had estimated that this is the cost of bringing up a child from birth to the age of five. But for the children in the above examples, it is appropriate to ask not what they cost, but what they contribute to a family's economic and social existence? How is one to estimate in economic terms the contributions of Madia and Man Kee to family life? Do these children simply act as an economic drain on their families or can one view their activities as having an economic benefit to the family, or even possibly the state? If Madia were not spending her time mediating British culture for her parents, who would do it? How would it be paid for and who would pay? What would the social consequences be of Madia not being available? In the case of Man Kee, his school experiences increase his mother's awareness of British attitudes to childhood, to social relationships and to education. It might be hard to assign a monetary value to these experiences, but they nevertheless contribute to the acculturation process, whether or not the parents like what they see.

Whether consciously or not, Madia and Man Kee seem to influence their parents' participation in mainstream society. Although both children and their parents tend to be of 'peripheral participation' in relation to the new society, the children appear to be more active participants in 'communities of practice' (Wenger, 1998) in mainstream society than their parents are. Children seem to pass their knowledge and understanding of the new society to their parents. What knowledge do children pass to their parents? How do children carry out their mediation? What kind of impact does children's mediation have on their parents? To what extent does children's mediation affect parents' participation in the new society? Or even simply, does children's mediation change their parents' lives in the new society? In this book, I will be exploring these issues in order to understand the nature of cultural mediation, how cultural mediation occurs and the role of children in Mandarin-speaking Chinese families in helping develop their parents' knowledge of what might be termed the 'hidden curriculum' for becoming British. Throughout the eight chapters, the book will endeavour to answer the following three questions:

- What is the nature of child cultural mediation in Mandarin-speaking Chinese families in Britain?
- How does child cultural mediation take place?
- How does child cultural mediation influence the relationship of parents to the new culture?

Chapter 1 provides an overview of migration and acculturation as a general context for child cultural mediation. In the process of adapting to a new society, parents and children may have different routes and draw on different resources for acculturation. In spite of multiple sources of information to help migrants adjust to the new culture, children appear to be a significant resource for their parents. Chapter 2 elucidates the theories arising from 'new' childhood studies. Both conventional and new paradigms about children and childhood are explained in order to demonstrate that children's roles cannot be restricted by children's biological immaturity, nor their dependent or subordinate status, but should be revalued as those of active social actors and agents. The theories of new childhood studies constitute a significant conceptual framework for my study. As a consequence of children's active roles in family life, power relationships change between parents and children, as demonstrated through mediation in migrant families. Chapter 3 is devoted to exploring the concepts of mediation and cultural mediation from the perspectives of different disciplines and reviewing the existing studies of child cultural mediation in literacy studies and language brokering. It then defines child cultural mediation into two types: explicit child cultural mediation and implicit child cultural mediation.

I introduce the six families who participated in my study in Chapter 4, providing detailed information about the young cultural mediators and their parents. The chapter also explains the situations in which the process of cultural mediation operates, and occurrences of the three levels of cultural mediation (assimilative, appropriative and accommodative) by children for their parents are examined in detail.

In Chapters 5–7, I analyse the data from these families and report the findings on child cultural mediation in Mandarin-speaking Chinese families at the three levels. Each of the three chapters relates to incidents and events happening in the everyday life of these families and finishes with a discussion of relevant issues about specific mediating events and a general understanding of child cultural mediation. Chapter 5 explains the key characteristics of the *assimilative* level: spontaneity, ephemerality, frequency of child cultural mediation, factual knowledge in the process and assimilation in polysemic events. It then illustrates these features with incidents that occur in home interactions. Finally, the chapter concludes that even though events at this level may be spontaneous, transient and oblivious, they are frequent and ubiquitous in families' everyday life, and that within the seemingly simplistic exchanges, parents gradually accumulate linguistic and cultural knowledge.

Chapter 6 explains the key characteristics of the *appropriative* level of child cultural mediation. It begins by explaining how the concept of appropriation is adopted and how it is used to describe this level of mediation. It then portrays two complex events relating to pocket money, eating and food choices, within the families. The issues that emerge about child cultural mediation at this level include, firstly, that knowledge transmission in immigrant families contrasts with that in indigenous families. While English children tend to receive knowledge and information from their parents, Chinese children appear to provide their parents with knowledge. This dependence on their children may apply to many immigrant families. Secondly, child cultural mediation inevitably depends on how much knowledge and information the mediators have gained from their sources, and how well they themselves understand a certain cultural activity. Child cultural brokers might not always mediate an event to the fullest extent. However, children's competency should be understood as situated within given circumstances, that is, children still tend to have more knowledge than their parents in a particular circumstance, and have more opportunities than their parents to experience the different cultural practices of the majority society.

Chapter 7 explains the key characteristics of *accommodative* mediation and how this concept of accommodation is adopted and applied in describing child cultural mediation. It examines two key events in depth – greeting cards and birthday celebratory rituals – to illustrate how children mediate card-related rituals in Chinese families, how children mediate birthday celebration rituals for their parents, and how children lead their parents to conduct the ritualistic practices. This chapter also discusses how children have introduced and consolidated their parents in an unfamiliar landscape through these two common cultural phenomena in the new society. It shows that, in spite of tensions and challenges in the process, parents appear to accept the embedded norms and values. Accommodative mediation happens as a gradual process. With implicit or unconscious guidance from their children, parents seem to have grasped the key points in coping with birthday party procedures, and have become able to organise parties for their children. The process of carrying out the ritual also highlights different cultural orientations between collectivism and individualism, and reveals distinct attitudes towards children and childhood in the two traditions. With their children's mediation and guidance, parents enact the new practices and manage their communication with the wider society more appropriately.

In Chapter 8, the general conclusion is drawn that implicit child cultural mediation offers more channels for parents to connect with the majority population, to get to know the society that they have just moved into and to evaluate their relocation experiences. With their child's mediation, parents may feel more intimately related to, rather than isolated from the new culture. Being positioned as the intermediary between parents and mainstream society, children create links, helping parents to understand the cultural phenomena and cultural practices of the new society and to appreciate the hidden curricula about living in the new country, thereby improving migrant families' social and emotional well-being in the new world.

Note

(1) In this book, the term 'migrant' is used to encompass both 'immigrants' and 'new arrivals'. 'Immigrants' refers to those who stay in the receiving country long enough to become permanent residents, whereas 'new arrivals' are those who have been in the country for less than three years and do not have permanent residence status.

1 Migration and Acculturation

As long as there have been human beings, there has been migration. Human beings colonised the land masses of the Earth by migrating from one geographical area to another. Migration has been continuous, for it seems that as long as people see opportunities in other places, or experience oppression, poverty or restraint in their own land, they will seek, or be forced, to migrate. Some of these migrations have been extensive, such as the Jewish and Irish diasporas, or the mass European emigration to the USA, while others have been more limited as individuals have sought opportunities to change their lives. Migration has been ranked as one of the most important factors in the global change and it appears to be one of the most salient phenomena in modern life (Castle & Miller, 2003). It has been studied from many perspectives – including psychological, literary and historical – but here we shall primarily draw on sociological analyses, linking the study of migration and acculturation with an analysis of concepts of culture.

Migration

Broadly speaking, population mobility changes demographic, social and economic structures, and facilitates cultural exchange and global integration (Castle & Miller, 2003). For the receiving countries, migration may give rise to cultural diversity and an evolving national identity, although problems may emerge when people who are culturally and socially diverse live together in one society. For migrants themselves, the experience of relocating may bring substantial changes and challenges as well as benefits to their lives, and lead to varying kinds of outcomes for them and their families.

As a consequence of their arriving in a new culture, migrants may have unsettling, challenging and traumatic experiences. Firstly, in daily life, they may experience differences in climate, food, language, living and work habits, ethics, religion and even dress (Berry, 1995); some of these differences will appear in later chapters as children deal with, for example, food and everyday habits and customs. Migrants may also experience difficulties in areas such as housing, transportation, shopping and schooling (Storti, 2001). Secondly, depending on how quickly they can find and hold down a job and enjoy economic stability, migrants may face difficulties in simply surviving in the new environment. Thirdly, lack of language skills may present difficulties in adapting to the new culture; some may encounter a totally new language and find communicating with others difficult, and thus may experience linguistic and cultural isolation. Every step of their daily life may become tough and complicated which may be compounded by difficulties in accessing appropriate social agency support and seeking advice for themselves or their families (Arthur, 2000). Fourthly, a migrant's previous educational backgrounds may be significant in his/her ability to take in new cultural knowledge and develop his/her attitudes towards the new culture. Those who are illiterate in their own mother tongue may encounter immense difficulty in learning and achieving understanding of the majority language. Bloch (2002) found that most Somali women arrived in the UK without formal education in their country of origin, and were the group least likely to acquire English language skills. Migrants' educational backgrounds may affect their job security and influence their social interaction (Kannan, 1978).

Due to cultural differences and racism, migrants may also experience misunderstanding or discrimination from the majority population. As a result, they may feel troubled by loneliness, or find it hard to establish friendships and achieve an effective social network. In a new society, lack of a sense of competence, control and belonging may lead to a sense of loss and disorientation (Suárez-Orozco & Suárez-Orozco, 2001). Thus, migrants must cope with sociocultural changes as well as economic difficulties.

However, despite its challenges and difficulties, migration may bring about benefits for new settlers. It may create advantageous life situations, such as better jobs and education. Migrants may have more opportunities to appreciate different cultures and enrich their life experiences. Depending on the circumstances, migration is seen as crucial to improving people's quality of life.

Castle and Miller (2003) classified migration into three types: economically motivated, forced and sojourners. Seeking more economic benefits, economically motivated migrants may be keen to improve their standards of living, set up a business, build a house and/or pay for education (see Garvey & Jackson, 1975; Kannan, 1978). Forced migrants move to avoid threats to life such as wars and political prosecution; they are often poor and their situations may be politically unstable in the country of asylum, particularly if they are being investigated by the government.

The focus of this book will be on sojourners. The experience of migration may be very different for sojourners from that of the economically motivated or forced migrants since they stay only temporarily in an unfamiliar environment (Furnham & Bochner, 1986; Ward *et al.*, 2001). Ward *et al.* (2001) identify many types of sojourners including business people, diplomats, technical experts, overseas students, missionaries, voluntary workers and so on. Sojourners relocate for various purposes and lead their lives in different ways. While they may experience some of the challenges mentioned earlier, such as inadequate finance and lack of support (see more in Arthur, 2000), sojourners may be more advantaged in other ways. They tend to be 'young, well-educated, highly motivated and adaptable' (Furnham & Bochner, 1986: 12). As Nauck (2001) finds, this educated group tend to assume an open attitude towards their migration, and this may lead to greater integration into both minority ethnic and mainstream cultures. Furthermore, some may already have knowledge of the majority language before their arrival and basic communication with the new population may help to reduce their sense of alienation and alleviate the pressure caused by their unfamiliar surroundings (Storti, 2001). However, due to variations in dialect, accent and slang usage, as well as local customs and codes of behaviour (Brislin *et al.*, 1986; Taft, 1966), speaking the same majority language does not guarantee a close relationship or identification with a new culture (Findlay *et al.*, 2004). In Bickley's (1982: 100) words, 'both cultural and linguistic barriers exist which may sour relations'. This may apply not just to migrating across countries and different speech communities, but also to moving within one country or one speech community. As Bickley (1982: 100) further argues, 'the fact that everyday things are done differently in different cultures often leads to misunderstanding, and even within an apparently homogeneous language community, varieties of the same language may be culturally divisive'. In other words, speaking the language may not be equivalent to knowing the values, world views and social practices of a culture (Katan, 2004; Suárez-Orozco & Suárez-Orozco, 2001).

While sojourners may intend to return to their home country on completion of their assigned tasks, they may have the possibility of staying longer in the host country. Whatever their ultimate destination, they may adjust rapidly to the new culture during their stay in the host society in order to operate effectively (Furnham & Bochner, 1986), e.g. in doing business or engaging in further studies, or they may have to start their journey of culture learning. Although their stay may be temporary, sojourners may still have to learn the key characteristics of the new society (Bochner, 1981, 1982) and the 'culture-specific skills that are required to negotiate the new cultural milieu' (Ward, 2001: 413).

The sojourners in question here are Chinese. Across its history, Britain has received immigrants from many parts of the world, but the history of Chinese migration to the UK can be dated back to the early 19th century when the first groups of seamen, recruited from Hong Kong and south-eastern China, settled in port towns such as London, Liverpool, Cardiff and Bristol (Chen, 2007; HAC, 1985).

In the 20th century, a large number of Chinese from the New Territories and Hong Kong emigrated to the UK, with most finding work in the food-related trades. This type of immigration continued until the 1980s due to the increasing popularity of Chinese cuisine in the UK (Li, 1994).

Up to this point, only a minority of the Chinese migrants were from mainland China, Taiwan and other Southeast Asian countries. During the 1990s, as the West established better relationships with mainland China, sojourners such as students pursuing their higher education and people working in commerce and industry started to form part of a new wave of Chinese migrants to Britain.

The families we will meet in the later chapters of this book can be most easily described as sojourners. They are an economically motivated and successful group who joined the post-1990s wave of Chinese migrants. Half the parents of the families were educated to university level before they moved to the UK, and each family has at least one member who has a full-time job in the UK, and a certain level of proficiency in English. They seem to take an open attitude towards the new society, but in spite of some advantages, they have, nevertheless, faced challenges and problems since arriving in the new country. Undertaking everyday living in a new culture and, in particular, having children who are being schooled and are growing up in this new culture create many issues for them, which, in some respects, forces them to engage with the new culture in ways that might be quite different from people without children. Once they stepped onto the new land, their journey of adaptation and acculturation began.

Acculturation

Acculturation is understood as the process that occurs when the characteristics of one cultural or ethnic group are changed as a result of interacting with another group. In this process, the interacting groups exchange cultural characteristics and are changed at the same time (Banks, 2002). Although the process can be reciprocal between the dominant and the minority groups, acculturation is mostly viewed as the minority group adapting to the habits and language patterns of the dominant group (Berry, 1995, 2003; Marín & Gamba, 2003). In most societies, the dominant ethnic or cultural groups are 'at least partially successful in getting other groups to adapt its culture and values because of the power that it exercises' (Banks, 2002: 59). As a result, acculturation may become the process of adapting to a new society, a process in which individuals of a minority cultural group come to change their behaviours, beliefs and values, cultural practices and identities as a result of continuous first-hand contact with the mainstream culture (Barry, 2001; Ward *et al.*, 2001). Thus, new immigrants may either seek absorption by becoming accustomed to the new culture, or find themselves under pressure to conform to the norms of the new society. Sometimes, these adaptations may be modest, as in moving from one part of a country to another; at other times, they may be huge as individuals and families face a new language, new ways of thinking and so on.

As a complex, diverse and long-term process of adaptation, acculturation may start as soon as the migrating population arrives in the new country and continue throughout their lifetime. It may even be a much longer process than this as several generations of families develop relationships with the dominant culture. All the possible changes in acculturation appear to be gradual, long term and ongoing (Bloch, 2002; Okagaki & Bojczyk, 2003). At the individual level, acculturation presents itself differently to different people, as individuals may vary in their ways of dealing with cultural influences. Berry (2003: 19) points out, 'not every individual enters into, participates in, or changes in the same way; vast individual differences exist... even among individuals who live in the same acculturative arena'. Even different members of a family may acculturate at different rates due to their amount of exposure to and interaction with the mainstream society (Gopaul-McNicol & Thomas-Presswood, 1998). As Berry (1995, 2003) argues, the process of acculturation may also appear different across several generations.

The variations in the acculturation process may derive from a multiplicity of factors. They may depend on the immigrants' status on arrival, their length of residence in the receiving country, whether they come as individuals or as families, the similarities to or differences from their original cultural values, the support they receive from agencies in the new country, the existence of people or communities from the original country, the degree of acceptance or discrimination by the majority population, the quality of their living environment, their age, educational background, proficiency in the majority language, urban or rural orientation, their goals, their personality and so on (Arthur, 2000; Costigan & Su, 2004). Given this variety of factors, how does acculturation take place?

The directionality of acculturation can be explored in two ways. An older view suggests that acculturation takes place in a linear and unidirectional manner; that is, the acquisition of the new culture is accompanied by the loss of the ethnic culture in a kind of zero-sum equation (see e.g. Birman & Trickett, 2001; Costigan & Su, 2004; Phinney, 1990; Trimble, 2003). This model seems to take assimilation to the new society as the ultimate outcome of acculturation, paying little attention to diversity in the acculturation process. However, while unidirectional assimilation was seen as a normative practice of some migrants in the past, recent research has suggested multiple models of acculturation.

A more recent approach suggests a bidirectional or orthogonal model of acculturation. Individuals may be attuned to both their native culture and the host culture, and retain their original ethnic identities and cultural values while adapting to the new ones of the majority culture (Berry, 2003; Costigan & Su, 2004; Phinney, 2003; Trimble, 2003; Tsai *et al.*, 2000). Buriel and De Ment (1997) found a bicultural pattern in Mexican, Chinese and Vietnamese families in their review of sociocultural change in immigrant communities in the USA. This view of acculturation seems to recognise the complexity and diversity of the process. In other words, the eventual outcome of acculturation may not necessarily be assimilation; there can be other pathways in the overall process.

Indeed, according to the degree with which immigrants adapt to the dominant society and maintain their home culture, as well as their psychological and cultural conditions, Berry (1988) suggests that there are four possible outcomes of acculturation: *integration, assimilation, separation* and *marginalisation*. While *assimilation* depicts those migrants who totally embrace the new cultural elements, its opposite category is that of *separation*, where individuals turn their back on the new society and just maintain their own original culture. This group remains monocultural, 'clinging to the culture of [its] origin and rejecting all the foreign influences' (Bochner, 1981: 12). There are others who may 'selectively engage with the new while merging it with the old' (Berry, 1995: 461), and this is termed *integration*, i.e. attaining a certain degree of adaptation to another culture while maintaining one's previous culture. The other outcome is *marginalisation*, which refers to those who disregard their own ethnic identity, cultural contacts and practices of their country of origin while resisting the adoption of the 'host' culture.

In addition, Bochner (1981) argues that there is another group that can be described as multicultural. They retain their culture of origin and learn several other cultures, particularly in a multicultural society. Among the aforementioned five groups, the integrated and multicultural groups are those likely to become mediators. They are more likely to be 'intercultural speakers' who are curious and open to the daily life experiences of other cultures and to the expectations of appropriate behaviours of people of different cultures. They have knowledge of both their own country and others. More importantly, they develop their skills of interpreting documents and relating events from their own culture to others, and the skill of acquiring new knowledge of different cultural practices and using them in everyday interactions with the majority group (Byram, 1997).

In addition to the directionality and degree of acculturation, how migrants acculturate to the majority culture can be seen from their changes in three dimensions: *cultural orientation, identity* and *cultural values*. *Cultural orientation* can be seen in behaviour, in how individuals participate in the cultural activities and actual practices of daily life, including language use, preference and proficiency; daily living habits in terms of food and music choices; and social interaction patterns (Zane & Mak, 2003). Relatively speaking, changes in this dimension may be more easily detected in the acculturation process because it is observable, although it may equally take time to measure and assess how the actual changes occur. Behavioural changes may result from deeper internal changes in other dimensions such as identity and cultural values, but this dimension may be misleading, since one's behavioural changes may be regarded as temporary outcomes of cultural learning, and tend to be subject to alteration when circumstances change (Furnham & Bochner, 1986). In spite of the importance of behavioural orientation, it cannot represent the whole acculturation process.

The dimension of *identity* refers to how migrants identify with their own culture of origin or the majority culture (Phinney, 2003). Identification is not fixed but fluid and dynamic (Nazroo & Karlsen, 2003; Ward, 2001). It can be assessed from affective aspects such as how migrants perceive their own sense of belonging, how strongly they feel that they are emotionally attached to certain cultures. This dimension is more subjective than behavioural orientation and is embedded within individuals' inner worlds and harder to measure precisely (Costigan & Su, 2004; Phinney, 1990). However, behavioural preferences tend to be included in judging identity (Felix-Ortiz, 1994). For example, how migrants feel the sense of belonging to the mainstream society may be associated with learning the majority language, developing a social network beyond their own ethnic group and becoming culturally competent in the social contexts of the new society (Phinney, 2003). Empirical studies also suggest that social relations can be associated with ethnic identity development (Ward *et al.*, 2001), that is, 'the internal process by which a person comes to feel like a member of a specific ethnic group' (Suárez-Orozco & Suárez-Orozco, 2001: 119). It may shift with individuals' awareness of ethnic differences and understanding what their ethnicity means in the larger social setting, and may also vary with age, over time, across generations and in different contexts (Phinney, 1990).

The third dimension, *cultural value*, refers to the cognitive aspects of acculturation. It entails beliefs, values and orientations, and relates to how migrants change their cultural values in the new society and/or retain their original ones (Tsai *et al.*, 2000, 2002). It is concerned with what obligations and responsibilities individuals have in relation to their families or to the society, how individualism versus collectivism is operated in daily living, and how migrants deal with their interpersonal relations in the new society (Marín & Gamba, 2003). Cultural values have been viewed as an important component of acculturation because beliefs and values are often used to identify certain ethnic or cultural groups and/ or differentiate between them (Marín & Gamba, 2003). A change in values may be related to a change in behaviour. On the one hand, it is likely that one's cultural values and beliefs may be modified and one's behavioural orientation may be changed in acculturation. On the other hand, it is also possible that one's values and beliefs may resist change as acculturation proceeds (Marín & Gamba, 2003).

How the acculturation process affects and is reflected in these different dimensions appears to be dynamic and complicated. Costigan and Su (2004) argue that there can never be one common pattern of change in migrants' cultural orientation, identities and values, which means that one simple model for the relation between ethnic and mainstream cultures can never explain the process. However, it seems important to understand changes in the three dimensions as a matter of *process*. First, change is embedded in participation. As Rogoff (1993, 1995) argues, change can be perceived as occurring in shared actions and interactions between individuals or between social partners. Such analysis presents development and learning as a process, rather than a product; Wertsch and Stone (1979: 21) claim, 'the process *is* the product' (cited in Rogoff, 1993: 139). Second, this view suggests that not all changes can be explicitly evidenced within a given period of time, but they can be viewed as constant in the dynamic of acculturation. The process tends to transmit different levels of culture and different cultural codes.

The Concept of Culture

Acculturation and the processes and dimensions discussed so far presuppose the concept of 'culture', which we have used thus far without problematisation. It is, however, a very problematic concept that we need to explore further in order to discuss later how Chinese people with their 'Chinese culture' acculturate to the culture of their new environment.

'Culture' has been conceptualised in a variety of ways in different disciplines, depending on the historical, social and political circumstances.

Even within a certain field, there is no agreement on the concept (Asher, 1994); Kroeber and Kluckhohn (1961, cited in Katan, 1999) have compiled 165 definitions of culture. There are also attempts to create models such as Hall's (1959, 1990) 'triad of culture', Trompenaars and Hampden-Turner's (1997) three layers of culture, Hofstede and Hofstede's (2005) 'onion skins' of cultures and Brake *et al.*'s (1995) 'cultural iceberg theory'.

In this study, we take the notion that culture can be perceived as 'the whole way of life of a people' (Jenks, 2005: 12), including 'values, beliefs, and standards that are learned, shared, adapted to particular circumstances, and continually changing' (Au, 1993: 92). As Willis (1979: 185) argues, 'it is one of the fundamental paradoxes of our social life that when we are at our most natural, our most everyday, we are also at our most cultural'. Culture can be regarded as daily human experience existing everywhere in our life (Jenks, 2005). Among the models of culture, Hall's (1959) triad of culture is of particular relevance, as it provides a meaningful basis for analysing parent–child interaction in migrant families.

According to this triad, culture can be represented at three levels: technical, formal and informal. At the technical level, ideas can be transmitted explicitly in oral or written communication. The word 'technical' here points not just to scientific fields such as engineering or physics, but also to situations where what is translated, interpreted or mediated denotes meanings that can be found in dictionaries, textbooks and manuals (Katan, 2004). Phenomena at the technical level can be analysed and explained explicitly in a certain linguistic form and can be taught and learned in a formulaic manner. They are explicit and 'the observable reality' (Trompenaars & Hampden-Turner, 1997: 21) of the 'language, architectures, … fashions and art'. As symbols of a deeper level of culture, they constitute semiotic systems, along with signs, gestures, pictures, artefacts and dress, as well as linguistic items (Hofstede & Hofstede, 2005). They can be relatively easy to manage and adapt to for those new to a culture or be copied by another cultural group. This suggests that the technical level of culture can be learned from reading or residing in the new society.

The second level in Hall's triad is 'formal culture', which refers to the accepted ways of behaving, standards of behaviour or 'formal tradition' (Hall, 1990: 64). While the formal level of culture can be articulated and learned by migrants, it entails phenomena that are more subjective and can be taken for granted, such as customs, rules, rituals and practices. They are assumed so much a part of everyday life that people may not be aware of them until they are violated (Katan, 2004). As Hofstede (1991: 8) points out, rituals or cultural practices are 'technically superfluous in reaching desired ends, but … within a culture, are considered as socially essential'.

Hofstede (1991) even took an example of the roles of real or imaginary heroes in a culture to illustrate that the meanings and beliefs attached to these heroes may not be understood or perceived by people from other cultures. Thus, not knowing about certain superheroes may be perceived as not belonging to that culture. For migrants, they may not appreciate the essence of the rituals, conventions or practices of the host society, nor share them with the majority population. According to Hofstede and Hofstede (2005: 8), the technical and formal levels are comprised of practices 'visible to an outsider observer', although their meaning can be partially invisible, because it 'lies precisely and only in the way these practices are interpreted by the insiders'.

The informal level of culture in Hall's triad refers to values and orientations that are invisible to the outsiders of a culture (though they may be visible to trained cultural observers). They are not explainable and overt even to insiders. There seem to be no 'rules' to the informal level of culture, but only purely personal ways of doing and behaving (Hall, 1990). As Hall (1959: 53) argues, 'culture hides much more than it reveals, and strangely enough what it hides, it hides most effectively from its own participants'. Informal culture, according to Hall, is not taught or learned, but acquired informally and unconsciously. In comparison with denotative meanings at the technical level, the informal level involves connotative meanings of linguistic forms, and implicitly reflects the culturally determined value system (Ulrych, 1992). It is 'the most powerful element of culture' in every interaction (Brake *et al.*, 1995: 34).

The informal level of culture is therefore associated with the values and basic assumptions that are core to a culture, though hidden from people within it. As a kind of 'hidden curriculum' of a culture, it may be dealt with automatically or obscurely in everyday life. Due to the 'out-of-awareness character' and the 'high degree of patterning' of informal culture, difficulties arise in cross-cultural situations (Hall, 1959: 96). The informal level of culture also seems to explain why cultural differences and cultural conflicts still exist even when different cultural groups have lived together in one society for a long period of time, and when migrant groups are in the process of adapting and acculturating to the dominant society.

Different Values in British and Chinese Cultures

The fact that cultural differences and conflicts still exist between groups even when they live together for quite a long period of time is explained by Hyatt and Simons (1999) in terms of groups following different 'cultural codes'. They define these as 'symbols and systems of meaning that are relevant to members of a particular culture (or sub-culture)'. These codes are utilised to 'facilitate communication within the "inside group" and also to obscure the meaning to "outsider groups"' (Hyatt & Simons, 1999: 23). As the central group of my study, Mandarin-speaking Chinese can be regarded as the outsider group holding different cultural values to the insider group, i.e. British people. Chinese migrants who have just come to Britain – though they are able to speak the language – may not share cultural values with the majority society. The differences in the two value systems can be explained on the basis of 'individualism' and 'collectivism'.

According to Triandis (1988), differences between individualism and collectivism tend to characterise, respectively, Western societies and the traditional East societies. According to Xiao (1999: 643), 'in collective culture, individuals are willing to subordinate their personal goals to the goals of various in-groups, such as the family, the tribe, or the work group..., but in individualistic cultures, it is considered acceptable for individuals to place personal goals ahead of the group's goals. Chinese culture in its traditional and still dominant form puts more emphasis on collectivism, whereas mainstream British (Western) culture is oriented more towards individualism. While the dominant Western cultural themes underscore independence and individualism, traditional Chinese culture values group solidarity and social deference (Triandis, 1988; Xiao, 1999).

The collectivistic orientation can be traced back to traditional Chinese culture, in particular, Confucius philosophy, which mainly advocates social harmony, hierarchy and learning or being educated. (This last characteristic may explain why Chinese parents pay substantial attention to their children's education.) In a philosophy of social harmony, man should exist only in harmony with nature and in relation to others. A harmonious whole, such as a family, is viewed as more important than its individual components, that is, each family member (Pleck, 2000). As Xiao (1999: 642) further argues, 'people are born into a family or a group and cannot prosper alone; the success of an individual depends on the harmony and strength of the group'. Therefore, like other Asian children, Chinese children tend to be more willing to place family well-being above their individual wishes (Feng, 1994).

Furthermore, under Confucian tenets, harmony can be achieved by implementing a well-defined hierarchy in social structures: governor over subjects, parents over children, teachers over students. Lower categories are supposed to show respect and obedience to the higher categories who are viewed as authority figures. Chinese children are taught to listen to their parents and elders and to follow their advice and guidance (Glenn & Yap,

2004). In fully respecting their parents as authority figures, children's individuality tends to be reduced and disregarded. Although Xiao (2000) does find a weakening in the influence of Confucian ideology on people's values and behaviour in Chinese urban areas, Confucianism has profoundly shaped traditional Chinese culture.

Incorporating the concept of culture with acculturation, we can see that adjusting to a new society entails acquiring different levels of culture and cultural codes, and producing changes in different dimensions of acculturation. The Chinese families in this book may have grasped the linguistic code of British society and continue to increase their technical level of understanding in their study and work, but due to their differences from the majority population in various cultural codes, their adaptation and acculturation may be much more gradual. How do these Chinese families in particular, and the immigrant community in general, manage the whole process? What resources can they possibly draw on?

Resources for Acculturation

Knowledge about a society at the three levels defined by Hall's triad may be explicitly taught, or it may be available through both formal and informal channels. As Rogers (2001: 111) argues, 'cultural models are not properties of individuals but are mediated across individuals, groups, and social institutions by various discursive means'. Living in a new culture, migrants may deploy a variety of formal and informal resources, and use multiple ways to gather information about the new society in their everyday life and verify or complement information from different sources, rather than depending on only one.

Organisational and institutional resources

Migrants may get formal support from governmental departments, local authorities, charities and other non-governmental organisations. These organisations or institutions may provide legal, welfare and housing information for migrants, as well as relocation advice. Some organisations, such as the Joint Council for the Welfare of Immigrants, specialise in information and knowledge about welfare and benefits; some are directed to helping certain groups of migrants, for example, the Council for International Education (UKCOSA), which provides professional advice and support for students who enter the UK for further studies.

Migrants who are sojourners include those who relocate for business purposes and who may be financed by their parent company to live in a new culture, having been offered some training for living and working in the new country (Brislin *et al.*, 1986; Storti, 2001; Ward, 1996; Ward *et al.*, 2001). For international students, a second group of sojourners, support at the institutional level may be available where they study. For example, many universities have international offices that help solve visa and accommodation problems for overseas students. Within those universities, there may also be services such as extra language support for those who use English as a second or foreign language. Under certain circumstances, migrants can also take classes in the local culture (Storti, 2001). These services may help reduce initial difficulties in living in a different culture, and provide an opportunity to learn about the new society.

The media

A major resource for immigrants is the media, although the impact of the media as a cultural resource may be rapidly changing in the digital age. The popular media, television, radio, newspapers or magazines, books, films, videos and DVDs, video games, advertising, etc., are not merely formal sources of information about news and products, but also effective providers of multiple levels of information, from the very explicit to the deeply subtle. Indeed, part of the power of the mass popular media is that they affect people's knowledge, attitudes and beliefs without people being aware of any change in themselves (Fairclough, 2001). For migrants with some language knowledge, the media, operating in the majority language, may provide cultural information (Berry, 1995) and can be a major resource for continuing to develop their oral and written language, particularly their vernacular use. Even if migrants have language difficulties, they may be influenced by the mass media because visual images themselves can be very informative. There are two reservations that must be made: first, in presenting particular images and views of a culture, the media may be heavily biased towards particular perspectives. Second, due to technological developments and the consolidation of migrant communities in a host society, some migrants prefer to access the media in their mother tongue. In so doing, the media may not play a positive role in migrants' acculturation to the host society (Ward, 2001), but may enhance migrants' connection with their original cultural values and identities (Liu, 2006).

Interaction, observation and community support

Another important resource for migrants is their tacit daily observations in their social interaction with local people, including their migrant community members in the majority society.

As with anybody new to an environment or experience, migrants tend to closely observe how local people conduct themselves in their daily living, including their dress codes, their hairstyles, their demeanour in public places and so on, and then they may make hypotheses and inferences for themselves (Storti, 2001). In certain circumstances, migrants may have to risk making mistakes, appearing stupid in public and explaining things away when being resented or laughed at. By so doing, they may learn the dominant social codes from experience.

In other situations, by asking questions and through conversations and non-verbal communication strategies, such as facial expressions, gestures or other body language, migrants may get a better understanding of the customs and conventions of the new society, although they may still be confused at times. New settlers can learn about rules, norms and conventions through general observation in mundane and everyday interpersonal encounters (Bochner, 1982).

As mentioned earlier in this chapter, migration is a key feature of contemporary life, and contact among people from different cultural backgrounds is increasing. In a new society, migrants tend to find local people who are from their own cultural origin by participating in community activities or by joining associations or societies comprised of people from certain cultural groups. It has been suggested that co-national relations and friends are one of the most salient and powerful sources of support for many migrants (Leslie, 1992; Li, 2002; Ward, 2001). Some migrants may start making their living within their cultural communities in the new society, and form social networks with those from similar cultural backgrounds. Their communication may transfer experiences and knowledge about the new culture, share information about coping with the new environment and provide an emotional channel to release frustrations and to gain encouragement (Adelman, 1988, cited in Ward, 2001: 431). Although migrant families living in denser communities may be less likely to become fluent in English (Birman, 2005), these communities may provide a lifeline, catering to the initial needs of some migrant, and becoming lifelong resources for others.

Children

This overview of resources identified in the literature serves as a contextualisation for this final section. What we shall discover in the following chapters is that, despite the existence of other resources, children are a crucial if not the most important resource. Parents use their children as a significant cultural resource. They learn elements of the cultural models presented and represented by their children who have acquired them unconsciously (Rogers, 2001). However, as we shall see in Chapter 3, it is not only in immigrant families that children act as cultural mediators or brokers; in almost all families, children bring important social, cultural and technological information to their family lives. It is, for example, no accident that parents always seem to know more about recent popular culture than do adults who do not have children. Children draw their parents' attention to the latest dress and hairstyles, the latest music trends, new technologies and new forms of language. These moves to mediate social change are not always good news for parents, and may put pressure on family budgets, but the result is that parents are forced to look differently at the ways in which the world is changing.

Nonetheless, while child cultural mediation can have an impact on all families, it is often vital in migrant families. Young children are adaptive and are usually enrolled in full-time schooling. Through this educational and social contact, children develop competence in the new language and take on patterns of behaviour that are highly influenced by their new experiences. Thus, they tend to enjoy more resources and be drawn into the majority culture more quickly and more intensely than their parents, who may struggle with ambivalence (Birman & Trickett, 2001; Perreira *et al.*, 2006; Suárez-Orozco & Suárez-Orozco, 2001). In other words, children's school learning improves their language proficiency and develops their familiarity with the dominant cultural values and norms of behaviours due to their broader exposure to the mainstream society and their higher expectation of assimilation with their peers (Chun & Akutsu, 2003; McKay, 1993; Nauck, 2001; Partida, 1996; Willett & Bloome, 1993). They develop their intercultural competence more quickly and more thoroughly than their parents do. As Garcia Coll and Magnuson (1997: 91) claim, 'immigrant children are often thought to be the first of their families to be socialized into the receiving community's culture'. The beneficiaries of this developing knowledge and preceding socialisation are the children's parents, and thus to varying degrees, family life. That is, as an important resource, children's contributions to their families in the new culture seem to play an indispensable role in the acculturation of parents and families. However, the significance of this cultural mediating role has been largely invisible or undervalued in research about immigrant families and children, although it is, of course, not always invisible to the participants in family events.

2 Understanding Childhood

In families in contemporary society, children may coerce their parents, consciously or not, to look at the world in different ways by bringing home updated technological and cultural information. As we saw in the previous chapter, in migrant families, parents may employ multiple ways to learn about the new culture, but for some newly relocated parents, their children become a significant source of knowledge and a resource for adapting to the new society. Children play indispensable roles in parents' day-to-day living in the new culture, and impact on their parents' acculturation to the new society. This positive contribution to parents and families leads us to different ways of looking at children.

Traditionally, children have been seen as subordinate to and dependent on adults, but this has proven to be an inadequate approach to depicting the whole of childhood because of its overemphasis on the biological reality of children and its total ignorance of social and cultural factors. In particular, this may lead to a lack of fuller understanding of children in various sociocultural contexts such as migrant families.

New childhood studies presented by James and Prout (1990, 1997) brought into focus the social aspect of childhood. The combination of the natural and the social in understanding children opens a pathway to understanding the diversity of childhood in different sociocultural contexts, especially children acting as translators and mediators for their family members (James, 2005). In order to recognise their contribution to families and society, and to re-evaluate children's roles in migrant family life, it is necessary to reconceptualise children and childhood.

The Developing Child

Children and childhood have often been perceived in terms of their biological development. As children are biologically smaller and mentally less mature than adults, childhood is seen as a transitional period to adulthood. Based on the biological immaturity of children, childhood is represented by naturalness, irrationality and universality (James & Prout, 1997).

The idea of naturalness derives from the observation of physical growth from infancy to adulthood. In Piagetian accounts of developmental stages, a child goes through predetermined stages; each phase of a child's intellectual growth is based on a specific way of thinking and 'a well-defined pattern' (Jenks, 2004: 81) which governs the child's direction to the subsequent phases and their particular structures (James & Prout, 1997; Thomas, 2004). This suggests that the child progresses to a subsequent stage only when a certain schema is ready in his/her mind; thus, in undergoing the particular stages, children develop their cognitive skills, grow up biologically and eventually enter into the social world of adults.

Based on this idea of natural growth, children's mental and social development into adults can be viewed as progressing from simplicity to complexity of thought, from irrationality to rationality of behaviour (James & Prout, 1990; Jenks, 1982), taking adulthood as the final stage and the standard of rationality (James, 2005). According to Piaget's theory of stages, the child may start with an *embryonic* mind, which then develops and transits from figurative to operative ways of thinking, and ultimately attaining the full status of adulthood and achieving adult intelligence or rationality (Gabriel, 2004a). Classical socialisation theory tends to reflect this conventional view and sees children as 'asocial [and] acultural', but adults as 'social and autonomous' (Mackay, 1973: 28, cited in Prout & James, 1997: 13). Thus, socialisation is the process by which the asocial child transforms into a social adult, which some see as a process of acquiring uniquely human attributes (Wrong, 1961, cited in Jenks, 1996). However, what is ignored is that the social transformation from child to adult may not follow the same route as physical growth (Jenks, 1982). Linked with naturalness, universality implies that children or childhood is invariable regardless of temporal and spatial situations (Gabriel, 2004a; James & Prout, 1997). This perceived commonality of childhood suggests that a child reaches a certain cognitive or emotional level at a certain age, irrespective of other factors such as culture.

However, a child's development is now considered to be much more complex. First, further studies suggest that logical operations appear inconsistent at the different stages that Piaget identifies in a child's cognitive development (Greig & Taylor, 1999). Some children are found to be capable of doing what surpasses their 'suggested abilities' at certain biological stages (Donaldson, 1978). Thus, the theory of developmental stages may not apply to all children even though they grow up in the same nurturing condition. Secondly, perceiving children collectively may result in disregarding diversities among individual children's experiences. Children tend to have various experiences in different social and cultural contexts. Finally, cross-cultural evidence challenges the universalist account of children's cognitive development (Levine, 2007). Childhood is far more complex than what the prescribed patterns and stages can depict.

Because of biological facts and the developmental concept, children tend to be positioned as incompetent and dependent, while they may in fact be more agentive and autonomous. Incompetence and dependence tend to be used to explain many social aspects of childhood, and children are often conceived as socially inadequate and lacking credibility (James & Prout, 1997; Qvortrup, 1997). Official statistics ignore children's contributions to society and limit their information sources to adults' activities and perspectives (Solberg, 1997). In everyday life, not only does the notion of social inadequacy influence some social, political, cultural and economic agendas (James & Prout, 1997), but many parents and teachers tend to find these conventional views straightforward and easy to accept. It is taken almost as a common belief that parents care for their children because of concerns about their incapability. Consequently, children are often positioned as 'burdens on their families or the state, who do little more than consume goods and services' (Morrow, 1995: 227). As aptly summarised in Qvortrup (1997: 90), children's status as dependents is 'so naturally ingrained in adult belief systems as not to be questioned at all'.

Given such conventional claims about children's incompetence and dependency on their parents, the protection of children has been taken for granted by parents. While it may be reasonable to protect children in many ways, there might be cases where overprotection may impinge badly on the child–adult relation and may give rise to a 'protective exclusion' of children in real life (Jenkins, 1993). As argued by Qvortrup:

> Protection is mostly accompanied by exclusion in one way or the other; protection may be suggested even when it is not strictly necessary for the sake of children, but rather to protect adults or the adult social orders against disturbances from the presence of children. This is exactly the point at which protection threatens to slide into unwarranted dominance. (Qvortrup, 1997: 86–87)

This suggests that with adults assuming their representative role, children may be deprived of access to their own interests and the opportunity to be heard in their own right. In the name of protection, children's freedom of independent mobility may be decreased and their contribution to family life and social worlds may be degraded or ignored (Qvortrup, 2005). Thus, parents may make decisions for their children on issues concerning the children themselves (Neale & Smart, 1998). It seems that children have to 'mature' before they obtain the freedom to act on their own behalf.

As a consequence, children's social life and childhood may be misrepresented or under-represented, and their positive roles undervalued. Children may become a marginalised group muted by the dominant adult group; children are 'not focused upon directly; they are most often represented by other agencies which means, at the same time, other interests' (Qvortrup, 1997: 101). As Hendrick (2008) points out:

> throughout the discourse, adult opinions and interests are always dominant; they are the ones which we know off by heart. As a result of this dominance, children are at an inherent disadvantage when talking to us and when they try to present themselves as self-conscious actors. (Hendrick, 2008: 58)

Despite the fact that many countries have ratified the UN Convention on the Rights of the Child, and in Britain the Children Act I (1989) has put this issue firmly on the statute book (Alderson, 1993), it is necessary to be cautious about how these regulations are interpreted in practice, and in whose voices the 'best interests' of the child are formulated (Boyden, 1997). Nevertheless, as Qvortrup (1997) illustrated, it is generally the case that children are perceived as 'dependents' and can be best served if they show appreciation and obedience towards adults' understanding of 'their best interests'. Thus, the emphasis tends to be put on the roles of the family and school as socialising agents, which may fail to consider the active role of children and the diversity of social contexts, i.e. how actively children are involved in their own socialisation and to what extent different arenas affect children's involvement (James & Prout, 1990; Thomas, 2004). Wittingly or not, children may be prevented from making decisions concerning their own everyday lives at home and school (Christensen & James, 2001). Parents may think they make decisions that are best for their children without consulting their children, but children are denied the opportunity to participate in this decision-making process (Lansdown, 2005). Therefore, the developmental perspective tends to endorse children's dependency and vulnerability for a considerable length of time (Gabriel, 2004b); children are socialised with the help of adults in the arenas of family, school, health care and other institutions and this seems to assume that children's interests can be integrated within these arenas (Gabriel, 2004a).

A preoccupation and emphasis on children's incompetence in making decisions also seem to prevail in society. As an age-graded institution, school has been perceived as an ideal place where children are nurtured and protected and where adults select what and how children should be taught. This seems to result from the obsession with the developmental model which is deeply rooted in the conventional schooling system, and which fails to acknowledge children's engagement with their own education. Children are perceived as the passive receptors of what the school system offers. In spite of school councils and peer mediation for example, education systems still seem to function largely on the basis that 'children are both ontologically absent and socially incompetent and therefore unfit to reflect on school choice and policy' (Wyness, 1999: 366).

Age-based demarcation affects not just how children are organised and streamed in school, but it also prescribes the stages of global literacy: at certain stages, children should be able to meet the targets of literacy appropriate to their age. This seems to suggest that beyond a certain age, literacy may become unachievable. In countries where schooling is heavily loaded with tests and examinations, children are expected to perform well enough to demonstrate that they are up to certain standards for their age in terms of literacy and numeracy. All children are expected to learn to count, speak the language of the country and respect traditional moral values at particular stages. In the UK, with the advent of the Education Reform Act 1988, the testing of young children's maths and English at the ages of 7 and 11 and then the national curriculum of literacy and numeracy have been direct outputs of uniformity. After they are tested against common standards, underperforming children may be labelled and marginalised as 'problem kids' with low ability. This educational ideology has been used to eradicate differences between children. However, a tension is caused by the 'universalizing intentions of current education policy to produce and maintain a commonality' (James & James, 2004: 120) in childhood and the diversity of social dispositions and cultural backgrounds that children have in their everyday lives at home and school.

In short, the conventional perception of children tends to stress their biological immaturity and positions childhood as dependent, inadequate and incapable both naturally and socially, and as only a transitional stage into adulthood. Although interest in childhood is not absent from the discourse of social scientists, early studies are marked by the silence of children (James & Prout, 1997). The developmental model can easily be challenged by the diversity of children's everyday experiences, and it ignores the agency that children actually exercise in their everyday lives. As James and James (2004) pointed out, positioning children as recipients may damage their potential for agency. More significantly, the age-based framework or the developmental paradigm ignores the social shaping of childhood, i.e. how childhood can be variably contextualised within different cultures, and fails to value the agency of children that is of central importance in the new paradigm of childhood.

Re-evaluation of Children's Social Roles

In the study of childhood, the 1970s was a watershed between the traditional and the new conceptual framework of childhood studies. During the subsequent decades of debate, the age-related traditional framing was challenged by a new paradigm of childhood study, which was referred to as an 'emergent' paradigm by James and Prout (1990) and a 'competence paradigm' by Hutchby and Moran-Ellis (1998: 8). The new paradigm can be traced back to Aries (1982) who argued that there was a lack of awareness of the nature of childhood as opposed to that of adulthood in medieval society. The later debate over his ideas led to a view that children's individual experiences cannot be explained purely by their biological processes, but rather by their social and cultural upbringing that tends to be characterised by diversity (James, 2004). As argued in Jenks (1992: 32), the child is 'a status of person which is comprised through a series of, often heterogeneous, images, representations, codes and constructs'. This suggests that there is not one childhood, but many, as a result of a variety of social, economic, cultural and political contexts in which children are located.

Thus, the new paradigm suggests that 'children's social relationships and cultures are worthy of study in their own right, independent of the perspective and concerns of adults' (Prout & James, 1997: 8). Looking at children as a separate category – in contrast to adults – may lead to a better understanding and recognition of children themselves (Vandenbroeck & Bouverne-De Bie, 2006). This shift leads to listening to children's voices and raising their visibility in a group as social beings (Vandenbroeck & Bouverne-De Bie, 2006). Led by these earlier fundamental arguments, James and Prout (1990, 1997) elaborated a series of issues for the new childhood studies, among which two key elements are highly relevant to the study of the families in this book – childhood can be viewed as a social construction and children can be seen as social actors and agents.

Childhood as a social construction

The new paradigm of childhood studies draws on the notion of childhood as a discursive formation (or formations) within which different types of childhoods have been constituted (Qvortrup, 1997). This recognises the increasing diversity in children's experiences, both socially and culturally. As Jenks (2004: 78) further argues, 'children, quite simply, are not always and everywhere the same thing, they are socially constructed and understood contextually'. Thus, awareness needs to be raised of the variety of ways in which 'the child' has been constituted in society (Qvortrup, 1994). The age-based concept of childhood becomes problematic when children's social and cultural contexts are taken into consideration; the emphasis on the biological processes leads to the inadequacy of the conventional framework. Childhood has social, cultural and historical dimensions. As Thomas (2004) argues, children undergo biological processes in growing up and getting older, but these changes are patterned and have to be understood within social and cultural positioning. Furthermore, variations may exist at different historical periods even within a societal system (Lowe, 2004). All this suggests that the emphasis should be shifted towards the social dimensions of childhood (Hutchby & Moran-Ellis, 1998; Woodhead, 1996) in order to fully understand children and childhood.

Secondly, cultural differences exist in understanding children and childhood within various social and historical contexts. In other words, the early years of human life are neither natural nor universal, but 'appear(s) as a specific structural and cultural component of many societies' (Jenks, 2004: 77). As James and Prout (1990: 8) argue, childhood cannot be seen as 'divorced from other variables such as class, gender or ethnicity'. In relation to children's ethnicity, cross-cultural comparisons can be made in terms of the interpretations that people from different cultural backgrounds place on childhood, and the beliefs they have about what children of certain ages and genders are capable of doing and should be expected to do (Sanders, 2004; Song, 1999). In Solberg's (1994) study, she found that Norwegian children, even at a young age, participate in the division of labour at home as collaborators with their mothers, in particular, they look after the family house for part of the day when their parents are out at work. Children in this case may become more independent than those who are prevented from being alone at home without parental supervision in countries such as Britain. In other studies, children have been found to act as child soldiers or as carers for parents (see e.g. Stephens, 1995). In some societies, children are expected to do far more physically demanding work. In many working-class and/or migrant families, children assume the responsibility of participating as needed and valued members of their households, and in some cases children's labour is necessary for the family survival (Song, 1999). This suggests that children's household responsibilities may vary according to family structures, finances and parental education (Zelizer, 1994). All these examples point to the cultural specificity or variability of particular childhoods.

Thirdly, the ways in which childhood is structured in any society are expressive of a particular view of children's competence, for as Alderson (1993: 158) argues, 'competence is more influenced by the social context and the child's experience than by innate ability'. This seems to resonate with the notion of what Hutchby and Moran-Ellis (1998) referred to as 'situated competence'. They emphasised that children's competence can be displayed and negotiated in actual arenas of activities instead of being innate to certain developmental stages. This also explains why Solberg (1994) talks about children's social age rising or falling in different social contexts. In other words, contexts in which children live tend to shape their social competence.

Families, as a significant arena, act as social units where children acquire and utilise their competencies (Hutchby & Moran-Ellis, 1998). With its particular structures and organisation, each family presents its children with resources in which different types of social competencies can be displayed and developed. Solberg (1994) argues that the meaning of childhood can be negotiated in social life and that the physical abilities and social competencies of children of the same age differ with different family expectations. Children in Mexican culture are expected to participate in household work, and rather than being burdens to their families or simply objects of adult care, these children are 'sources of deployable labour' (Orellana, 2001: 376). Their social competence may appear higher than those of the same chronological age in another society. In other words, their childhood can be constructed differently given their particular social circumstances.

Children as social actors and agents

The second key element of the new childhood studies is that children can be perceived as social actors and agents in different cultural contexts. The notion of agency, as opposed to structure, indicates activeness and initiation involved in one's social action, and it is the capacity of individuals to act independently within certain social structures and organisations rather than being constrained by them (James & James, 2008). According to Giddens (1979), structure and agency are intertwined; human beings act in ways provided by social institutions/organisations, but the form of social institutions may change as a result of actions.

As far as children are concerned, there are two approaches to the notion of agency. One approach positions children in their own developmental contexts, i.e. children have the ability to exert some control over their own lives, in, for example, schooling and any social structure relating to themselves; in peer interactions, children take their own initiative to make sense of their social worlds, rather than just being recipients of outside influence. The other approach locates children within a broader social context where they can play certain roles in the changes taking place in society. This approach seems to reconcile the notion of agency with concepts of social inequality and power relationships with adults at home and at school (Vandenbroeck & Bouverne-De Bie, 2006), that is, children may exert their agency over their parents in their everyday relations and interactions. While the two approaches appear complementary to a better understanding of children's agency, both are complex and can become problematic within the developmental paradigm where children are assumed to be in an inferior and exploited position in relation to adults. Within the structural constraints, children's agency can be ignored by adults and even downplayed by the children themselves. As a minority group in society, children may not give any credit to their own ability to act as agents (Mayall, 2002). In such a subordinate position, to what extent can children contribute to social change?

As Prout and James (1997: 8) argue, children 'are and must be seen as active in the construction and determination of their own social lives, the lives of those around them and of the societies in which they live'. As Lloyd-Smith and Tarr (2000: 69) claim, 'children experience a wide range of social relationships and engage in life experiences which are often quite independent of adult concerns'. This makes any claim to a naturalised incompetence increasingly hard to sustain. In other words, although children are influenced by conventional structures, we should recognise from the lived experiences of various childhoods that children are constantly exercising their agency (James & James, 2008). They can be their own agents: actively influencing the events in their social worlds, making their own choices and decisions as independent social actors and 'making the environment what it is' (Greig & Taylor, 1999: 160). Focusing on agency will allow us to turn our attention to the diversity of individual childhoods and recognize children as competent social actors (James & James, 2008).

The beingness of childhood

In order to understand the nature of children's agency, it is important to pay initial attention to the beingness of childhood rather than just to its becomingness, or a child's growing and maturing. The conventional perspective on childhood based on age stresses that children are considered to be in a state of permanent transition, either within or between stages. Thus, children tend to be defined as potential persons and valued more for their future as adults than for their 'present day-to-day lives as children' (Gabriel, 2004b: 65).

According to James and James (2004), childhood is still seen more as the preparatory stage for adulthood than as a stage of life that deserves to be valued in its own right; attention has even been paid to the establishment of indicators to predict the contribution that children will make to society on becoming adults. As a result, there is no space for a 'present' of childhood, and this leads to an underevaluation of the child's competence in his/her everyday situations. The new childhood studies suggest that children should be viewed not only as 'protoadults, future beings', but also as active 'beings-in-the-present' in here-and-now situations (James & Prout, 1997: 245). In other words, despite the fact that children will step into adulthood biologically and mentally, we still should not ignore the presentness that children experience in their everyday lives. As Greig and Taylor (1999) claim, viewing children as social actors suggests an emphasis on the present 'tense' of childhood, on children's specific characteristics and on their active participation in constructing their own lives and their relationships with their family and friends.

Children as active participants

Children, though having different experience from adults, can be considered as active participants in the same social and cultural world as adults (Sealey, 2000). Children's participation should be viewed in relation to complex economic and cultural changes (Stephens, 1995). Under various social contexts, children are attributed certain abilities and competencies so that they can be recognised as active and influential participants (Vandenbroeck & Bouverne-De Bie, 2006). Currently, there is a great emphasis on an ethical stance that gives even the youngest children the right to participate and to have their voices heard, and a number of programmes have been developed to help practitioners working with children explore ways in which this can be achieved (e.g. Lancaster, 2003).

Children can also be seen as active participants in their socialisation and development (Thomas, 2004), as is shown by studies in developmental psychology. According to Rogoff (1990, 2003), children's socialisation and development can be seen as joint efforts between adults and children. She uses the concept of guided participation to indicate the interrelatedness and complementarity of children and adults' roles. According to her, an adult partner may guide a child's participation in explicit and tacit or 'distal' ways, but the child may also play an active role in managing such guidance from the adult. For example, children, even from their earliest period of life, appear to be active participants in their social and cultural activities. Very young toddlers may manipulate their social partners to satisfy their own needs or achieve their aims by tuning their caregivers to arrange the activities in a way that is comfortable for them. Even babies may adjust adults' assistance through eye contact, smiles and cries. This suggests that children may make efforts to 'enlist adult involvement in their activities and observe or force their way into adult activities according to their interests' (Rogoff, 1990: 20).

Rogoff's emphasis on children as active participants contrasts with previous sociocultural theorists (e.g. Bruner, 1997; Vygotsky, 1978, 1986) who stress the leading or guiding roles of adults as the more experienced partner in children's development, which has been termed scaffolding. It has been suggested that scaffolding will occur ideally where there is a zone of proximal development, i.e. 'the distance between the actual development level as determined by independent problem solving and the level of potential development as determined through problem solving under adult guidance or in collaboration with more capable peers' (Vygotsky, 1978: 86). While many studies within a sociocultural framework further establish that adults (teachers or parents) or more experienced peers play the roles of guiding children to learn new skills and initiating them to conduct new cultural practices (Gregory et al., 2004), children's active role in relation to adults' appears to have been overlooked.

Rogoff further proposes that children's relationships with others in joint activities can be seen as interdependent, rather than purely dependent on others. In her study she presents an example of a nine-year-old boy taking control of managing the instruction in a laboratory classification task when his mother claimed that she was confused. Although the mother was assigned responsibility to get the child ready for a test and had access to a cue sheet with the correct placement of the items, the child led the mother through the checking process, and he seemed to have assumed a more responsible role in the activity. This example suggests that while adults tend to be regarded as knowledgeable enough to adjust their support in developing children's skills, children simultaneously adjust their own pace of learning.

While Rogoff herself did not claim that scaffolding may occur in guided participation, other researchers (e.g. Li, 2002; Ma, 2004) point to the 'bi-directional' and 'reciprocal' manner of scaffolding. Although here the concept of scaffolding seems to be used in a looser sense than it was originally termed, it seems to provide a wider context for scaffolding. That is, scaffolding may not only be generated from a more experienced partner in the shared actions, but it may also originate from child to adult when the child's knowledge or skill is higher than the adult's in the joint activity. Many studies on literacy (e.g. Gregory, 1998; Gregory et al., 2004) provide empirical evidence for the importance of the child's role, and suggest that children's scaffolding occurs in shared activities with their siblings, peers and grandparents. Thus, scaffolding can be seen as dual and reciprocal, involving both parents and children; children may not just play an active and important role, and engage themselves to joint activities, but they may also build scaffolding for their adult partners in certain circumstances.

Although it has not been specifically mentioned in the literature, this might well apply in migrant families where the parents are less knowledgeable and experienced than their children in certain areas, and the children may thus take more responsibility in mediating their parents' lives or in shared activities with their parents. We shall thus be able to refer to this perspective in later chapters.

Children as negotiators and decision makers

From the examples listed in the previous sections, we should also note that in participating in joint activities with their parents, children may deploy freedom of action and negotiate the directions favouring themselves in spite of their weaker status (Solberg, 1994). Children can be perceived as competent social and moral agents who negotiate their daily lives while participating in them in much the same way as adults do (Alanen, 1998). It is generally believed that unequal social ranking determines parents' high level of power and authority in their relationships with children. However, when parents' higher social rank enables them to impose their will or authority on their children at their own discretion or in the name of benefiting their children, parents may have to face resistance from their children, and resistance has to be seen as an act of agency. Negotiations may become more serious and more intense when certain kinds of punishment are present. In some families, parents may negotiate with their children on subjects such as holidays, television, clothing, leisure time and so on, while in others, parents may be found to please their children (Jing, 1990, cited in Luk-Fong, 2005). This suggests that shifts have been made towards negotiation as a norm for the relationship between parents and children (Du Bois-Raymond, 2001; Vandenbroeck & Bouverne-De Bie, 2006).

In addition to being negotiators of their social lives and social world, children can be viewed as decision makers, together with adults; or they are at least entitled to participate in any consultation about decisions concerning them (Lloyd-Smith & Tarr, 2000; Rogoff, 1993). While the dependency model downplays children's ability to make self-conscious choices due to their immaturity, incompetence and lack of experience and knowledge, the new paradigm acknowledges children's capacity as agents in making decisions that shape their daily lives, social relations, identities and futures (James, 2004). Although adults may still assume responsibility for them, children tend to demand the right to exert agency in achieving their own purposes and constructing their own world (Lloyd-Smith & Tarr, 2000). Consequently, schools have used techniques such as 'circle time' and 'playground peacemakers' to allow children to be the central decision makers and arbiters of their own behaviour (James & James, 2004). The children in Corsaro (2011) were also found to make adjustments to school rules, on the one hand to avoid being detected, and on the other, to engage teachers to enforce or modify the rules. In some families, parents may change the way in which they treat their children; for example, they may treat their children as conversational peers, advocate children's autonomy and allow decisions to be made by their children or in consultation with them (Edward, 1989; Vandenbroeck & Bouverne-De Bie, 2006). As Prout (2002: 75) claims, 'children have valuable insights and perspectives to offer on many aspects of their lives'. Empirical studies on children's culture (e.g. Enerstvedt, 1971; Kvideland, 1979, both cited in Solberg, 1994) have illustrated how children make choices and decisions among available possibilities, or supplement and recreate materials in outdoor games, narrative tradition and singing, instead of passively receiving what adults transfer to them. The children in Solberg's (1994) study organised their own time when they are 'homestayers'. In migrant communities, children have been found to make decisions on behalf of their parents, for example, in communicating with public institutions such as solicitors, bankers, doctors, inspectors, and so on, in the new society (see e.g. Hall & Sham, 2007). For these families, children's agency has actively and aptly displayed them as being not just active participants but also negotiators and decision makers in their everyday living.

Children's work

Children's work is another strand that embodies children's agency. Traditionally in Western societies, work is perceived as paid employment or a job that results in some form of economic value or reward, and which belongs almost exclusively to the adult world, whereas children's activities in schools or families are regarded as play or learning, not as work (Orellana, 2001). Children are thought of as small, young, dependent and incompetent in some families, and in others as the 'problems of parents seeking care for them' (Solberg, 1997: 142). At the societal level, the regulation of a child's life tends to give priority to making childhood 'a carefree, safe, secure and happy phase of human existence' (Sommerville, 1982, cited in Boyden, 1997: 191).

The traditional view of children's activities as 'play' to some extent hides their contribution to society and their family. Historically, the term 'child labour' was used up until the 1980s to describe all kinds of adult work activities conducted by children, including bonded labour, slavery and long hours of working in unregulated sweatshops. Outside the domestic remit, children have been involved in agricultural and industrial work, but their work has always been associated with low pay and low status, and hence can be perceived as marginal and insignificant (James et al., 1998).

In addition to the jobs outside family, children were historically involved in helping with household and farm chores, hunting and fishing, which required skillful and time-consuming preparation when modern technology was not widely used (Corsaro, 2011). In modern society, work of this type has been condemned as incompatible with childhood, as it is perceived as exploitative and detrimental to children's social, physical and psychological development (James & James, 2008). If getting paid is the only criterion for work, this conception becomes problematic when children perform unpaid work. Many feminist researchers have criticised this notion of work as it excludes housework or other unpaid work (James & Prout, 1997).

In many cultures of the modern world, children are often seen taking care of their siblings, doing general housework such as cleaning and running errands. There are also child carers who look after their sick or disabled parents as part of their daily life; a task that they might find both physically and emotionally demanding (James & James, 2008). These examples may acutely challenge the developmental paradigm in that children are not always vulnerable, incapable and looked after, but are responsible and competent to care for adults (Wyness, 2006). Solberg (1994, 1997) explores how children's work in and outside the home in Norway contributes to their families. Song (1996, 1999) also reports that children as young as age seven or eight start to help their parents with kitchen tasks in their family takeaway shops and gradually deal with customer orders in the evenings after school or during weekends. In the above examples, children may receive little payment in monetary form. It has been argued that these domestic endeavours can be considered as educational or culturally expected, rather than exploitative, as children fulfil their familial responsibilities in specific cultural contexts. Boyden *et al.* (1998) say that working children in many countries can go to school only as a result of their contribution to family life from work. Not only does their work support their own access to education, but it also adds substantially to their family well-being. So these kinds of work actually carry financial value as they are contributing to families and the wider economy. If children did not carry out these tasks, adults would have to spend time and energy on them (Morrow, 1994). Hence, children's work 'may or may not generate income', but it is 'economically significant in the here and now' (Morrow, 1995: 210).

The failure to recognise the economic value of children's work can be due to the fact that children carry out these tasks mostly at home, a private venue that is dominated by parents. However, in some households, children perform other tasks, taking over the conventional parental roles, not only without payment in most cases, but also largely taken for granted. Both Walsh *et al.* (2006) and Puig (2002) have termed this phenomenon as 'parentification' and 'adultification', respectively. In their studies on immigrant or refugee families, children were found to become consolers or advisors to parents. There are similar examples in Valenzuela's (1999) study where children of immigrant families work as carers or surrogate parents in managing a range of household tasks such as cooking, cleaning and looking after their younger siblings. In these studies, children were also found to help their siblings with their homework and even their parents with their English homework, translating official business documents for their parents. Rutter and Candappa (1998) describe how refugee children act as translators and mediators for other family members as part of their domestic duties. Orellana (2001, 2009) examines children's work in their immigrant households as helpers and brokers for their parents, making children's immigrant experiences visible. She illustrates how children's present living, rather than their past and future, impacts on family life. Hall and Sham (2007) argue that children's language brokering for their parents could also be counted as young Chinese adolescents' work in immigrant families. The children in their study actually contribute positively to the administrative and social well-being of their families, which can often be indirectly related to the economics of family life, as children carrying out the tasks may save parents' time and enable them to do other activities. Moreover, parents in the study did not have the linguistic ability to perform the tasks well themselves.

Therefore, through working for or on behalf of their parents, these children are actually making economic contributions to their family life. However, the roles that children play in participating in adult space are concealed because their status is that of a dependent (Wyness, 2006).

The invisibility of children's work at home requires a reconsideration of the concept of work. The traditional conceptualisation has rendered invisible the wide varieties of children's work, thereby undermining the value they produce. This may stem from the conventional perception of childhood as a phase of play and free of responsibility. However, these studies demonstrate the importance of children's contribution to their family enterprises and economy, although the significance of children's work in families may or may not be evident in monetary terms. Children make decisions, take responsibility, demonstrate commitment, and exercise their agency, completely differently from the irrational and immature images in a developmental model.

Thus, the concept of work should be extended beyond paid employment (James et al., 1998) and into domestic duties and responsibilities. Work can be reconceptualised to 'include all activities which involve the production, management and conversion of resources' (Wadel, 1979, cited in James & Prout, 1997: 241) and 'the performance of necessary tasks and the production of necessary values' (Wallman, 1979, cited in Morrow, 1995: 210). These resources and values may or may not lead to immediate economic and financial benefits and may or may not be recognised by the adults or even the children themselves, but participation in adult space, exertion of social agency and execution of adult responsibility are essential to the production of resources and values. Within this conceptualisation, work may include a wide range of activities that are not conventionally viewed as employment, but are economically or emotionally significant, contributing to personal and family capital (Zelizer, 2005). What children do for their parents or on behalf of their parents can be counted as work since children are converting resources, producing value and performing tasks for their parents, without which parents' everyday living and functioning can become challenging and disturbing.

To summarise, we have presented key elements of the new childhood studies while discussing the conventional view of children. Just as it is too limited to emphasise only the biological reality of children, it is equally incomplete to place the focus purely on the social aspect of childhood. While it is not possible to neatly separate the biological and the sociocultural aspects of childhood, analysing the hybridity of the natural and the social is more helpful in understanding children and childhood. As James (2005) argues, childhood can only be understood in its heterogeneous complexity especially in the context of migration and contemporary globalisation. The meanings of childhood may vary with time and space and with the social and cultural construction of childhood, and children can be seen as social actors in their own right, not just actively participating in their social life, but also acting as agents for other participants. How they exercise their agency in their everyday lives may vary in different social and cultural milieus. Specific cultures and communities shape and are shaped by children's actions. The re-evaluation of children's roles also suggests a new dimension of parent–child relationships in migrant families. Children, in particular, rather than their parents, become the source of knowledge and norms of behaviour in the new society, which offers children ample opportunities to mediate for their parents. These new childhood studies provide a framework in this book to understand children's mediation in migrant families. With the expanded conceptualisation of work, child cultural mediation can be counted as work as they exercise their social agency and produce social and emotional values for their parents living in a new land. The following chapters of this book will demonstrate how these children perform their work in mediating for their parents.

3 Cultural Mediation

Migrants draw on different resources in their acculturation to a new society, and children tend to be one of the main resources that parents rely on in their new situation. Children play active and agentive roles in immigrant families, and the role of the child in linguistic and cultural mediation has been increasingly noticed.

Mediation and Cultural Mediation

The notion of mediation has been used in many ways, and various disciplines within the social sciences have approached it from different perspectives. We shall see in the following sections that, for the purposes of this book, we need to adopt the broadest and most open definition of mediation in order to fully investigate the roles that children play in mediating the new culture for immigrant families.

Some researchers, particularly in sociology, define mediation in broad and general terms. For example, Simmel (1950) treats it as an almost ubiquitous aspect of social interaction. He claims that mediating activities exist in

> ...all groups of more than two elements ... From the conversation among three persons that lasts only an hour to the permanent family of three, there is no triad in which a dissent between any two elements does not occur ... and in which the third member does not play a mediating role. (Simmel, 1950: 148–149)

This suggests that mediation can take place in a wide range of social practices. Kurin offers a series of examples to illustrate this multiplicity of contexts, objects of mediation and types of mediator:

> ...peace treaties by peace brokers, presidencies by power brokers, corporations by stockbrokers, houses and buildings by real estate brokers, spouses (at least some) by marriage brokers, international shipments of goods by customs brokers, the best books by literary brokers, and the last remnants of personal wealth by pawnbrokers. (Kurin, 1997: 20–21)

Thus, many social transactions become more complicated than just a straightforward dyadic interaction due to the involvement of a third-party mediator (Knapp-Potthoff & Knapp, 1986; Wadensjo, 1998). Also referred to at times, as in the previous quotation, as an intermediary, an interpreter or a broker, the mediator occupies a middle ground, playing a linking role between the other two parties of a group or exerting influence over them. The mediator may use a variety of means, both tacit and explicit, and verbal or non-verbal, when carrying out mediating activities. Mediators may facilitate an agreement between two parties by way of 'a gesture, a way of listening, [or] the mood that radiates from a particular person' (Simmel, 1950: 149). From this perspective, mediation is viewed as a universal, constant and complex social phenomenon in human interaction.

However, though broad and encompassing, this perspective predominantly sees mediation as happening between two individuals or groups of people and this is a limitation if we take into consideration the issues raised for immigrant families in Chapter 1. There, we discussed how migration brings culturally diverse people together, living in one society. Cultural borders may emerge wherever cultures run into each other (Szasz, 1994). While there is a need for the whole population to adapt to a multicultural environment, migrants may find it necessary to adapt to the majority culture in order to be successful. Although this situation may result in mediation between persons or groups, it is likely to involve mediation between persons on the one hand, and more abstract and less tangible elements on the other: national culture, history and identity as well as socially accepted cultural practices. While these are often embodied in persons, they are also expressed in normalised ways of being, appearing and acting that can be seen as entities in themselves. We can clearly see this type of mediation in the case of Man Kee cited in the introduction to this book.

How, then, has mediation of culture, as a distinctive practice, been addressed in the literature? Some authors define mediation as a wide and extensive practice. Kurin (1997) claims that culture can be mediated always, though variably, by countries, organisations, communities, groups and individuals. Brown (1992) argues that cultural mediation occurs in all cross-cultural situations. Similar to Simmel's conceptualisation of mediation, Taft (1981) defines cultural mediation as happening between two persons or groups of people who differ in their language and culture. Despite being more specific, this perspective still appears to exclude other forms of cultural mediation and there are researchers who emphasise another form of cultural mediation, i.e. the one that takes place between two cultures. For example, Gentemann (1983: 119) argues that cultural mediation could happen 'between the mainstream culture in a pluralistic society and the various sub-cultures'. Although this may entail any two cultures, e.g. mainstream culture versus youth culture, in a multicultural society it may also refer to the majority culture versus the minority ethnic cultures.

While the above two perspectives appear to overlap each other, they stress different dimensions of the cultural mediation dynamic. However, just as in Simmel's definition of mediation, neither of them seems to highlight the form of cultural mediation that happens between people and culture. On the other hand, there are empirical anthropological studies that describe this form. In his writing, John Macgowan, who was a missionary, mediated Chinese cultural values, social behaviours and habits of thoughts for Westerners (Cheng, 2002). As McLeod (1981) argues, acting as a channel of information, the mediator may aid in the development of certain cultural practices, attitudes or identities in another group of people. At the same time, the mediator may inform outsiders about the religious or symbolic content of their own people's traditions (Hinderaker, 2002). This seems to suggest that cultural mediation may occur between a group of people and the cultural practices, traditions or attitudes of another group. What is mediated appears to comprise both tangible and less tangible entities. It is this form of cultural mediation that is of more relevance to examining how children mediate new cultural practices for their parents.

Previous studies have also described cultural mediators by their characteristics and their functions, stating who can be mediators and what they do in practice. According to Taft (1981), a cultural mediator is

a person who facilitates communication, understanding, and action between persons or groups who differ with respect to language and culture... In order to serve as a link..., the mediator must be able to participate to some extent in both cultures. (Taft, 1981: 53)

This suggests that the mediator must be to a certain extent bicultural, playing a bridging role. As mentioned in Chapter 1, people may mediate if they are cognitively and behaviourally multicultural or integrated, or linguistically and culturally competent in two languages and cultures (Bochner, 1981; Dennis, 1994). Mediators may disseminate their own culture and import others' (Cheng, 2002; Murphy, 2003; Szasz, 1994). They may facilitate business relationships and be responsible for interpreting diplomatic and political concepts (Hinderaker, 2002). Geertz (1960: 228) showed that mediators can perform 'an altogether critical function' and 'communicate both with the urban elite and with the rural followers of a particular local tradition'. Acting as 'agents of modernity', mediators also help to build up effective communication networks between the regional and the central systems (Robins, 1996: 124). Therefore, we can see that cultural mediators may create and maintain relationships between open social systems even within one socially, culturally, religiously and politically diverse country (Bochner, 1981; Richter, 1988).

The question then arises as to how conscious mediators are of their own practices. Different situations precipitate the roles of cultural mediators. While some mediators may be fully aware of their own roles and endeavours, others may just play the mediating role alongside their daily working and living, without being conscious of their behaviour. In Alred and Byram's (2002) longitudinal study, the Year Abroad experience gradually turned undergraduates into intercultural mediators and impacted on their career choices, but these individuals were not fully aware of their changed roles and competence.

Some people are involved in mediating activities through their livelihoods, or when doing their job, such as carrying out the mission of a religious or educational organisation, business or government (McLeod, 1981) or being sojourners involved in job-related technical projects or international educational exchange programmes, and others mediate due to their bicultural childhoods (Bochner, 1981; Taft, 1981). As Bochner (1981: 28) claims: 'cultural mediation is not a recognized profession', but 'throughout the world there are a great many individuals who, whether they know it or not, are practising cultural mediators'. Therefore, some mediation tends to be conducted explicitly while some may be implemented implicitly.

Under different cultural, social and political circumstances, mediating individuals tend to vary in terms of their social status, educational experience and age. However, studies on cultural mediation tend to have focused more on adult mediators than on children, even where children are participants, for example, in the fur trade (see Szasz, 1994). Studies have included mediation between adults within an immigrant community who make meaning from written texts and exchange meanings in daily communicative practices (Baynham, 1993; Baynham & Masing, 2000) or between literate and illiterate prisoners (Wilson, 2000) and between scribes and their clients on the plaza in Mexico City (Kalman, 1999). An important point that has emerged from this research is that studies of mediation have focused predominantly on linguistic and literacy brokering. What we need to recognise is that these studies have almost exclusively focused on adults. Children as mediators seem to have been largely ignored and the possibility that children can act as cultural mediators remains to be explored.

Why have child mediators been ignored? How are children positioned in relation to adults in mediation? Cole (1996) explained mediation by placing human action in its environment, and claimed that there exists a triadic relationship of subject–medium–object. The object can take different forms such as concrete and tangible entities or abstract and less tangible ones. Human subjects may 'incorporate auxiliary means (including, very significantly, other people) into their actions' (Cole, 1996: 119) in order to understand or approach objects. Thus, this suggests that mediators are more experienced people who provide assistance for subjects. In studying children's acquisition of reading, Cole (1995, 1996) claims that adults play a mediating role for children to make sense of the world, although simultaneously children may have other contacts with the outside world. Schieffelin and Cochran-Smith (1984) also provide similar evidence that story readers, who are usually parents or other adult carers, take on the roles of intermediaries between children and print. Mediation of this type can be found in an adult's scaffolding for a child in his/her zone of proximal development (Gillen, 2000). Linking with the childhood studies discussed in Chapter 2, we can see that the way this triadic relationship of subject–medium–object has been used incorporates the conventional view of childhood, that is, the child–subject tends to be positioned at a dependent and less agentive status, with the parent as the mediator in the middle.

However, as explained in Chapter 2, Rogoff (1990) suggests that while children's participation can vary with how responsible the involved parties are for the joint activities, children can be perceived as playing active roles in mediation by shaping the way that adult mediators relate to them. Thus, the process of mediation appears to have reciprocal aspects for both adults and children. While this construct allows for the role reversal of conventional relations between parent and child, the child is still positioned as a less knowledgeable recipient who depends on the adult mediator. What this model does not explore in depth is the possibility of children being more knowledgeable than adults and playing more active and agentive roles. Drawing on the new childhood studies, we can see that this needs to be perceived from a wider perspective. In immigrant families, might it not be possible that children mediate the new society for adults such as parents, due to their different degrees of access to the new society and their diverse sources of knowledge about it? How might the dynamic of mediation operate when children help the parent–subject understand their new society?

Child Cultural Mediation

Those who have a bicultural childhood may become cultural mediators. Previous studies suggest that child cultural mediation is prevalent and 'a common practice' (Weisskirch & Alva, 2002: 369) among linguistic minority communities, starting from a very early age and continuing into adulthood (Hua & Costigan, 2012; Jones *et al.*, 2012; McQuillan & Tse, 1995; Tse, 1995, 1996a, 1996b; Valdés, 2003; Vasquez *et al.*, 1994; Weisskirch, 2005, 2006; Weisskirch *et al.*, 2011; Wu & Kim, 2009). As Hall claims:

> the extent to which a young person takes this more powerful role may well depend upon particular children or particular settings, but it is clear that in some circumstances, this role is exactly that undertaken by children. (Hall, 2004: 286)

Children's mediating roles may add to patterns of family interaction and become an aspect of life in migrant communities (see e.g. Baptiste, 1993; Gopaul-McNicol & Thomas-Presswood, 1998; Kibria, 1993; Menjivar, 2000; Portes & Rumbaut, 2001; Valenzuela, 1999). It is one of the adaptive strategies to living in a new society, or an adaptive response to societal and cultural pressures generated by migration (Garcia Coll & Magnuson, 1997; Jones *et al.*, 2012; Morales & Hanson, 2005). In other words, to help the family survive, children use their growing linguistic and cultural competence, whether or not parents and they themselves are fully aware of its existence, benefits and outcomes.

Child cultural mediation entails not just translation, interpretation and paraphrasing of 'single words, whole phrases, extended text or discourse, and conversation' (Orellana *et al.*, 2003a: 15) from one language to another, but also explanation, transmission and negotiation of culturally responsive messages or information in a variety of ways. It can be intentionally set up or 'spontaneously offered, with or without the support of other people or tools' (Orellana *et al.*, 2003a: 15). That is to say, child mediators may facilitate intercultural communication by interpreting linguistically, conveying cultural cues and imparting information (Chu, 1999). As Jones *et al.* (2012: 182) summarise, child cultural mediation plays a unique role in immigrant families to 'help their parents and others navigate the new culture and language'.

We should note therefore that it is unhelpful to discuss different types of cultural mediation as if they were separate practices, and more relevant to conceptualise cultural mediation as spanning a whole continuum, in which particular practices may overlap or even merge. Moreover, we can identify two ends of that continuum – explicit and implicit – according to the visibility of child cultural mediation in family life, children's awareness of their own mediation, challenges for child mediators and parent–child relationships within mediation in families. The term 'explicit child cultural mediation' designates those transactions in which children tend to take over responsibility, and their agentive roles appear to be intentional, conscious and more visible in family life; 'implicit child cultural mediation' signifies those occurrences where children carry out their agentive roles in a less intentional, less visible and less conscious way.

Explicit child cultural mediation

Explicit child cultural mediation lies at one end of the continuum and is characterised by a number of features such as visibility, self-awareness, level of challenge and changes in child/parent power relationships. Explicit child cultural mediation has been studied more than any other kind, and the most frequently studied form of explicit cultural mediation is what has come to be termed 'child language brokering'. In the 1970s, Harris and Sherwood published an article on what they termed 'natural translation' and the topic began to receive some academic notice. Natural translation was defined as 'translating done in everyday circumstances by people who have had no special training for it' (Harris & Sherwood, 1978: 155); their article contained a number of short descriptions of events in which children acted as interpreters or translators for their parents. Despite some controversy about the use of the term 'natural translation', the role of children as interpreters and translators was thereafter neglected and it was not until Shannon (1990), while studying Hispanic migrants in California, brought it back into focus, although the restricted scope of the journal meant that relatively few people discovered the article. Shannon was the first person to publish an extended transcript of a child language brokering event. It was only when McQuillan and Tse (1995) published in a major international journal a study of younger adults' memories of what they termed 'language brokering' that the topic seriously impacted on the research community. Within a few years, an increasing number of studies began appearing and the topic went from academic invisibility to a fashionable research topic.

Visibility of child cultural mediation in family life

Despite the long-term neglect of this topic by researchers, explicit child cultural mediation is actually often highly visible. Mediating events often occur in upfront circumstances where children are positioned, often physically, in the middle between their parents and other institutional personnel such as doctors, solicitors or bankers; in such circumstances, there is nowhere for a child to hide (see e.g. Abreu & Hale, 2011; Cohen *et al.*, 1999). For the participants, explicit cultural mediation events are highly visible because they force themselves into people's lives; it would be very difficult, if not impossible, for many families to survive without such mediation from their children. No matter what supports can be provided, the number of translators and interpreters is always going to be limited and may be unavailable when needed. Therefore, families will try to liberate themselves from their dependency on outsiders (Abreu & Hale, 2011) and continue to rely on their children because of the privacy of family events.

These events are often marked by clear boundaries, both temporal and spatial. The language brokering event documented by Shannon (1990) is a very clear example of this – where a Spanish-speaking mother visited a chiropractor. Although she knew a small amount of English, she still felt she needed to take along her 11-year-old daughter, Leti. This event took place in a very specific space, the chiropractor's office, and was bounded by set times for starting and finishing. Thus, it was in effect a quite self-contained event. Although defining boundaries is not always easy, even in the event just described, for a researcher interested in language brokering, the interpreting role of the child took place at a particular time and in a particular space and could therefore be more easily studied than other kinds of cultural mediating roles. It was for this reason that Shannon was able to get the agreement of all parties to allow a tape recording of the event and she was able to produce a detailed transcript of the conversation. To a large extent the huge increase in studies of language brokering is a consequence of the relatively clear framing of such events, something that makes the topic more manageable for researchers.

The visibility of child language brokering also comes about in many cases because of its frequency and its penetration into all aspects of family life. Brokering can occur in almost every aspect of daily interaction and occurs in a wide range of domains such as education, health, commerce, law, finance, everyday living and entertainment (Orellana *et al.*, 2003b). This frequency and penetration makes a child's translation and interpretation of vital importance to the family's social, economic and administrative activities and in linking families productively to the various resources and services of the new society (e.g. McQuillan & Tse, 1995; Tse, 1995, 1996a, 1996b). What is clear from the now extensive research on child language brokering is that this activity is usually highly visible to parents, but how visible is it to children themselves?

Children's awareness of their own mediation

In explicit cultural mediation, children tend to have a clear awareness of their brokering roles in helping adults. First, due to the predictable nature of some language brokering, parents may invite, request or demand that a child acts as a cultural broker for them. They may even be quite selective about this, choosing either a more experienced child or one who actually enjoys such participation (see e.g. Abreu & Hale, 2011; Orellana *et al.*, 2003a; Vasquez *et al.*, 1994). In such circumstances, the child chosen will be very conscious of his/her own intermediary position in the triadic interaction and even of the consequences of his/her own behaviour on families or parents. For instance, a Chinese teenager in Hall and Sham (2007: 23) commented that 'If I interpreted wrongly my parents would get trouble from it...'. Many children may be well aware of the deeper aspects of their mediating role such as the Vietnamese adolescent who made a poignant request to teachers at a local school conference: 'If I translate for you when you talk to my mother, don't look at me, look at her when you speak' (Weinstein-Shr, 1995: 119). He was clearly sensitive to the position of his mother in these transactions, recognising that in many cases involving inexperienced interpreters the conversation often ends up as a two-way interaction between the main language speaker and the interpreter, and the other party is left out.

Secondly, child mediators' self-awareness can be seen from their different attitudes towards their own endeavours. For some children, perhaps a minority, their brokering activities are anything but a pleasant task and they find the role very stressful. In Tse's study (1995: 188), more than half of the 35 student respondents liked brokering activities, less than half felt 'proud to be brokers' and less than 20% felt that brokering was burdensome and embarrassing. However, children often feel they cannot refuse to broker (Weisskirch, 2007; Weisskirch & Alva, 2002), and in Valdés (2003) some young interpreters or translators regarded their brokering as a responsibility to their families. For them it was not remarkable but just an everyday, natural experience that was an inevitable part of their growing up. Among their Chinese American adolescent language brokers, Wu and Kim (2009) found that young people who were more oriented towards Chinese cultural values tended to have a stronger sense of efficacy. Young Portuguese immigrants living in England became more aware of their bicultural identity through acting as translators for their families, which impacted on their self-development (Abreu & Hale, 2011). These children may become more connected to their culture of origin and understand more of its values and norms (Jones *et al.*, 2012). The benefits of speaking the two languages and understanding the two cultures also improved their academic performance

(Corona *et al.*, 2012; Dorner *et al.*, 2007). Thus, children may be called to broker for their parents from a very early age, and gradually brokering becomes a natural thing for them to do. As Orellana *et al.* (2003b: 516) report, children think of their own translating or interpreting experience as 'just normal'. It seems that children's brokering may shift from being very conscious to being almost subconscious to them.

Challenges for child mediators

Explicit cultural mediation tends to present different challenges for child mediators. As can be seen from the previous section on awareness, some children may have a positive attitude towards it, while the reaction of others may be just the opposite (see also Acoach & Webb, 2004; Buriel *et al.*, 1998; Walichowski, 2001). The challenges may stem from different factors, ranging from the inexperience of the children, their limited language skills, the technical complexity of the language being used and failing to understand the subtleties of the social interaction in particular circumstances.

Because much of the work in language brokering events is to comprehend vocabulary and messages, reformulate messages and judge the accuracy of this reformulation in the two languages (Malakoff & Hakuta, 1991), the linguistic demand becomes highly significant. Since they are children, whatever their language capabilities, child language brokers are inevitably still learning not only the new language but their first language as well, and may well have to start their brokering within a very short period of time after their arrival in the majority language community (Tse, 1996a). For a child broker who normally does not receive any relevant training, interpreting and translating tasks can be very demanding. In Corona *et al.* (2012), adolescents talk about their difficulties with complex words beyond their own English and Spanish language abilities, especially in medical settings. Their difficulties exist in both languages in terms of vocabulary, pronunciation and comprehension (see also Villanueva & Buriel, 2010). In another study, nine-year-old Jasmine wrote in her journal that 'I felt so nervous to translate for the doctor because I thought I would not be able to understand the big words doctors use' (Orellana *et al.*, 2003b: 516). It is clear from a number of sources that these children do make errors, sometimes so significant that the lives of family members may be threatened (Wagner, 1993) or the family's financial circumstances may be damaged (Kaur & Mills, 1993). Children may or may not be aware that they are making errors as mistranslations can occur even though a child is acting in good faith.

Furthermore, explicit cultural mediation can be socially and cognitively demanding for children, as child brokers may have to deal with complex social events that are often beyond the normal chronological age expectation. Compared with their peers in a majority group, these children may be confronted, much earlier in their life, with not only complicated vocabulary about institutions and systems, but also knowledge about complex social bureaucracies (Vasquez *et al.*, 1994; Weisskirch, 2012). With their insufficient knowledge and experience of the world, child mediators may find it challenging just handling certain social interactions. Hall and Sham (2007) reported the brokering experience of a Chinese teenage boy who says:

the inspectors from the health and safety department and the fire station came to our chippy. I am an interpreter for my dad and inspectors. It is all about regulations and guidelines which are so confusing. I could not understand it. It seems to be so complicated. (Hall & Sham, 2007: 23)

In Hall's (2004) study, child interpreters were posed challenges that potentially pitted adults against each other, for example, disagreements between adults about how children should be educated. Despite this being a very socially demanding situation, the 10-year-old interpreters operated highly strategically and successfully, carefully lubricating the social relationships between the adults.

A further point is that challenges for children can be physical and emotional not just because of the visibility discussed above, because they are often involved in public conversations about subject matters that generally belong to adults, but also because they may be pressurised to make quick responses in the swift flow of talk or debate between adult groups. Madia, the 11-year-old mentioned in the introduction to this book, recounted that 'the first time I had to speak publicly I was really embarrassed'. While it might be the case that she was conscious that her interpretation may make a difference to her family's future security, as probably the only child between groups of adults, the physical difference might be formidable enough to make a child nervous. It would be very unusual if she had been able to keep calm during her first experience of public speaking for her family on a matter of high importance. In many cases, it is not simply embarrassment about performing in a more public arena, but also because the children are sometimes mediating between adults who do not understand each other's position and move towards confrontation. In the Hall and Sham (2007) study, one 13-year-old girl reported:

One afternoon, a big tall man came to our take-away shop and showed his identity card and said that he came from the Health and Safety Environment Department to do the inspection. My mum and dad could not understand what he was going on about because they could not speak English. The man spoke to me instead of my dad. He asked me to interpret between them. I was shaking with fright. My dad told me, 'Don't answer his questions because we can lose our shop and business.' Every time it's something like this. I could not sleep for nearly a week for worrying about what the report would be. (Hall & Sham, 2007: 23)

When a child finds himself/herself in the middle of a confrontation between adults, it is not unknown for the child to be blamed for the tension that has arisen. As a consequence of cultural brokering, children may feel burdened, obligated and stressed about carrying out brokering activities, and feel resented by their parents especially when parents do not appreciate the difficulty of brokering, nor provide sufficient support (Dorner *et al.*, 2008; Orellana, 2009; Portes & Rumbaut, 2001; Weisskirch, 2012; Wu & Kim, 2009). They may experience emotional distress resulting from their involvement in cultural brokering events (Puig, 2002), and it has been found that the high demands in brokering due to high levels of family disagreement lead to high levels of child emotional distress (Jones *et al.*, 2012). These negative emotions tend to result in poorer family relationships between young Latinos and their parents (Weisskirch, 2007) and poorer adolescent adjustment to the mainstream society (Martinez *et al.*, 2009). In the case of the female culture brokers investigated by Sy (2006), they were found to experience a high level of school stress and lower academic achievement, and it can be argued that acting as a language broker is related to depression among young people (Love & Buriel, 2007).

The negative feelings such as stress and tension in children brokering can be caused by adolescents' understanding of the material to be translated, the setting of the brokering, youth brokers' cultural values and the extent to which parents and children share the efforts in the brokering events. According to Corona *et al.* (2012), stress tends to occur when adolescents' fluency in both languages is less developed, as they worry that their family members' health problems may be wrongly treated if their translation of medical terms is incorrect. When they understand their original cultural values such as *familismo* (meaning a strong sense of identification with, and loyalty to, the nuclear and extended family), their reactions to brokering tend to be less negative. Wu and Kim (2009) found similar reactions in Chinese American adolescents' brokering. In situations where parents understood English but did not speak English well, child brokers felt the spirit of 'team' work with their parents, rather than stress. Similarly, a 14-year-old girl in Corona *et al.* (2012) said, 'Sometimes I did not understand something but my mom did understand', thus it was 'easier' to translate for her mother; but the mother expressed the embarrassment that her daughter felt when she (the mother) asked her daughter the meaning of another word.

Changed parent–child relationships in cultural mediation

In explicit cultural mediation, conventional power relations between parents and children tend to change and instead of the child being in a typically subordinate and dependent position within a family, the parents become dependent on their children because of the children's higher level of language skills and privileged access to social resources. As Acoach and Webb (2004) suggest, children tend to become more adept than their parents at functioning in the new society. Even parents who are able to communicate in the majority language may still be dependent on their children for translating or interpreting in more specific or technical circumstances (Jones & Trickett, 2005; Orellana *et al.*, 2003a); the children help their parents navigate through the new social system (McKay, 1993). The changed power relationship can be embodied in several ways.

Firstly, by language brokering for their parents, children appear to be participating in an adult world, and take control of how information should be presented and what information can be passed to their parents. They may become the gatekeepers of information and access. According to Chu (1999), 70% of Korean American children in brokering events did not impart all the information to their parents. A 13-year-old Mexican boy even told his parents that the 'F' on his report card stood for 'fabulous' (Suárez-Orozco & Suárez-Orozco, 2001: 74). In Weinstein-Shr's (1995) study, one Cambodian father was shocked to know (from his neighbour) that his son had been expelled from school six months earlier. It suggests that, as holders of different kinds of knowledge, children may filter what to inform and what to interpret for their parents, and that it may not always be to the advantage of the parents (Partida, 1996).

Secondly, child language brokers do not just affect their parents' perceptions of the new society, but they may also make decisions for their parents without consulting them (McQuillan & Tse, 1995). With parents' weakening and compromised authority and control (Kibria, 1993; Zhou & Bankston, 1998), child language brokers may become more powerful, and may totally take over from their parents under certain circumstances. This process has been termed 'parentification' and 'adultification' (Oznobishin & Kurman, 2009; Puig, 2002; Titzmann, 2012). One teenager in Hall and Sham (2007: 25) said,

> Yes, you know... I cannot consult my parents all the time. The situation does not allow you to do it. I know what my parents want anyway. I took some decisions on behalf of them and they did not even know. I have trained how to deal with that kind of situation since I was seven so I have the confidence to make decisions. (Hall & Sham, 2007: 25)

In explicit child cultural brokering, it seems that children may be more in charge than their parents (Baptiste, 1993). This suggests that in taking over the responsibility and making decisions at their own discretion, child cultural brokers translate linguistically for their parents and at the same time amalgamate their understanding of the societal operations into their task performance.

Thirdly, explicit child cultural mediation may lead to role alteration and even role reversal, as a result of inevitable parental dependency and increased child responsibility (Chu, 1999; Portes & Rumbaut, 2001). As one parent in Kaur and Mills (1993) commented:

> In the Punjab, parents don't need to involve children in decision until they are much older. In England it is necessary to involve the children even when they are young, because there are some things that the parents don't know about. (Kaur & Mills, 1993: 116)

This suggests that children tend to facilitate their parents' entrance and adaptation to a new society, contrary to the traditional model of socialisation in which adults are assigned authority and privileges. Living in a new society and not mastering its language and culture, immigrant parents' pride and privacy are affected since they are not as self-reliant as they were in their own country (Abreu & Hale, 2011). According to Schieffelin and Cochran-Smith (1984: 15), brokering children tend to act as 'socializing agents'. In their study, children transmitted linguistic and institutional knowledge about the new society, e.g. in dealing with a variety of forms related to schools, jobs, medicine and tax. They also took the initiative in developing social resources and networks for their family. Thus, the socialisation sequence between adult and child appears to be reversed. In Suárez-Orozco and Suárez-Orozco's (2001) study, a Vietnamese refugee who arrived in the USA as a child commented:

...when we stepped into the exterior world, I was the one who told my mother what was acceptable and unacceptable behaviour... And even though I hesitated to take on the responsibility, I had no choice. (Suárez-Orozco & Suárez-Orozco, 2001: 75)

Thus, children's guidance may be significant for those who have little direct access to new practices in the dominant culture (Rogoff, 2003). In Nsamenang's words (1992: 137), 'children, not parents, are the ones who explain how the world functions'. Although parents may feel uncomfortable, ashamed and embarrassed about their children translating for them (Corona *et al.*, 2012), and may have a sense of frustration about not being undoubted mentors anymore (Chun & Akutsu, 2003), they may have to adjust themselves to the possible power shifts, power conflicts and role reversals.

In concluding this section on explicit cultural mediation, what must be said is that the various negative elements of the examples above should not obscure two important positive points. One is that most child cultural mediators operate sincerely and honestly for their parents, and that they make their parents' lives much easier. The second is that while the experience is stressful for some children, for others it is immensely rewarding. As a result of participating in family cultural mediation, children's language, cognitive and social skills may dramatically increase, along with achieving greater maturity more quickly than other children, and positive relationships have been found between levels of brokering, academic performance and social self-efficacy (Buriel *et al.*, 1998; Wu & Kim, 2009). It may also be very satisfying for the children whose self-esteem can be raised by knowing that they are helping their parents, for as one child said:

I feel I am useful. I can help my parents and that is a son's responsibility. With my peer group I can speak and understand two languages, so I feel I am better than my friends. My 'gweilo' friends also think I am clever because I can speak two languages. (Hall & Sham, 2007: 26)

These experiences may even contribute to greater family integration as they work together to understand their lives in a new society.

Implicit child cultural mediation

In the previous examination of explicit cultural mediation by children, I was able to support my writing at all times with many references to studies that were mostly specifically about child language brokering. However, studies on cultural mediation should go beyond linguistic translation in order to describe more accurately the unique and complicated role that children assume in immigrant or refugee families (Jones *et al.*, 2012). This has proved much more difficult for it is almost impossible to uncover studies that focus on what I have termed 'implicit cultural mediation', despite approaching many people working in related fields. Because of this, I want to approach my discussion of implicit cultural mediation in a different way. To a large extent, what follows in this section is hypothetical. Based on very limited evidence, I will be exploring what might be some of the significant features of implicit mediation, and in later chapters we shall see empirical evidence of what implicit cultural mediation looks like.

In a Canadian ethnographic study, Li (2002) portrays the home literacy practices of four new immigrant Chinese families to Canada. Li spent considerable time working inside families while studying how parents' literacy experiences, educational backgrounds and cultural values impacted on how they supported their children's learning. This study, although not setting out to examine cultural mediation, nevertheless describes some examples that might be associated with implicit cultural mediation.

Firstly, Li describes how all the parents wondered why homework was not given everyday and why the storybooks that were read at home tended to have no moral values. They were surprised to find that Canadian teachers had the freedom to choose the teaching materials, and often did not use textbooks, and that Canadian primary school children did not have many examinations. Secondly, although Yang's parents knew about the curriculum through the school newsletters, Yang's talk about school, his occasional work samples that he brought home, his school report cards and annual parent conferences, they thought this information too limited and too general. Yang's mother did not understand what to do even after reading the school newsletters. Although they did not understand why there were school activities such as a cake contest on Valentine's Day and Halloween traditions, the parents tried to work out their own ways of participating in the activities. For example, to enter the competition, they bought a cake instead of baking one, as they did not want their child to feel different and isolated from the other children. Thirdly, one father realised that as an approach to learning in the new system, his son did a lot of drawing at school; being unsure if this was a good practice, he did not encourage his son to draw at home. Another father doubted the value of drawing in literacy learning in the higher grades, although he thought it acceptable in kindergarten.

It might be asked 'Where is the child cultural mediation in these examples?'. They do not seem to show the children doing anything related to mediation, since all the children do is go to school like all other children, arrive home and talk about school like all other children, and the parents are sent official documents as all parents are with children at school. However, the parents of these children did not grow up in Canada, did not share the cultural capital of most native Canadians and, in particular, did not start with understanding Canadian school practices or the values, attitudes and beliefs that underpin Canadian schooling. The parents' own school and cultural practices did not fit in with their children's learning in the new system (Willett & Bloome, 1993). To Chinese parents, memorising and copying from books are considered the ways to acquire literacy; correct spelling, good pronunciation and standard grammar are viewed as important; students are expected to spend time doing homework and practical exercises, reciting and copying texts. From conversations with their children and from the school literature, etc., the parents did not observe these practices taking place in their children's schooling. What they were seeing represented something of a cultural shock as it contested most of their own beliefs about schooling and how children should be educated. The experiences of their children were mediating and influencing the parents' understanding of what counted as 'good education'. The parents may not have felt comfortable with what they were perceiving, and ultimately may not have changed their own beliefs, but they were nevertheless now attending to different notions of curriculum, delivery methods, textbooks, homework and evaluation. Like it or not, they were learning a lot about local social customs and practices as they related to schooling and childhood, and the principal conduits in this learning were their children.

For the parents, supporting their children in the new system was a learning experience for themselves (Li, 2002). However, in the families studied by Li, it was not only learning about schooling that resulted from these experiences, but also the language of the new land. One mother learned from her son, firstly, because she liked reading his books after him, and practising with him, since his books were children's books with everyday language, which made the mother feel that she was learning real English. Secondly, the son read while the mother listened and looked up any new words in their dictionary. After this, they took turns in reading and listening to each other. There are descriptions of the son correcting his mother's pronunciation in their taking turns at reading his Halloween storybook.

The parents in Li's study did have some knowledge of English, but this is not the case in many other immigrant and refugee families. McQuillan and Tse (1995) reported that immigrant parents often do not seem to have much effective communication with their children's schools. To start with, limited understanding of mainstream schooling may exacerbate their lack of confidence in using the majority language. Also, in some cultures, parents assume that educating their children is the teachers' responsibility. They see their own intervention in their children's education as inappropriate and disrespectful to teachers (Weinstein-Shr, 1995). Even when they may be keen to help their children succeed in school, parents can be puzzled or frustrated about how to do so. This frustration and confusion may cause a sense of isolation among parents (Delgado-Gaitan, 1994). Therefore, parents of school-age children may rely on their children to decipher communications from school (Weinstein-Shr, 1995), or to act as cultural mediators to help parents with the cultural and linguistic sophistication of schooling (Vasquez *et al.*, 1994). As Yang's mother admitted, 'most of what they learn about school is from Yang' (Li, 2002: 71). She got to know what Yang had been doing and learning at school from his explanation of his days, which was the most direct way for her to be connected with her son's schooling, and to link their home with school. Thus, the role of children in mediating not only school but also many of the values and customs associated with it, may be of great significance for parents in immigrant and refugee families.

In referring to Li's examples, it should not be thought that implicit child cultural mediation relates exclusively to schooling. Mediation pervades many aspects of everyday life, as will become evident in Chapters 5-7 of this book.

Visibility of child cultural mediation in family life

The characteristics of implicit cultural mediation become evident by comparing them with those of explicit mediation. The question that was considered earlier, 'Where is the child cultural mediation?', clearly relates to the visibility or invisibility of child cultural mediation. The examples above suggest that the visibility of child cultural mediation at the implicit end of the continuum is considerably lower than that at the explicit end, in that implicit mediation tends to occur in the course of everyday activities, often within home settings. Unlike the public occasions that involve a third party, implicit mediating events often occur in dyadic interaction between parents and children, and may thus be either visible only to them or even remain invisible to them. Although 'much interpretive work goes on behind closed doors in immigrant homes' (Orellana *et al.*, 2003a: 16) in conversations between family members, not all conversations will be goal oriented (Vasquez *et al.*, 1994) and visible. Consequently, the everydayness of the events obscures the significance of a mediating activity, or a child's mediation may be glossed over in everyday routine talk.

This relative invisibility also occurs because often the mediating events may not be clearly framed or marked by strong boundaries nor involve any language interpretation. While explicit mediating events are usually framed by time boundaries, place shifts and personnel changes, implicit mediating events are often deeply embedded in ongoing activities, and may remain subtle and intangible. In explicit mediation events, it can be clearly recognised that there are at least two clear purposes. The first is the overall and primary intent of the event, e.g. going to a doctor to be treated for an illness, or meeting with a social worker to gain a benefit. The second is equally clear to the participants: it is the facilitation of the event by the language and cultural activity and interpretation of a child mediator. In implicit mediation, the event in which the mediation occurs may still have a clear overall function or purpose, e.g. a parent and child arguing about whether the purchase of particular clothes is permissible or discussing what has been going on in school, but the cultural mediation may be unrecognised by both parent and child. To the parent and the child an argument or a discussion may be about whether clothing is appropriate or not, but in the process it is competing cultural values, beliefs and attitudes that are being explored, as the child brings to the debate his/her wishes to dress in the same way as his/her mainstream peers at school. As the child argues, so the parent is exposed to these different sets of values; the new culture is being mediated by the child, but neither she/he nor the parent may be conscious of this deeper meaning in the event.

Children's awareness of their own mediation

As indicated above, in explicit cultural mediation, the child may have a high level of awareness of most aspects of the event as she/he is having to think about how to move from one language to another and she/he is very aware of her/his social role in a triadic interpretation event. The limited school-related evidence from Li's study suggests that in implicit child mediation, the children may not even be aware that they are mediating and this might be the case across all implicit mediation, hence the choice of the word 'implicit' to represent the other end of the cultural mediation continuum from the explicit language brokering examples. In Li's examples, the child may simply be talking about the events and actions at school in the same way that all children do when parents ask 'What did you do in school today?'. These reports may comfort or disturb parents, but they convey information not just about schooling, but also about the new society's concepts of childhood, or many other aspects of the new culture. In many cases, these do not derive directly from the organisation or curriculum of schooling, but from the peer groups to which children are exposed. Li reports how one boy, as a result of his school peer-group interaction, became a pop fan and was familiar with the Spice Girls. Like his classmates, he collected hockey cards and popular stickers, and he even asked his mother to buy a particular cheese package that had these stickers. In all these cases, the boy is not setting out to mediate language or culture, nor is he aware of doing so, but the effect is that the parents begin to assimilate considerable knowledge about many aspects of the new culture.

Challenges for child mediators

In explicit mediation, the cognitive and social challenges for child mediators can be quite intense and highly demanding. As is suggested above and evidenced from Li, in implicit mediation this is much less likely to be the case. There are a number of reasons for this. One is that most implicit mediation occurs in homes within everyday family life and the only participants are likely to be the children and their parents. Thus, the social context is not one that is demanding for the children. Secondly, in implicit cultural mediation, the children are often not even aware that mediation is taking place; all they experience is the everyday discussions and arguments that occur between children and parents in all families. Thirdly, the areas being mediated are those which derive from the children's experience and knowledge, and do not normally demand that they use technical language or complex concepts, and are thus less cognitively complex. Fourthly, as events are not usually bounded by time, role and place frames as is often the case in explicit mediating events, there is often discussion across longer periods, topics get revisited, and at the same time several family members may work together in using reference sources or simply discussing topics (see Hall & Sham, 2007; Kibria, 1993; Vasquez et al., 1994). Lastly, in explicit cultural mediation there are often very tight goals for mediating events, while in implicit mediation the goal is seldom specifically to mediate; the cultural mediation may happen as a by-product of achieving other goals, such as children asking their parents to cook Western dishes and insisting on eating with forks and spoons rather than their hands (Kannon, 1978).

Parent–child power relationships

In looking at explicit mediation, it is clear that in many cases the children's role shifts from a subordinate one to a superordinate one; the parents become more reliant on their children than would normally be the case. Given what has been said in the preceding paragraphs, it seems likely that in implicit mediation the shift in power is less and, as in almost all normal family situations, more conventional parent/child power relationships are maintained. Much of the reason for this is that implicit cultural mediation is disguised; it tends to look like the events that occur in all families. However, in immigrant or refugee families, parents often find such events more confrontational than parents in mainstream families do. Prior to their migration, parents often have an unquestioned authority over their children not just because of their financial status, but because children may follow the traditional values such as respect for their parents and elders particularly in collectivism-oriented cultures. However, as children quickly take in new beliefs and values such as individualism, freedom seeking and equality in a Western society, so cultural conflicts may arise. Migration may lead to a decline in parental authority. As Hoffman (1989) points out, parents do not know the norms for living in the new society, and tend to be confronted by them through their children, often when demands are made that reflect the values of the new society. The awareness that their children are becoming familiar with the new culture, and the parent's wishes not to have their children embarrassed or humiliated, put the parents in difficult positions. They want their children to fit in, are aware that their children hold the knowledge of what is required to fit in, but are often uncomfortable with what is required. This puts parents in a position of having to trust their children and their doubts about the truth of what they are being told often lead to confrontations or disputes, as well as anxiety for the parents. Such confrontations are typical in all families, but the lack of cultural capital of immigrant and refugee parents makes it much harder for them to judge the validity of their children's claims. Thus, while implicit cultural mediation does not result in the same level of parental dependency as explicit cultural mediation, the issue does not go away.

The discussions in the two previous sections have principally sought to explore the ends of a continuum and again it must be stated that the exploration of the implicit end of the continuum is tentative. Nevertheless, this polarisation must not obscure the fact that there is a continuum and that at different times and on different occasions the degree of explicitness or implicitness will vary, but also that both may be present in any one event or series of events. However, for this book, the most important finding in this review of child cultural mediation is the almost total absence of research into implicit mediation.

It is the everydayness of these mediating occasions, the fact that there are no clear boundaries, and the fact that the cultural mediation may not be explicit, that probably account for most research into child cultural mediation within immigrant or refugee families being focused on explicit mediation, as in typical language brokering events. It is difficult to collect data that do not occur in clearly framed events, it is difficult to encourage participants to reflect on cultural mediation when they are not even aware that it is happening, and it is time consuming to spend long periods with a family on the off chance that an implicit mediating event will occur.

Yet, the analysis of implicit child cultural mediation suggests that it is much more frequent than explicit child cultural mediation, and that it occurs in all families, not just immigrant families. To some degree and in many different ways, all children are mediating changes in culture for their parents. It is no coincidence that parents almost always know more about many aspects of popular culture than do adults who are not parents. The big difference for immigrant parents is the lack of cultural capital relating to the new society. In these families, it is likely that implicit child cultural mediation plays a hugely significant role in the acculturation process, yet it appears to be the least studied and understood form of child cultural mediation.

4 Child Mediators and Their Families

As mentioned in Chapter 1, the six families who are the subject of this book were sojourners who had come to the UK initially for the purposes of work or higher education. Five of the families were new arrivals who had been living in the UK between six months and four years; the other family had lived in the UK for more than 10 years. The six families are the Yangs, the Tangs, the Zhaos, the Zhous, the Shis and the Lis, living in five towns within Greater Manchester, England. All the names given here are pseudonyms. My introduction to the child mediators and their families will include the parents' educational and occupational backgrounds, the children's education in both China and the UK, and the children's likes or interests and their after-school or weekend activities.

The Yang Family

The Yang family started their life as migrants in 1988 when Mr and Mrs Yang came to a British university for further study. They decided that they wanted to stay in the UK after their studies partly for personal reasons and partly because of the political changes in their home country at that time. Mrs Yang was offered a job, first as a systems developer for an information technology (IT) company in the north-west of England, and then as a computer officer permanently in the university where she had been a visiting scholar. Mr Yang had been working from home as a stamp dealer since the early 1990s. They both registered themselves as freelance translators and interpreters. Mrs Yang also worked as a freelance traditional Chinese music presenter. They moved to their mortgaged four-bedroom, two-storey house in a town near Manchester in 1992, where their sons, Fan and Hai, were born. Mr Yang's mother lived with them and she helped with the cooking. The three adults in the family looked after the two children, though Mrs Yang took the main responsibility for them and spent all her time with the children after she came home from work. Table 4.1 shows some of their personal details.

Table 4.1 The Yang family

Family	Age	Education level	Previous occupation	Years in Britain[1]	Current occupation
Hai Yang	5	Year 1, Britain	n/a	5	n/a
Fan Yang	9	Year 5, Britain	n/a	9	n/a
Mrs Yang	45	MSc in Systems Engineering, China	University lecturer	15	Computer officer, freelance translator and interpreter, Chinese music presenter
Mr Yang	57	MSc in Control Systems, China	University lecturer	15	Self-employed, freelance translator and interpreter
Mr Yang's mother	79	Secondary school graduate, China	n/a	5	n/a

[1]Years in Britain and age were recorded when the family first joined the study.

Both Fan and Hai loved playing computer games and they sometimes fought over their father's laptop when they were downstairs. One of their favourite computer games was 'The Age of Mythology'. Fan also played virtual online games via his computer and his mobile phone. They both liked reading, watching television, popular literature and movies such as Harry Potter and Lord of the Rings, stories about aliens and horror stories. Both children were in the top group in their class and got on very well with their classmates. Fan was assessed as talented in mathematics and had started having maths lessons with Year 6 children when he was in Year 4. He has won several medals in maths since 2002.

On normal weekdays, the family members briefly met in the dining room for breakfast at about 8am and for dinner at about 6pm when they chatted about their day. Information also flowed unpredictably at other casual encounters between the boys and their parents. Their father often took his children to and from school, but Fan usually went to school and came home on his own, since the school was close by. The two boys attended the school's after-school clubs during the week, with Fan involved in the computer and football clubs and Hai in the singing and Spanish clubs. They did not return home until around half-past four on those days. During their time at home after school, both children practised their piano and played their computer games, surfed the internet or watched television, with their father nearby. When Mrs Yang came home, she read books from the school library with five-year-old Hai in both English and Chinese, and she kept an eye on Fan's homework should he have any. During the week, she drove the children to different activities such as swimming lessons, football sessions, scout and cub activities and sometimes birthday parties. During the weekends, the boys had private piano lessons at home and went to Sunday Chinese school.

The Tang Family

The Tang family relocated from Taiwan in June 2002 because of a change in Mr Tang's occupation. The family lived in a house subsidised by his company and he drove a company car (Table 4.2).

Table 4.2 The Tang family

Family	Age	Education level	Previous occupation	Years in Britain[1]	Current occupation
Liang Tang	5	Year 1, Britain	n/a	1	n/a
Ming Tang	8	Year 3, Britain	n/a	1	n/a
Mrs Tang	42	College, Taiwan	Primary schoolteacher	1	Dinner lady
Mr Tang	42	BSc Mechanical Engineering, Taiwan	University lecturer	1	Projects manager

[1]Years in Britain and age were recorded when the family first joined the study.

According to Mrs Tang, the whole family had to face up to massive differences in daily living for the first three months. The two children, their five-year-old son Liang and eight-year-old daughter Ming, went to the same primary school near their home. Mrs Tang stayed at home, as she had done in her own country over the last eight years, taking care of all the household issues and the children's education at home. At that time, Liang cried almost every day (according to accounts given by Mrs Tang and the language support teacher). His response may have been because he had never been away from his mother or gone to school or nursery of any kind. Ming, who had no school experience either, seemed to be settling in very well. She not only became a comfort to her little brother when he cried, but she also picked up English very quickly and excelled in class. In February 2004, the children transferred to a Catholic school that had both infant and junior levels. They both seemed very settled. Liang had become a popular playmate among his peers, and Ming participated in the community football team, football becoming one of their main leisure activities. For some reason, the family did not have a television even when they were in Taiwan. If requested by the children, Mrs Tang would rent discs of popular programmes to play via their computer.

One common practice of the family, which they did in both Britain and Taiwan, was to go to church on Sundays because both parents were Catholic. The family had made friends with neighbours and people in the church. Mrs Tang was a volunteer at the church and other community activities. She invited the children's school friends to a party at their home, and the children also went to friends' parties during the year.

As Mrs Tang explained, the children were used to doing some coursework that she would set during term time and the holiday period. She had slightly different timetables during the school term and school holidays. During term time, all the 'learning activities' were done between about half past three and five in the afternoon. During the holidays, their learning sessions were in the morning after breakfast. This routine facilitated learning at home between Mrs Tang and the children. During term time, after the children had returned from school and had a snack, they went to the study next to the kitchen, where they did exercises in English and maths before they went out to play football or to go cycling. As for the sources of these exercises, Mrs Tang bought activity books (e.g. the Key Stage 1 Level 3 activity book) from charity shops even though she did not really know what 'key stages' meant. For some writing tasks in the book, Mrs Tang encouraged the children to do the same topic. Her rationale for doing this was that both children created different versions of the same task, which was interesting to her. There were occasions when Ming role-played a teacher for Liang, e.g. he designed maths problems and checked the results for Liang. In addition, the children read books from the school or the local library. Since June 2004, they had been going to a private tutor for piano lessons, so they spent about 15 minutes every day practising on their newly bought second-hand piano.

Both children loved playing the piano, and reading and writing in English. After two and a half years in Britain, both children had become very fluent in speaking English and quite accurate in spelling and writing. They played at being writers and selling books to their parents, and earned a lot of pocket money in this way. According to their school reports, both children were excellent in their academic achievements.

The Zhao Family

The Zhao family moved to Britain because Mr Zhao was promoted to branch manager by his company based in Taiwan. Being subsidised by the company, the Zhao family rented a three-bedroom house in a small town and drove a company car. Mrs Zhao took care of all the household issues and looked after her son Lin since Mr Zhao had to travel a lot on business. She did not enter employment until she had been trained as a language support teacher (Table 4.3).

Table 4.3 The Zhao family

Family	Age	Education level	Previous occupation	Years in Britain[1]	Current occupation
Lin Zhao	4.5	Year 1, Britain	n/a	4	n/a
Mrs Zhao	38	College. Taiwan	Air stewardess	4	Support teacher
Mr Zhao	41	BSc Mechanical Engineering, Taiwan	Department manager	4	Branch manager

[1]Years in Britain and age were recorded when the family first joined the study.

Lin went to a private school in a small town, where the class was very small. Unlike the children of the other families in this study, Lin was regarded as a slow student in his class and was put in a group that, according to the class teacher, needed encouragement and help to finish their work. Lin did not speak much in school, though he understood well. It seems that he did not have many friends at school and only occasionally invited his classmates to his home. Lin did not like drawing, colouring or music, but he loved playing with different kinds of toy vehicles; almost all the stories that Lin told his parents were related to vehicles. Lin's parents had high expectations for him and helped him with his spelling and reading at home in order that he would measure up to the teacher's high requirements.

Lin did not go to after-school clubs or anything other than the Sunday Chinese school. He stayed at home with his mother most of the time, doing the coursework from school every weekday and reading children's books in both Chinese and English. At home, his parents spoke Mandarin primarily, but Lin spoke more English than Mandarin. He talked a lot before going to sleep, and according to his mother, this was his 'story-time', when a lot of information flowed from him to his mother and sometimes to his father.

The Zhou Family

The Zhou family came to the UK because Mr Zhou got a job as a research associate in a university in the north-west of England. He had done his postdoctoral study in a Hong Kong university the year before. Mrs Zhou, along with her five-year-old daughter Hong, joined Mr Zhou later, in 2002, when he had settled into a house near the university. Even though Mrs Zhou had worked as a university teacher in China, she could not find a job using her previous skills because, according to Mrs Zhou, her spoken English was poor. She looked after the family and the household, she had a part-time job in a hotel and learned English in a local college four hours a week. She learned to drive in England and collected her daughter from school and her husband from the university every day. The general information about the family is shown in Table 4.4.

Table 4.4 The Zhou family

Family	Age	Education level	Previous occupation	Years in Britain[1]	Current occupation
Hong Zhou	5	Year 2, Britain	n/a	2	n/a
Mrs Zhou	35	BSc Mechanical Engineering, China	University lab assistant	2	Part-time hotel staff
Mr Zhou	38	Master in Mechanical Engineering, China	University teacher	2	Research Associate

[1]Years in Britain and age were recorded when the family first joined the study.

The family shared a three-bedroom house with another overseas student. Hong sometimes spent a short time in the common living room downstairs, watching television while Mrs Zhou prepared dinner in the kitchen. Hong also liked going to the supermarket and bookstores with her parents. Feeling that after-school time was being wasted since Hong's school did not give homework, her parents bought some books related to school coursework in English and maths. On returning from school every day, Mrs Zhou arranged for Hong to do a certain amount of work from the books they had bought, and to write diaries in Chinese and in English about her school day, as well as doing some reading from school. Mrs Zhou corrected Hong's spellings and monitored her neatness in writing. Routinely, Hong and Mrs Zhou spent about an hour reading and writing each day. Hong did not go to any after-school clubs during the week but she went to a dancing school and Chinese school at weekends.

At school, Hong was very active in the classroom and in the playground. As Hong was able to work on her own, she sat in the 'yellow' group who, according to the class teacher, were best in maths and quite good in literacy. Having been in Britain for two years, Hong understood English very well, and her English had become more fluent than her Chinese. She got along very well with her schoolmates and the teachers, and her best friend was an English girl in the year below. They liked playing games such as play house and hide-and-seek, together with other children at playtime.

The Shi Family

The Shi family came to the UK in September 2000 when Mrs Shi started her Master of Business Administration course at a university in north-west England. After her first degree, she had worked for 10 years in a college in China as a teacher of Economics and ran her own business with her relatives in her spare time. The family drove their own car in China. After Mrs Shi had successfully completed her postgraduate study two years later, she got a job in an import/export company with a five-year work permit. Gang Shi, her six-year-old son, joined his mother when she was about to graduate. They shared a house with other Chinese overseas students near the university in an inner-city area. Mr Shi had travelled several times from China before the family eventually reunited and started their project of buying a new house in a small town, where Mr Shi set up a joint venture restaurant with a Chinese friend. Gang went to a local primary school that had a good reputation, which was one of the reasons for the family settling in that area. The whole family spent Christmas 2003 together in their new house, with their first Christmas tree decorated by Mrs Shi and Gang, who had strongly requested this. The general information about the family is shown in Table 4.5.

Table 4.5 The Shi family

Family	Age	Education level	Previous occupation	Years in Britain[1]	Current occupation
Gang Shi	8	Year 3, Britain	n/a	2	n/a
Mrs Shi	35	BSc Business Administration, China; MBA, Britain	College teacher	3	Shipping manager
Mr Shi	35	Diploma Commerce, China	Department manager	3	Restaurant manager

[1]Years in Britain and age were recorded when the family first joined the study.

Mrs Shi looked after Gang's education and most of his daily activities. Gang preferred spending more time with his mother than with his father who disciplined him very strictly. Mr Shi's English was more limited than Mrs Shi's. According to Gang, his parents sometimes asked him the meaning of new words, as his own English was much better than theirs.

Gang was at the preschool stage in China and started his Year 2 primary schooling directly on coming to England. He developed his English by being entirely immersed in an English-speaking world. Mrs Shi did not do much to help Gang's English except to read books from school with him. Even though she used English in her job, she did not think her own English (particularly pronunciation) was good enough to teach Gang, and she wanted to avoid as much confusion as possible. Gang's English progressed so much that his level of spoken English soon went beyond that of his mother. When he was in Year 3, he was able to read English books on his own and became a conscientious reader.

Although Mrs Shi depended largely on school for Gang's English development, she took her own initiative to keep and develop Gang's Chinese language. On coming to the UK, she brought the maths and Chinese textbooks that were currently used in China and pushed him to do a certain amount of coursework from these textbooks. On weekdays, there was usually an hour in the early morning and half an hour in the evening before dinner, when Mrs Shi and Gang spent their home time together; this time was usually accompanied by Gang complaining about too much work, and ending up with a compromise between them. On Monday evenings, they usually did homework from Gang's school together. Gang was allowed to play computer games only during the weekends and holidays, and so he got up much earlier than usual on Saturday mornings.

Interested in a variety of subjects, Gang took part in after-school clubs, learning to play the guitar and French, and sing in a choir. During the weekends, he went to a private tutor for piano lessons, and he also did swimming lessons, Chinese school, and sometimes horse riding or a Chinese martial arts training session. His mother tried her best to benefit Gang in different ways; for example, she booked a trip to Egypt after Gang learned about Egyptology at school. Gang was easy-going and sociable, and had many friends at school; he liked playing football as many British boys do. At the beginning of Year 4, with a new Chinese boy Hao Li (one of my most recent participants who will be introduced later in this chapter) joining his class, Gang became a helpful friend to the new boy, particularly when the teacher failed to make herself understood.

The Li Family

The Li family came to Britain with Mrs Li arriving first. She had worked as an assistant manager at a foreign venture company for 12 years in China. Coming to Britain, she worked part-time in a restaurant. As an outgoing and sociable lady, she took charge of the household, as her English was much better than that of her husband. Mr Li joined his wife seven months later, and became a chef at the same restaurant. He was very hard-working and did not speak much. The whole family spoke both Cantonese and Mandarin, but mainly Cantonese among themselves (Table 4.6).

Table 4.6 The Li family

Family	Age	Education level	Previous occupation	Years in Britain[1]	Current occupation
Hao Li	9	Year 4, Britain	n/a	0.5	n/a
Mrs Li	33	BA Public Relations, China	Assistant manager	1	Counter assistant
Mr Li	40	High school diploma, China	Car dealer	1	Chef

[1]Years in Britain and age were recorded when the family first joined the study.

The Lis lived and worked in the same town as the Shi family in the north-west of England. Renting a terraced house in the town centre, the Li family used the ground floor as the restaurant and the first floor as their living area. Even though Hao had his own bedroom, the family of three shared the parents' bedroom as a living room which had the basic necessities for living. The room had a large desk, on which there was an up-to-date computer with a small, old monitor, and a big box of books and magazines mostly in Chinese. On the wall beside the desk hung posters, a Chinese calendar and pictures that Hao drew at home and at school. Pieces of paper with English words were hung on the doors of the wardrobe that stood near the desk. Hao was expected to learn these words by heart every day to improve his English.

Hao was in Year 3 of a primary school in a medium-sized city in south China. He read and wrote well in Chinese and liked drawing. He enjoyed playing computer games and football, and only learned the English alphabet in China. Relocating to England, he was placed in a Year 4 class, the same class as Gang Shi in the local primary school. Mrs Li tried her best to find time to help Hao with his English but sometimes did not do as much as she hoped due to the nature of the restaurant business. The common period of time during the day when Mrs Li and Hao were both awake was between half past three and half past five during which the whole family usually had dinner. Sometimes, Mrs Li would ask Hao to stay downstairs when the restaurant was not busy so she could help him with his homework. Aware of her lack of time, Mrs Li turned to three friends for help on different days of the week. They worked together with Hao on different days of the week to finish his homework assignments and to read books from school. In addition to doing work in English, Mrs Li asked Hao to keep doing coursework in the maths and Chinese textbooks. During his first months, Hao either did Chinese coursework or read some story books in Chinese when he was alone upstairs in his own room. He did not watch a lot of television, as he did not understand much English, according to him and his mother.

In spite of his limited English during his first three months of school, Hao did very well in maths because he had done similar tasks in China many times. He had two support teachers to help him with his English, one was a Cantonese-speaking lady who gave Hao three hours of support teaching a week and the other was an English-speaking lady who had an hour session helping him with his English separately from the whole class. At school, Gang Shi used to help Hao when the class teacher failed to make herself understood.

This chapter has provided vignettes of the six Mandarin-speaking Chinese families from whom I collected data for my study. The parents had different levels of knowledge of English and their proficiency in English allowed some of them to work professionally in the UK, e.g. as researchers in universities or engineers in companies, while others had manual and temporary jobs in the catering services.

What we shall see in the following chapters is how, whatever the language levels of the parents, their children were often able to help with understanding the society around them.

5 The Assimilative Level of Child Cultural Mediation

Living in a different culture from their source culture, migrant children and parents face challenges in adjusting to the new society; they have different kinds of exposure to the new culture and may achieve different degrees of acculturation. In terms of the positioning of bilingual children in the two cultures, although Weisskirch and Alva (2002) claim that they live in and, to some extent, are caught between two cultures, Harris (2006: 34) suggests that bilingual children 'inhabit a number of ethnic and cultural subcommunities which they articulate together in the flow of everyday life'. In Kenner's (2004: xi) words, 'these children live in simultaneous worlds rather than two separate worlds', and it is in the flow of their everyday life that children's mediation between their family/community culture and the mainstream culture takes place.

In spite of the variety of channels through which acculturation occurs, the parents described here draw extensively on their children. They also realise that while they may rely on their children for particular language-related knowledge, their children also offer assistance in the larger challenge of understanding a new culture. On my first visit to her family, Hao Li's mother said, 'learning the language is one thing, but learning about the culture is another. I feel my son will learn about the culture better than I do' (translated fieldnotes 12/09/04). Ming and Liang Tang's mother also wrote similar comments in her diary, which was requested by the researcher, stating even more explicitly: 'I learn about the English culture from my children' (translated diary 16/01/04). Therefore, it seems that the significance of children's cultural mediation is clearly recognised by their parents. Mediation, as a widespread common practice, happens frequently in everyday life in immigrant communities. However, to what extent does child cultural mediation affect family life? How does it impact on the parents' adaptation to the new country? What exactly is being mediated by the children? How does cultural mediation happen? These questions will be addressed in this and the following two chapters.

Hall's (1959) triad of culture analyses culture at three levels, technical, formal and informal, and child cultural mediation can be investigated in terms of these three levels. More precisely, what the children are mediating to their parents and its impact on the family's daily life and the parents' acculturation to the new society, can be analysed in relation to these levels. I will use the term 'assimilative' to refer to mediation at the technical level of culture, 'appropriative' to refer to mediation at the formal level and 'accommodative' to refer to mediation at the informal and conceptual levels (see also Guo, 2007; Hall & Guo, 2012). These terms seem to reflect the characteristics of the technical, formal and informal levels of culture most accurately and to encompass the occurrences of mediation in these families. Although the three terms may carry connotations of policy, they are not of relevance to the analysis here. The terms 'assimilation' and 'accommodation' stem from Piaget's classification in that assimilation does not lead to changes in quality, but in numerical accumulation, whereas accommodation leads to a fundamental conceptual alteration in one's schema. The term 'appropriation' originates from the sociocultural understanding that changes may occur while interacting with social partners in shared activities without stressing the type of changes (Rogoff, 1993, 1995). However, it should be emphasised that the levels of mediation are only loosely linked to Hall's three levels of culture, and that mediation at the assimilative, appropriative and accommodative levels does not strictly cover the technical, formal and informal cultures, respectively. That is, the technical culture may not be exclusively mediated at the assimilative level, but rather it may also be communicated across the appropriative and accommodative levels. Similarly, mediation at the accommodative level may entail elements of the technical, formal and informal cultures. The three levels of mediation and the characteristics of each level emerged from of my data, and Hall's terms are a useful starting point though not more, as we shall see in the detail of description of each level.

It will become clear, therefore, that an analysis of mediation according to these three levels serves a heuristic purpose and does not imply that they are completely distinct from each other. Nor does it imply that they always occur discretely. Indeed, all three levels may be found within one event, and it is more appropriate to view these levels as a continuum on which they may overlap and merge with each other. Although each level can be characterised by a number of attributes, some of these may be shared with other levels. For example, aspects of the assimilative level of mediation may be accompanied by those of the appropriative and accommodative levels. It is also likely that an event at the accommodative level may derive its source from assimilative mediation; for instance, a word that the parents learn from events at the assimilative level may lead to deeper changes at the accommodative level. The appropriative level of mediation may lay a foundation for accommodative mediation to happen. Thus, each level of mediation can be transformed into another, and blurred and overlapping transitions may exist between them in real life.

Nevertheless, as I shall show, these different levels of mediation can be characterised to a certain extent according to their collection of dominant attributes. It is according to these that I place each one on the continuum of cultural mediation, and it is, therefore, for the purpose of analytical clarity that I will discuss each level separately. It is important to note that as essentially analytic categories, these levels may not exist as a conscious reality. In the busy everyday lives of the families, mediation just happens at various spatial and temporal points in the middle of different activities where it is unlikely that the parents or the children realise what is going on. However, from a research perspective, the demarcation of the three levels provides a starting point for a better understanding of child cultural mediation in immigrant families. In this chapter, I will explore how the assimilative level of mediation can be understood and how it manifests itself in the families' everyday life.

Key Characteristics of the Assimilative Level

Three major characteristics can be identified in child cultural mediation that take place at the assimilative level. First of all, at this level, child cultural mediation happens in everyday life spontaneously, ephemerally and frequently within families. This type of mediation might almost be seen as incidental. Whenever parents and children encounter each other, a mediating event may happen, whether or not the participants are conscious of it; events at this level can happen at almost any moment during parent–child interaction, and do so frequently. However, due to their deep embeddedness within swift, ongoing and hectic daily lives, they can easily be overlooked. They are often of very short duration, and occur as momentary one-off events and this is why they are either almost unnoticed or can be swiftly forgotten and hard to recall as other events succeed them in daily interactions.

The second characteristic of mediation at this level is that instances involve mainly factual knowledge; for instance, the meaning of single words or specific facts that may have literal meanings and which might be found in dictionaries or manuals. The words are often what Halliday (1975) would term 'field vocabulary', i.e. specific language associated with particular domains of life. The facts are mainly straightforward, relating to historical, geographical and other types of knowledge about events, occurrences and places, such as that there was a man called Guy Fawkes, that there is a place called Hastings, or that Jews celebrate Hanukkah by lighting the nine candles on the Menorah.

Thirdly, this level is predominantly assimilative, hence the title I have ascribed to it. Originating from Piaget, the terms 'assimilation' and 'accommodation' distinguish between new knowledge that simply adds to a list of facts about an existing schema and new knowledge that leads to changes in conceptual understanding, which in turn leads to a modification of a schema. That is, assimilation tends to lead to quantitative accumulation, but accommodation leads to qualitative changes to or transformations of the existing conceptual structures (Greenberg, 2006). The term 'assimilation' is used at this level to represent perhaps its most fundamental characteristic: that the acquisition of facts from the events does not, in itself, result in significant conceptual change, but rather, the new knowledge or experience gained can be incorporated or fitted into parents' existing cognitive structures or schema about certain fields. For example, parents may learn from their children the English names of mathematical shapes or names of different plants without changing their understanding about the nature of the shapes and the internal biological processes of the plants. Thus, under the straightforward transmission of factual knowledge, the parents seem to be accumulating knowledge rather than radically and significantly changing their understanding of certain fields.

Spontaneity/ephemerality/frequency of child cultural mediation

Spontaneity

Events at the assimilative level tend to happen in very casual situations where children and parents are having conversations in the middle of other actions. Mediation appears to be so embedded within the conversations-in-action and to happen in such an 'all-of-a-sudden' way that neither the child nor the parent might realise that it is happening. There are numerous situations in which mediation happens spontaneously. At the breakfast table with the television on, the mother may be puzzled about some words from the morning news, and the child will tell her immediately what they mean. Mrs Yang learned what *talisman* meant when, one morning, Fan hurried back from school to fetch his talisman and claimed it was his *lucky charm* for his examination that day. When Ming and Liang told their mother about their school day, they had to explain what she did not understand. Mrs Tang may have forgotten that she had first learned the English expression *relay race* as Ming explained excitedly to her father about her sports day at school. On the way to their friends' house, as hailstones fell on Mr Yang's car, Fan's parents heard him exclaim 'hailstone', and thus learned how to name that kind of weather in English. At the lunch table during their holidays, Fan's parents were astounded when he explained a kind of British currency whose value was even less than a penny. At the Tangs', the teaching of football terminology and regulations frequently happened as they watched a match on television together at home.

All of these events just happened without any planning on either side, as can be seen from the following dialogue, which arose as Ming, Liang and their mother were going home from school in their car. While driving, Mrs Tang was asking about the children's school day.

Extract 1
Note: **M**: the mother, Mrs Tang; **G**: the eight-year-old girl, Ming; **B**: the five-year-old boy, Liang. The text in italics is the translation from Chinese.

B: Mum, a poet came to our school today, and he has got a book of poems.
M: Poem, *what it is like?*
G: Poem, **p, o u i m**, not **p o i m**.
M: Poem (repeating the word).
B: Poem, **p, o u i m**, not **p o i m**.
M: Poem (repeating the word).
B: not **p o i m**.

In the rest of their dialogue, their correction of their mother's pronunciation continued to occur now and then. It is at the moment when the children told their mother about the poet and poems, and the mother responded with some error, that the mediating act started. None of them was intentionally creating the occurrence until the children's critical ears caught the difference in their mother's pronunciation of the word 'poem'. The two children corrected their mother's way of handling three vowel sounds in the English word when they spotted that their mother only pronounced two of the three vowels. It is probably due to first language influence that it is difficult for parents to pronounce the three vowels together in one word. From the last turn of Extract 1, it is evident that Mrs Tang still did not pronounce the word correctly.

As the children speak English fluently in most cases unless required by their parents to speak Chinese, the children seem to provide for their parents a model of standard English pronunciation, which they pick up from school. As a consequence, receiving constant pronunciation input may raise parents' phonological awareness. This awareness appears important in parents' improvement of their English pronunciation, as the ways in which they pronounce certain sounds may have stuck in their minds for so long that they do not realise their mistakes until they are pointed out. Children's correction appears to be critical, since parents may not have opportunities to listen to and notice sufficient English themselves, even though they live in England. As Mrs Tang herself admitted, her children proved to be a direct audio guide to pronunciation and much more useful than her dictionary.

Ephemerality

From Extract 1, it seems clear that the spontaneity of mediation is accompanied by unexpectedness and ephemerality. That is, spontaneous events tend to be unexpected on both sides. They may occur just once, and pass by swiftly in the ongoing flow of everyday life, before either party becomes aware of them, so that, when asked, neither party can recall them. This can be exemplified from the following.

The event in Extract 2 happened in very informal and unexpected circumstances in the Yang family. This extract was part of the conversation at the dinner table when I was visiting the family (observation notes 14/10/04).

Extract 2

Note: The text in italics is the translation from Chinese.

Researcher: *The pine and the grass are really nice in your garden.*
Mrs Yang: *They were there when we moved here five years ago. Yes, they are quite good.*
Mr Yang: *We have to buy some tools to trim them when they grow too high.*
Fan: Dad, they are called conifer.
Mr Yang: *What does that mean?*

This extract suggests that the context of the parents' learning from their children occurs in an unexpected manner. None of the adults anticipated any comments from Fan. He did not appear to be listening to the adults' conversation, and Mr Yang did not know this word before his son uttered it, as he later admitted, although he guessed it might be the name of that kind of tree. Almost immediately after the short transaction between Fan and his parents, the whole family went inside for dinner and the conversation moved on to other topics. This suggests that eight-year-old Fan did not intend to teach his parents, neither did he realise that he was offering a new word to his father; however, for Mr Yang, remembering this new word may become easier with the child's timely contextual cues. It seems that children's spontaneous offering in their conversation provides parents with vivid contexts for language learning, yet such brokering events happen transiently without any planning or arrangements. In these kinds of implicit and unpredictable ways, parents tended to learn numerous words.

Frequency

Such mini events at the assimilative level may happen at any moment during daily parent–child interactions within the families, and they also occur frequently. For example, over a period of two weeks (10–25 February 2004), eight-year-old Ming Tang wrote in her diary 15 words, 2 doggerel rhymes and 1 game that she thought she had taught her mother. Mrs Yang recorded six instances of such events in her diary over a period of a week (21–26 September 2004). We should note that the frequency of these events has to be viewed in the light of the spontaneity and the ephemerality that I discussed earlier, i.e. many of the events may occur at an almost unconscious level, and these are what the parents and the children can recall and then remember to write down. It is, therefore, inevitably an underestimate of the number of times such minor events occur. In one of my own observations, I found a number of brokering incidents happening during a two-hour visit to Mrs Tang's home. When the two children came up to Mrs Tang at home time, Liang explained to her that he had got a sweet from one of his classmates because it was that child's birthday, giving Mrs Tang some idea of how a child celebrates his/her birthday in England. (The details will be explained in Chapter 7.)

Seated in the car, the two children were talking about the scores in a recent football season. From their conversation, Mrs Tang overheard how to say 'draw' in English when two teams in a game get the same score. At home, Mrs Tang learned how to say the names of animals when reading storybooks together with her children and when to say 'it' when playing a game called 'tag'. In the conversation at the dinner table, Ming told how one of her classmates' parents had grounded her because of her very bad behaviour. The discussion provided an opportunity for Mrs Tang to learn how to say the word 'ground', a new meaning for this word, and how some British parents use grounding to discipline their children. This suggests that the frequency of the mediating incidents at the assimilative level is high, and much higher than parents themselves can remember.

These types of occurrence are so frequent that they tend to become part of daily living. This suggests that learning from their children is a most convenient and direct channel for the parents. Some parents wrote in their own notebooks the words they learned from their children. Mrs Zhao wrote in her diary:

> Today while I was in the kitchen, Lin sat on the top of the sofa. Hanging his legs from there, he said to me, 'Mum, do you know what I am doing.' I said, 'what is that'. 'This is called dangling, you know?'. I immediately learned this word, much more quickly than I learned it in other ways. (Translated diary 12/01/05)

Similar to the events in Extracts 1 and 2, this event presents a good opportunity for parental language learning. It also suggests that children initiate brokering events with a better awareness of their own roles, which might result from frequent occurrences of mediation in the families. Briefly, these data on mediating events illustrate the point that 'countless exchanges, experiences and observations [are] accumulated in the routine ordinary intercourse of everyday life' (Harris, 2006: 34).

Factual Knowledge in the Process

What is also manifest from the previous illustration is that factual knowledge tends to be brokered in routine family activities, i.e. facts are mainly taught or learned at the assimilative level. They may comprise various kinds of knowledge such as historical or more linguistic items of field vocabulary and even child discourses such as *give me five, by the side, up above, you're in love, I am super, I am wicked* and *I am coolest man*. For example, when the families are strolling in the park, the children initiate the brokering by asking the parents if they know the names of blossoms, plants, trees or birds. When doing homework together, the parents ask their children about the names of different shapes in mathematics and thus get to know how to say them in English. Similarly, the parents get to know or recollect their own historical knowledge by asking their children.

Extract 3 shows how Mrs Yang learns historical knowledge from her son. The dialogue took place at the breakfast table on 1 April 2004, eight months after the family's trip to Hastings. I happened to be there for my observation since I had slept over at their house the night before. Their trip to Hastings was purely Fan's idea. It was his great enthusiasm for Hastings and his insistence on going there that enabled the trip to happen.

Extract 3

Note: **M**: the mother, Mrs Yang; **F**: the eight-year-old Fan. The text in italics is the translation from Chinese.

Turn/Interlocutor/Transcript

1 **M**: *What you mentioned yesterday, what, how many years did France and England fight, how many years?*

2 **F**: *116 years.*

3 **M**: *Who won, who really won?*

4 **F**: *The truth is, I tell you, England fought with France.*

5 **M**: *Yeah, really?*

6 **F**: *That is England wanted to control France.*

7 **M**: *Really? Englishmen wanted to control France.*

8 **F**: *Right.*

9 **M**: *Frenchmen wanted to control France.*

10 **F**: *Right.*

11 **M**: *That sounds Englishmen were not very reasonable.*

12 **F**: (giggle) *as a result, France drove Englishmen back to England.*

13 **M**: *The French drove away the English.*

14 **F**: Yeah.

15 **M**: *But when we went to see* Battle of Hastings, *wasn't that the French called* Norman *run up to, and won the Englishmen?*

16 **F**: Yeah, I know.

17 **M**: *Then how come was this?*

18 **F**: (laugh)

19 **M**: *This is before that, or after that?*

20 **F**: Mm, two or three hundred years later.

The first thing this extract illustrates is that there is often an explicit invitation from parents to their children to contribute knowledge that is helpful to the parents, and it is certainly the case at all levels of mediation that the construction of understanding may be cooperative as parents and children prompt each other. By asking Fan questions, Mrs Yang was trying to recollect her knowledge of British history around 1066 along with the period around the Hundred Years' War between England and France between 1337 and 1453. Fan was quite precise in telling his mother the length of the war (turn 2). My later inquiry revealed that Mrs Yang already knew about the Hundred Years' War, since Fan had told her something similar the day before, but that she was confused about the relationship between the Norman Conquest and the Hundred Years' War. Her memory of the invading side in the Battle of Hastings reminded her of the question about the invading side in the Hundred Years' War (turn 17), which was only answered with a non-verbal sign (laughter) from the child. Fan had convinced his parents at the end of the whole conversation (not shown above), that he had learned from his history class that there was a very famous battle in Hastings in 1066, and he learned about the Hundred Years' War not just from school but from playing his computer game 'Age of Empire' and reading a history book called *Horrible History*. Whatever the source of Fan's knowledge, the above extract seems to help Mrs Tang connect the two historical events together.

Extract 4

Note: **M**: the mother, Mrs Tang; **G**: the eight-year-old girl, Ming. The text in italics is the translation from Chinese.

Turn/Interlocutor/Transcript

40   **G**:   If you are inside the goal, you mustn't use hands; if you use hands, the ball will become the other team's.

41   **M**:   Mm.

42   **G**:   *Then you become a foul. Then you will* get a yellow card. *If you* get a red card, *then you won't play anymore, you have to walk away.*

43   **M**:   *Which one?* Red card, *then you can't play anymore; if you've got one* red card, *then you can't play.*

44   **G**:   *Right.*

45   **M**:   *[It]/just means* out, *just means* out.

46   **G**:   *If you get* a yellow card, *you continue doing bad things, you get a* red card, *if you do it again, just* foul people, *this* yellow card.

47   **M**:   *What* people?

48   **G**:   Foul people.

49   **M**:   what is {what is it?

50   **G**:   {push people over, trip people over, *in the middle* pushing people over, *he wants the* ball, *he is called* 'foul'.

51   **M**:   *This is called* foul. [He] *will* get a yellow card.

Parents' learning from their children may cover various areas about which children tend to have more knowledge. Mrs Tang learned about football terminology from her children. During one conversation, the children explained football terms such as *tackle, goalie, head the ball* and *foul* in a detailed way to their mother. On another occasion, the children, in response to requests from their mother, taught her what *penalty, free kick* and *corner* were while they were watching a football match. Both conversations are very typical of the way in which mothers accumulate their English vocabulary, gradually picking up cultural elements. The event in Extract 4 happened in the previous conversation when the children were reading with great interest a football magazine that their mother had bought them to share. Initiated by their mother, in the original full conversation there are 71 turns altogether, with Mrs Tang having 36 turns, Ming having 28 turns and Liang having 7 turns. Mrs Tang took 19 turns of questioning and another 13 turns of repeating the children's English. Nevertheless, it only lasted about 4 minutes. The children's turns are mostly answering or explaining, providing feedback and confirmation such as 'yes, right', as their response to Mrs Tang's previous turns.

In turn 40 of Extract 4, it seems that Ming is introducing a new topic of conversation, which not only arouses her mother's interest but also offers information. Her mother responds to this by asking questions on the basis of the information provided (see turns 43 and 47). She also repeats the information as her way of learning (turns 43 and 51). Getting to know the rules about the yellow and red cards, Mrs Tang encounters a new word *foul*, which was first introduced by Ming at turn 42 and was mentioned again at turn 48. However, Mrs Tang does not raise the question about this word until she hears it the second time. It might be the case that she did not catch the word when it was first uttered, or that she only had time and opportunity to ask about it during the consecutive turn-takings. At turn 50, Ming provides an apt description of what a *foul* is, by paraphrasing in simpler English and code-switching between English and Chinese in order to get it across to her mother. Speaking more English than her mother does, Ming switches to English when it comes to anything related to the topic of football even though there are Chinese equivalents for these words. It may be the case that Ming did not know the Chinese words or that she felt more comfortable using English words for these football terms because it was in English that she first heard them. While the code-switched conversations (Baynham, 1993) between English and Chinese may help develop Ming's Chinese, she also seemed to be providing English language input for her mother.

The research on language learning has established that a high frequency of input leads to acquisition of both first and second languages (Duran, 2003; Gathercole *et al.*, 1999). We can note here that Mrs Tang's English words were mostly repetitions of those spoken first by her children, suggesting that there is an effort on Mrs Tang's part to assimilate these terms into her language and knowledge repertoire. Mrs Tang may not offer any other responses, but just repeat what her child tells her, and straightforward acceptance may not generate further discussion. However, when parents ask further questions about the pronunciation, spelling and/or meaning of words, more clarification from their children may lead to further discussion. When the above conversation happened, the family did not have a television at home and the children appear to be the only source of this knowledge for their mother. She said that the basic knowledge she got from her children helped her understand more about football and enabled her to make better sense of football matches, and she also found herself more aware of important matches that her children would be interested in.

Assimilation in polysemic events

The previous extracts suggest that children transfer different types of factual knowledge to their parents in everyday situations. The transmission may not cause any conceptual change in the parents' knowledge repertoire. This is one of the main attributes of the assimilative level of mediation. It suggests that parents tend to accept what is being mediated by their children with little disagreement, and may apply the knowledge learned from their children to different contexts. However, as noted at the beginning of this chapter, we can understand mediating events as located on a continuum. That is to say, learning of factual knowledge at the assimilative level may be accompanied by discovering the deeper cultural meaning of a social phenomenon, as the following example shows.

Ming's parents learned the word 'idol' from Ming and Liang attending a school activity based on a television programme called 'Pop Idol'. Since the family did not have a television set at home, they did not know about the programme 'Pop Idol'. A school letter came home, saying that those who wanted to participate in 'Pop Idol' could put their names down and take their music cassette to school. Lack of the related cultural knowledge and not knowing exactly what to do after reading the letter compelled Mrs Tang to start using her own previous experience and imagination (see Li, 2002, for similar examples). Mrs Tang thought it was like a singing contest as a child had to enrol first to sing a song. She therefore taught the two children to sing two Taiwanese children's songs 'Mum's eyes' and 'The cart is running fast', because it was close to Mother's Day, which, Mrs Tang assumed, was the point of the activity. However, when they went to watch it, they were very shocked to see many other children wearing heavy make-up and elaborate clothes, singing rock and roll or pop songs, while Ming and Liang went up to sing children's songs. Both parents were so embarrassed that they wished they had not been there watching. However, the result of the activity was not too bad since the children got certificates for their performances. This event left a deep impression on both parents. Later, they understood that it was just an entertainment activity that related to popular culture within a school. However, what confronted the parents and clashed with their cultural values was the association of such a popular cultural practice with school contexts, which probably never happened in their home country, and thus they learned not just the words but also something about British schooling.

The lesson of 'Pop Idol' made such an impression on the parents that they remembered the word 'idol' from then on. After learning it from this activity, Mrs Tang attempted to use it in other situations. The three turns in Extract 5 show that she used the word 'idol' when talking to her children about their favourite footballers.

Extract 5
Note: **M**: the mother, Mrs Tang; **G**: the eight-year-old girl, Ming. The text in italics is the translation from Chinese.

M: *who is your that* idol? *who is your that* idol?
G: *What is* idol?
Here is a one-second pause since the girl did not seem to understand her mum.
M: *Your* pop idol, no, *your* football idol,
Mum bursts into laughter. Both Mum and the children laugh.

This again suggests that the assimilative level of mediation may add more items to the parents' knowledge repertoire but may not lead to conceptual changes. However, a mediating event at the assimilative level may have multiple meanings, and thus allow it to be entwined with the other levels of mediation, as we shall see in Chapters 6 and 7.

Three issues emerged from these examples: the relation to classroom discourse, the reciprocity of scaffolding and the boundedness of events at the assimilative level.

The relation to classroom discourse

At the assimilative level, words or facts tend to be explained explicitly by verbal means such as questioning and answering or feedback. Different from the conventional learning direction from parents to children, it is apparent that the parents receive pieces of knowledge from their children, just as students do from classroom teachers. But to what extent is the conversation similar to or different from classroom discourse? Extract 4 suggests that the conversations between Mrs Tang and her children appear to be learning experiences for the mother. She used questioning and repeating to initiate and respond to the children's answering. Ming then provided confirmation feedback such as *right, yeah*. At first sight, the whole process appears to be similar to the initiate–respond–follow-up (I-R-F) model (Coulthard, 1985) of classroom discourse. However, in a classroom, the teacher who elicits the pupil's response usually knows the answer to his/her own questions, whether open or closed. The follow-up that the teacher gives tends to be evaluative, such as confirmation, comments like *right, good, excellent* or other feedback such as correcting the pupil's answer. The conversation between Mrs Tang and Ming here seems different from traditional classroom talk.

Firstly, Mrs Tang does not know the answer or the exact answer to her own question. Although her questioning might be seen as her deliberately leading the child to say more about the topic, she admitted that it was not until the moment of their conversation that she knew most of what the children were talking about. Her questioning in Extract 4 was intended to achieve her aim of acquiring more knowledge about the sport. She admitted that all her knowledge about football, particularly the English terminology, came from her children. She asked the questions because she really wanted to get more information about football as her children were fascinated by it and she was keen to have as much shared language as possible with her children. Thus, the questioning is led by Mrs Tang as a learner rather than in the more traditional role she may have had as a teacher of her children. Thus, a form of role reversal takes place.

Secondly, children who responded to the question knew more about the topic, in contrast to the situation in the classroom where the teacher knows more than they do, or in traditional settings where the adult/parent knows more. However, here, Mrs Tang does not know if the children's answer was correct or not, nor does she have any way of checking it. She just has to accept it. Nevertheless, her children check if she has understood the information they provided. She seems to stand in the position of a student in the classroom, who depends to a certain extent on the teacher, but here the 'teachers' are her children. Unlike in classroom interactions, the children do not expect any correction from their mother, the adult. All in all, it is the children who provide the information, answer the questions and correct the information, i.e. they follow the IRF model like a class teacher, while the parents play a subordinate learner's role, detached from their usual position of authority. This differs completely from the normal model of learning that happens between parents and children, and the conventional role patterns of parent and child are subverted.

The reciprocity of scaffolding

From a sociocultural perspective, the conversations between parents and children may be seen as joint activities in which scaffolding takes place

As previously explained in Chapter 2, scaffolding refers to the provision of adult help within the child's proximal zone of development in the context of adult–child interaction. It can also be understood as guidance and collaboration that more experienced adults or teachers provide for children or learners in classrooms. The event occurring in Extract 4 challenges the mechanism of scaffolding in the conventional sense. In the conversations between parents and children at home, scaffolding is set up by the children. For example, in Extract 4, Ming helps her mother to understand what *foul* is by paraphrasing the word in various ways. This highlights the possibility that scaffolding is not only generated by adults, who are conventionally viewed as the more experienced partners in shared activities, but also originates from children, who are generally considered less experienced than their adult counterparts in many ways. There exists a 'bi-directional' and 'reciprocal' way of scaffolding in the adult–child interaction (Li, 2002; Ma, 2004), which in effect means that such events are co-constructed. As discussed in Chapter 2, Rogoff (1990) points out that children, from their earliest period of life, are active participants in their social and cultural activities, and children take different degrees of responsibility in shared activities. This study suggests that reciprocal scaffolding emerges when the child's (language) skill is higher than that of the adult and where children have more knowledge and better understanding than their parents do. That is, there are moments when bidirectional or reciprocal scaffolding comes into play in child cultural mediation for their parents.

The boundaries of mediating events at the assimilative level

Most of the events explained at the assimilative level tend to happen in an unpredictable manner, emerging from everyday family situations and embedded within the routines of family life. For parents and children, the boundaries of these occurrences may be blurred or even invisible in the 'messiness' of everyday family life, so that it is difficult for participants to discern the start and end points. Immersed in their activities, they are not thinking about such boundaries in their interactions. For the researcher, it is equally hard to discern boundaries but, as the boundary itself is an artificial construct and is subject to purposes and circumstances, the researcher may have to define and apply the boundary according to a certain research context. Thus, the notion of a mediating event is, in most cases, an artefact of the analytical process and may be unrecognised as such by the actual participants. This is, of course, the same for all levels of mediation.

To summarise this chapter, acts of mediation at the assimilative level arise from the rapid convergence of a number of eventualities. In spite of the short duration of the mediating process and the unexpectedness of the knowledge to be mediated, child cultural mediation at the assimilative level happens with high frequency. During the process of the families adjusting themselves to the new society, any assistance from the children may be timely and helpful. In other words, though events at this level may be spontaneous, transient and oblivious, they are frequent and ubiquitous in families' everyday life.

In spite of its ostensibly modest effects, the assimilative mediation is informative and meaningful to parents' gradual integration into the new community. Within the seemingly simplistic exchanges, parents gradually accumulate their linguistic and cultural knowledge. Parents learn new words and activate old receptive words in their repertoire and may become more engaged in some activities, such as watching football matches with their children, and further enrich their cultural experiences. These mediating occurrences are invaluable for parents and become part of everyday life in these families. Although most of the events at the assimilative level do not change parents' conceptual schema or attitudes, they are likely to have multiple meanings, some of which challenge parents' previous cultural values. In this sense, the assimilative level of mediation can be linked with other levels, which will be examined in the next two chapters.

6 The Appropriative Level of Child Cultural Mediation

As discussed in Chapter 5, the levels of cultural mediation tend to overlap, with the distinctions between them often blurred, and are part of a continuum. The assimilative level and the accommodative level may represent the two extremes of the continuum, with the appropriative level positioned somewhere across or between them. The appropriative level appears to oscillate between the assimilative and the accommodative levels, floating between the two ends that they represent as we shall see below.

Key Characteristics of the Appropriative Level

The appropriative level of mediation can be identified as having four main attributes. First, the term 'appropriation' means 'taking something that belongs to others and making it one's own' (Wertsch, 1998: 53). It suggests that individuals apply what they have learned to practice in ways that might be different from the original form. In Rogoff's (1993, 1995) work, the concept of appropriation refers to how individual social partners change through their interaction with each other in different sociocultural activities. She argues that changes seem to occur while people are participating in shared activities, i.e. 'participation is itself the process of appropriation' (Rogoff, 1995: 151). In this study, parents participate in their own ways in activities that take place in the new society and make changes in the process. They only participate to meet their children's requests or demands, without fully understanding of events.

Secondly, mediating events at the appropriative level tend to have a greater effect on families' lives in the new society than do those at the assimilative level. Unlike the spontaneous and ephemeral events at the assimilative level, what is being mediated at the appropriative level happens in an ongoing manner and may have accumulating effects. Instead of being a one-off, a mediating event at the appropriative level will have a number of instances, which occur over a period of time. Thus, parents do not just remember what the instances are about but they may also gain a better understanding of the event at each occurrence. Despite some events at this level generating information of the kind seen in the assimilative level, events at the appropriative level tend to have a more powerful impact on parents; this level of mediation is more complex than the assimilative level.

Thirdly, mediating at the appropriative level may confront or challenge parents and cause uncertainties, confusion, tension and ambivalence; events at this level almost always elicit a response of some kind, often either change or resistance. What is being mediated at this level is not simple fact or terminology, but things that have the potential to become significant issues for parents because they bring the parents face-to-face with deeper-level cultural conceptions. They meet these through the experiences and views of their children who are accommodating swiftly to the new culture. It is at this level that the children's accommodation can become problematic for parents who may find the cultural assumptions underpinning their children's requests and demands, or those of the agencies with which children are associated, challenging their own deeply held cultural beliefs.

Fourthly, given these complex feelings produced in parents, we cannot rule out the possibility that the appropriative level of mediation may open up a path to accommodative changes. In other words, recurrent mediating instances may offer parents constant access to their embedded meanings and motives. Thus, even when parents make some alterations to their daily arrangements simply to suit their children's proposals or ideas, they may well come to appreciate the more profound significance of these changes and embrace them. Mediating events at the appropriative level may offer the potential for accommodation, to which we shall turn in Chapter 7.

Examples of the Appropriative Level of Mediation

Poppy Day

As part of the education that schools in Britain offer, they tend to integrate significant national events into both their curriculum and extracurricular activities. Although parents themselves may have access to such events from other sources, they are often brought into direct contact with them through their children's experiences at school.

As a symbol of Remembrance Day – on 11 November each year when the dead of previous wars are commemorated – red paper poppies are widely sold and are pinned to one's clothes. Parents new to the country may not know why many people wear a small, red, paper flower every

November; why it is this little red flower rather than any other flower; or even what people call it in English. In the Tang family, when Ming brought home a poppy of red paper that she had made during her art lesson at school, Mrs Tang did not know what it was called. She admitted that she had never bought any poppies since coming to England. She said, 'I have never seen a Chinese wearing a poppy since I came here' (translated fieldnotes).

I happened to be observing in Hai Yang and Fan Yang's classrooms on 3 and 11 November 2004. On 11 November 2004, at 11am sharp, the whole school observed a two-minute silence. Glancing at Hai, I noticed that he still wore a smile for the first second but suddenly his facial expression changed. His immediate shift into a serious expression almost made me laugh in the silence. The school's other related activities started much earlier. On 3 November, during the last 20 minutes of school the junior children on the school council carried a collection box into each classroom, collecting money in exchange for poppies. They were selling them at 20 pence each and the money went straight into the box. The children who had bought poppies pinned them on their sweaters, with the teacher's and my help. Hai did not do anything but watch since he had not brought any money with him. Five minutes later, another boy who had bought two poppies, pinned one onto Hai's sweater. The class teacher told them:

We buy the poppies to remember those who fight and die for their country. The seeds of red poppies grew everywhere in the mud of the trenches at the battlefields.... Money raised by selling poppies will go to the Royal British Legion and they will look after the money. So 11 November is a special day to remember. There will be national services ... *(inaudible)* all over the world. (Classroom observation fieldnotes 3/11/04)

When Hai's mother came home that day and saw the red poppy on his sweater, it became a topic of conversation.

M: Hai's mother; **H**: Hai. Note: words in italics are translated from Chinese.
M: *How do you have a* poppy?
H: Adam *gave it to me, it's* free. *Tomorrow I want to buy another one.*
M: *How come is the use of* poppy, *I still don't know.*
H: *In the* trench, *there is* Yuk mud, *nothing grows but only* poppy *grows,* and poppy is pretty.
M: Ah, *really.*

Hai used what he had learned from school, particularly the piece of information about *trench*, but in his explanations he had created two of his own reasons, one was *in the yuk mud only poppy grows*, the other was that *the poppy is pretty*. Simpler than the teacher's explanation, Hai has added his own imagination to his explanations. Although children may mediate cultures, they often have only partial knowledge and the result may sometimes create more confusion than understanding for parents.

At first glance, this seems to be an assimilative event; after all, Hai's mother had little more than some factual information about the poppy, and it did not last very long because immediately after the above transaction, their conversation switched to the topic of Hai's reading book for that day. However, the significance of this event is its potential for a change in understanding. While Poppy Day in the UK marks the end of two major wars, Chinese parents bring some background of national reminiscences from their own culture, such as 1 August, which commemorates the foundation of the People's Liberation Army in mainland China, or 10 October when Victory Day and National Day in Taiwan are celebrated. Thus, in some ways, Chinese parents can understand why such an event in the UK is highly significant culturally. However, children's mediation seems to confront parents with their non-identification with the new society. When such an event takes place annually, parents' identification with the majority is repeatedly challenged. As migrants living in a foreign country, these Chinese parents may not have assumed the same national obligation as the local English people. In other words, their identity as Chinese people living in England might have been questioned and pondered over and again each year. One year, Mrs Tang wanted to buy a poppy, but eventually she did not, as she thought that she might look strange because mostly English people wear them. Thus, unlike most of the mediating events that occur at the assimilative level, which may be obliterated in the bustle of everyday life, mediation at the appropriative level tends to produce more profound effects.

Fundraising at school

Another set of examples can be found in the parents' experiences of fundraising at school. One afternoon, Lin arrived home with a letter from his school soliciting donations for a school collection that would be donated to the 2004 tsunami disaster appeal. On one level, this was a straightforward appeal that, given the publicity around this event, would have been easily understood by the parents. However, the school made it rather more complicated because instead of simply asking for a donation, they suggested or requested (for the mother perceived it as a request) that parents use a Smarties tube in which to place the money, probably as a way of involving children in the activity. Lin's mother had no idea what Smarties – a well-known sweet – were, but with Lin's guidance she went to a shop and bought a packet. It took her 60 twenty-pence coins to fill the tube. Although this was quite a lot of money to his mother, she still did it because, as she explained to me, she was concerned that children would compete with each other, she did not want her son to feel excluded, and it might not be good for her son if she did not respond to the school's requests.

The issue of fundraising appeared again, but in a form that was even more perplexing to the parents. Just before Christmas 2004, Gang's family got a school letter about a new activity. There were two requirements: one was to donate non-perishable goods purchased from a Marks & Spencer supermarket to fill a hamper that had been bought and was displayed in the school; the other was to buy raffle tickets in order to win the hamper. Through this activity, the school raised money for its resources.

The following extract comes from a conversation between Gang and his mother who was reading the letter.

M : Mrs Shi; **B**: Gang. Note: words in italics are translated from Chinese.
M: *What is this for? What should I do?*
B: *It is just a basket, the school will send it to* Marks and Spencer
M: *What do you mean? Can you be a bit clearer?*
B: Get all the jars from Marks & Spencer, which they washed for new goods.
M: *What thing is* Non perishable? *What should Mum do with it?*
B: *Get some* Marks & Spencer's *jars and tins, take them to school office, sell them.*
M: (She still looks unsure. The mother looked up in her electronic bilingual dictionary). Hamper *is a big basket with a lid; Raffle is getting lottery. Here at the bottom it says selling tickets, when doing raffling, is the prize going to be something of* Marks & Spencer *that everybody donates?*
B: (No response from the boy)

From the above extract, it is clear that Gang's mother did not understand what she should do in response to the school letter. The school seemed to have assumed that all parents understood what *hamper* meant. For Gang, it was the first time that he had come across this school activity related to a Marks & Spencer hamper, as he had just moved to this school from another area. Thus, he could not clearly explain to his mother what the underlying purpose was of this collection and raffle. From Gang's turns in the above conversation, it is clear that he himself did not understand it and he even gave his mother totally wrong answers, except to explain the meaning of *hamper* as a *basket*. Not having understood her son's explanation, she had to use her bilingual dictionary to look up the words *non-perishable, hamper* and *raffle*. However, even with the meanings of all three words, she was still not very sure about what she should do. As Ming's mother commented in a similar situation, 'I know every single English word *(in the school letter)*, but just can't make sense of what I should do with it' (translated fieldnotes). Later, Gang's mother told me that she bought two raffle tickets to satisfy the requirements mentioned at the end of the school letter. Not being very sure about what to do with tins and cans from Marks & Spencer, she did not buy any, but she guessed that they might be sent to poor countries in Africa since she remembered a similar activity in Gang's old school in another area.

The actual purpose of the activity was to raise money for the school, and as the activity proceeded, so this function gradually became clear to both Gang and his mother. The difficulty was not in understanding the notion of a raffle, but in understanding why the school needed to raise money. In China, most primary schools are fully funded by the national or local government and are supported by parents who pay directly for their children's textbooks, stationery and some educational activities. Thus, Chinese schools do not raise money indirectly from parents, nor do they raise money for the general use of the school. For the parents, it was something of a revelation that a school might need to solicit money for general purposes as they had assumed that British schools, like Chinese schools, were fully funded. In this way, an activity deriving from their child's experience in school confronts them with a cultural challenge. They would not participate in such an activity in China, nor did they feel confident enough to ask the school about the reasons for the activity, and relying on their child's testimony led to perplexity and confusion. Mrs Shi admitted that she had not thought that English schools had to raise money for themselves from students and parents. But after many of these activities, she gradually understood how and why such activities occur in English schools, and that it was considered part of the school ethos that parents contributed in many ways to the collective life of their children's school.

In both the above examples there is a strong assimilative element in that the parents are gaining quite a lot of factual knowledge about Poppy Day and school fundraising activities. However, both sets of events also have deeper cultural knowledge running beneath them. In the case of Poppy Day, it relates to British history and identity and ways of holding onto powerful collective memories. In the fundraising example, it could enhance knowledge about the place of schooling in British culture and how schools constitute themselves as a collective and caring community. However, these also offer the potential for a change in deeper-level cultural understanding. Although actual change may not necessarily take place, this powerful potential marks a move away from a simple assimilation of factual knowledge. In the final example, one mother began to understand how an activity that originated with her children actually had the potential for making her feel more of an insider at work.

Dr Who

This experience arises not directly from the children's schooling but from their participation in the wider context of children's popular culture (although this participation is certainly influenced by peer culture at school). Researchers (e.g. Marsh, 2004a, 2004b) have found that popular culture plays an important role in children's identity formation and peer and family relationships. Where children's popular culture is concerned, it is the children who are the experts rather than the parents (Mitchell & Reid-Walsh, 2002). In the Yang family, watching the television programme *Dr Who* had become a shared family experience. It was initiated by Fan, who had heard about it at school and wanted to watch it at home. For Fan, this was important, as being an insider at school demanded that he developed shared popular cultural reference points with the other children. *Dr Who* is the world's longest-running science fiction television programme and it has captured the imagination of at least three generations in the UK. As a result of Fan watching the programme, his mother became interested and used to sit with her children every Saturday evening. If, for some reason, one of the children was not at home, the programme would be recorded and watched later. Led by Fan, his mother became aware of its influence over his classmates' parents' generation. For instance, in each episode there are evil monsters that cause trouble so that the Doctor can display his bravery and authority. After watching one episode about the evil creatures called the Daleks (one of the Doctor's most famous nemeses, metal-cased mutants well-known for their exterminating battle cry), Fan told her that 'your webmail is called dalek, did you know?' 'Really?' his mother was very surprised. She went to check the address of her webmail and found that her son was correct. Actually, she always used to misspell this word whenever she checked her email at home, e.g. she tended to transpose the *a* and the *e*. After Fan drew her attention to this, she did not make a similar spelling error.

Relating to her job as a computer officer, she recalled many other web server names used in her department, such as Sontarans (a warlike evil in the story). Her curiosity drove her to ask her colleagues, who were in their late thirties or forties, about their naming system on their servers and she found that all the names derived from *Dr Who* characters. The consequence of the child's identification of the server names was that Mrs Yang developed a much better sense of belonging at her workplace. She said:

> We parents did not grow up in the UK, so we did not have the same kind of childhood experiences as Fan's classmates' parents in terms of popular culture. It is no wonder why I could not understand the chat between my colleagues sometimes. I don't have the same kind of knowledge background as my English colleagues. I am not British even though I hold a British passport. (Translated fieldnotes)

Thus, the child's interest in *Dr Who* seemed to enable his mother gain a deeper insight into some aspects of her workplace. She claimed that it helped her develop a more positive relationship with her job and her colleagues because she was able to participate in workplace conversations with a better level of understanding.

Complex Events from the Appropriative Level

This last event has moved from the assimilative to the appropriative level in that the mother's behaviour has changed (albeit in a limited way), and that she seems to appreciate the significance of what is being mediated and open to the possibility of acceptance, in spite of confrontation and challenges. In the next two more substantial examples, this move towards appropriative changes in behaviour is examined in more detail.

Pocket money

Pocket money is a weekly or monthly allowance given by parents to their children either unconditionally or for doing some work, and through which parents tend to socialise their children in monetary and economic matters (Furnham & Thomas, 1984). Pocket money can be a valuable way of helping young children start to understand money and to practice their ownership and spending of money, and it is also an important way to foster independence and decision-making skills (Spungin, 2006). How much pocket money is given to a child seems to depend on the family finances and the peer community. In different countries around the world, pocket money takes various forms. In the USA and the UK, some children are given pocket money in return for doing household chores. In Holland and England, children are encouraged to save at least some of their pocket money in a piggy bank or its equivalent. Pocket money can become a battleground between parents and children. The issues tend to focus on how much children get from their parents and what choices are legitimate for children's purchases with the money. Handling these issues properly can be a problem for native parents, and even more so for parents from cultures where there is no tradition of giving pocket money.

Chinese parents' experience of pocket money

The Chinese parents in my study did not have much experience of being given pocket money when they were children. Most of them did not receive pocket money regularly from their own parents as their needs were more often met as and when their parents thought appropriate. It is rare for children in China to receive a regular sum of money from their parents, as children do in some Western countries. There is one occasion when children get money from parents or other relatives as a gift, and that is at Chinese New Year. This is known as the custom of giving the red envelope to children. However, children cannot spend the money as they want to. Usually, they have to ask for parental permission before they can spend it. Some of the parents in this study recalled that they did not have ownership of their savings until they went to college or university. While in England, the Chinese parents may have heard about pocket money through friends or colleagues, but it is probable that the first time they really had to think about issues related to pocket money was when they were confronted by a request from their own children. This is very different from British parents, who tend to see pocket money as a natural or inevitable gift to their children, even if sometimes it is given reluctantly. However, it is one thing to be confronted by the demand for pocket money, it is another to work out how much children should get. Even British parents struggle to make decisions on the amount that children should be given, as there seems to be no rule about it. This is the case at least from my personal experience.

Children's request for pocket money

In British families, the pocket money practice tends to start with children in primary school or even slightly earlier. Like other British cultural phenomena, it is something that Chinese children hear about at school. It is inevitable that children exchange ideas about what to buy with money given to them by their parents and about how much they regularly get. Peer culture becomes an important motive for children in making requests to their parents for pocket money.

In the Yang household, the younger son Hai did not ask his parents for pocket money, even at the age of seven, so his mother was very happy not to give him any. However, she had started to give her elder son Fan pocket money at that age because of the strong request he had made. Fan may have become aware of pocket money issues from his classmates and realised how significant it was for his peer group. As with other situations where they relied on their children as a resource, the parents did not seem to have other reference points to help with the decision about the amount of pocket money to give, and therefore had to be guided by their children. As Mrs Yang commented,

> I don't know how much pocket money I should give to him and from what age shall I give pocket money to a child.... Fan told me that his classmates get fifty pence or one pound, and even two pounds a week. (Translated fieldnotes 13/04/03)

While Mrs Yang might have been able to check this information with other parents, approaching strangers and asking for personal advice may not have been comfortable. The information provided by Fan guided Mrs Yang in her own practice when dealing with this issue so that Fan would not find himself incompatible with his school peers. Mrs Yang was not only giving her child pocket money but she also seemed prepared to accept the possibility of increasing the amount. The pocket money she gave Fan started with 50 pence a week when he was in Year 3 (aged 7), increasing to 1 pound a week for a while and only rising to 2 pounds a week after he had finished Year 4. Although Fan had asked for a rise a few times during that year, his mother's reasons for not increasing the amount related to the family's expenditure on birthday parties and on going back to China or holidays. Later, due to Fan's request and the parents' acknowledgement of the possible need to contact him in an emergency, his mother bought him a mobile phone. The purchase package stipulated that the mobile phone was free on condition that the user (officially the mother) signed a 12-month contract with the mobile network and paid an equal amount of money every month by direct debit. It allowed the user to make a certain number of minutes of telephone calls or send a certain number of text and voice messages each month without extra charge. If these limits were exceeded, the user had to pay extra money. Fan and his parents made an agreement that he could use the mobile phone for his purposes, but he had to pay with his pocket money if he exceeded the limit.

The following three extracts are from a conversation between 10-year-old Fan and his mother on a Friday afternoon during a half-term break. The conversation happened when Fan's mother opened a telephone bill. It contained clear evidence that Fan had exceeded his free call allowance by a considerable margin. His mother could not stand this overspending particularly since Fan had lost his keys two weeks earlier. She summoned Fan, who was in his room upstairs, to explain the bill. Looking quickly at the bill, Fan realised that the cause was his computer game, Habbo Hotel, which he played online via his mobile with another unknown player. Although it was his mistake in exceeding the agreed expenditure, Fan defended himself vigorously, and we can see how Fan engaged his mother and got his argument across to her, step by step, in order that the outcome was favourable to him.

M: Mother (Mrs Yang) **F**: Fan. Note: words in italics are translated from Chinese.

Turn/Interlocutor/Transcript
20   **M**: *Fan, this money you must pay yourself,* £ 15.82.
21   **F**: *Mhm, I tell you, Mum, I don't want to argue with you, but because you forgot many many times* [to give him the pocket money].
22   **M**: *What many many times?!*
23   **F**: *That will be almost equal to this amount.*
24   **M**: *No, it won't be.*
25   **F**: *Yes, it will. When you should have given me ten pounds, you did not give me.*
26   **M**: *That ten pounds, last time the remaking of another key cost ah, ah, how much, 6 pounds, deduct it, is this right?*
27   **F**: *Is that 4 pounds a key?*
28   **M**: *I had two keys remade this time, in case you lost it again, 6 pounds for two, 6 pounds, then if we count that ten pounds, there should be 4 pounds left, right? This is* £ 15.82, *I won't count this 82.*
29   **F**: *That ten pounds is what it was a long time ago, after that there was something else.*
30   **M**: *What something else? No, there wasn't.*
31   **F**: *Yes, do you know, you are not being fair, there is still something else, the ten pounds I said is long time ago, the early of September, so.*
32   **M**: *Then, 6 pounds for the keys, and this 15 pounds, 21 pounds*
33   **F**: *Deduct that 10 pounds, then, there is another almost 10 pounds*

34   **M**: *According to what you said, there is another 11 pounds, right?*
35   **F**: *No, not right, not right! It is another 10 pounds after that 10 pounds, because you still did not give it to me. Right?*
36   **M**: *How come I am always forgetting another 10 pounds?*
37   **F**: *Mum, when I mentioned 10 pounds, it is long time ago. Then from then till now, there is another 10 pounds, do you know or not?*

When his mother had calculated his total expenditure and claimed that what Fan had spent on his mobile phone must be paid for by him, Fan unfolded his arguments by claiming that his mother was not giving him his pocket money on time. From turn 23, it seems that Fan had very swiftly done his own calculation, and was trying to persuade her that she actually owed him 20 pounds in unpaid pocket money. Fan was diplomatic by saying 'I don't want to argue with you, but...'. In turn 25, Fan seemed to lay a sound basis for his later argument, implying that it was not just once that his mother had forgotten. Seeing that his mother was not ready to admit that she might have made a mistake, Fan kept on explaining why she actually owed him money. It seems that his mother had to admit to one occasion when she forgot the money, but then reminded him of his recent history of losing his house key. Fan remembered clearly how much each key cost (turn 27), and virtually compelled his mother to explain how much money she had actually spent on having the new key cut (turn 28).

Between turns 29 and 35, Mrs Yang and Fan were doing different kinds of calculation. While Mrs Yang only counted once when she forgot to give him pocket money, Fan insisted over and again that there had been two occasions (turns 29, 31, 33 and 35) and he attempted to make his case more powerful by listing exactly when and how each occasion when she forgot had occurred. From turn 36, Mrs Yang was probably feeling somewhat browbeaten and appeared to move towards being persuaded by Fan's case. Furthering his argument in turn 37, Fan made a last but strong impact on his mother's memory, and almost forced her to give in. However, Mrs Yang suddenly seemed to think of something else that might win her whole argument (see the next extract with turns 38–55).

38   **M**: [pause for a second] *how about the last bill, you did not pay that either?*
39   **F**: *Last time, there was not anything to pay.*
40   **M**: No, there was one, you sent pictures, this or that
41   **F**: *That was just 50 p*
42   **M**: *No, several pounds last time, I can get you that bill* [She goes and looks for the bill].
43   **F**: *That may be 1 pound.*

44   **M**: *No, it's certainly not.* [Then after a few seconds the last bill was found].

45   **F**: 1 pound, look, 1 pound

46   **M**: [looking at the last bill] Mhm, 1 pound, all right, *you did not even give me that 1 pound*

47   **F**: *I will have to give you 2 pounds.*

48   **M**: *How come just 2 pounds?*

49   **F**: Because 20 pounds deducted, 20 pounds deducted

50   **M**: *You just simply say 10 pounds , how come another 10 pounds?*

51   **F**: *There is, Mum, I have already calculated.*

52   **M**: *All right, then. You gave me two pounds, and we are clear to each other.*

53   **F**: OK.

54   **M**: *Then from the next bill, you have to pay all by yourself if you still spend money like this, you know?*

55   **F**: Mm. OK. [He goes upstairs to his room to fetch money for his mother].

Fan's mother started to defend herself by remembering the last mobile bill when Fan also exceeded the limit, but not by as much as this current bill. She found the last bill, which showed that Fan's memory was better than hers. Although it might be the case that Fan took advantage of his mother's poor memory of how much pocket money she owed him, Fan appeared to be logical and strategic in manipulating his mother to accept his arguments throughout the process. Although his mother kept mentioning his previous carelessness, Fan appeared to be very clear about his own standpoint. Eventually, Fan's mother once again had to acquiesce that Fan might be right, particularly when he stressed again what he had calculated (turn 51). It seemed that Fan achieved what he expected from the situation and he then only needed to pay two pounds for the bill. I also noticed that Fan made a mischievous face to himself when he went upstairs to fetch his money, and a cheeky, victorious smile appeared on his face. While Fan was upstairs fetching the money for his mother, Mrs Yang, a bit embarrassed, explained to me how she and her husband had agreed to cut two new keys, just in case Fan lost the new one again, and that her husband had reminded her to give her son pocket money on time to avoid these kinds of arguments, but she kept forgetting to do so. It seemed that Fan took advantage of his mother's forgetfulness, and perhaps her unwillingness to get into a full-scale argument. The arguments over the mobile phone bill seemed to end with a mutually satisfactory solution, but another argument was ignited. An argument commenced over the amount of pocket money (see turns 56–75).

Turn/Interlocutor/Transcript

56 **F**: (Giving the two pounds to his mother) *Mum, I tell you, I think, Mum, two pounds you give me per week is a bit less, others are all given more, everybody, everybody.*

57 **M**: *Say it in Chinese.* (Louder voice)

58 **F**: *Everybody all.*

59 **M**: *How do you know?*

60 **F**: *I asked, others are all given more than that*

61 **M**: *Who are the others?*

62 **F**: *The people in my class*

63 **M**: *How many in your class did you ask?*

64 **F**: *Many of them*

65 **M**: *How many?*

66 **F**: *Most*

67 **M**: *How much are they given?*

68 **F**: *Almost 5 pounds*

69 **M**: (thinks for a second) *I will discuss with Dad when he comes back.*

70 **F**: *Arg.*

71 **M**: *What?*

72 **F**: *But you should give me more.* (running upstairs)

73 **M**: *I tell you, Fan, I will discuss with your Dad about your pocket money, but you should lay out the bowls and chopsticks for dinner each night.*

74 **F**: *But you'd better call me.*

75 **M**: *All right.*

Although Fan ended up paying his mother only two pounds, his negotiations did not stop, but accelerated. It may be the case that when Fan took his money from his wallet, he realised that he did not have much money because he was not given as much pocket money as his peers at school, or he thought that it was a pertinent moment to reiterate his request for an increase in pocket money. However, it may not be too strong an argument to suggest that Fan, maybe almost intuitively, knew that when an opponent is weak it is probably the best time to seek further advantage, a highly tactical approach to negotiations. So, he embarked on another argument by citing his peers' experience of getting pocket money (turn 56), but with a relatively soft start. Then, his emphasis in English on *everybody* seemed to allow his mother to slightly divert the conversation to the topic of speaking Chinese. However, Fan did not give up on his point of insisting on an increase in his pocket money. His mother did not oppose this proposal since Fan based his request on referencing his peers' amount of pocket money, but neither did she concede his point.

The short consecutive turns bouncing back and forward between Fan and his mother suggest that Fan was taking advantage of the fact that he, rather than his mother, had hold of the source of accurate information. His mother then took an escape route (one that has, unfortunately, been adopted by many mothers in many households for years) by using the delaying tactic of referring the subject across to Fan's father (turn 69). Not being successful straight away, Fan ran upstairs in disappointment (turn 70). As a point of return for a discussion with his father, Fan's mother set up a light household chore for Fan to do (turn 73), but Fan bounced the responsibility back to her by saying that she had to remind him to do the chore (turn 74).

Mediated in the pocket money event

Several issues emerge from the above three extracts. Firstly, the transactions between Fan and his mother suggest how a child can act as a skilful negotiator in handling an adult. Fan's negotiation is based on two arguments. Referencing his peer culture appears to be an initial and potent argument. As many children do with their parents, Fan made good use of his peer culture to precipitate his mother's response to his proposal and to influence his parents' practice (Parke & Ladd, 1992). He was successful in steering his mother towards the pocket money issue, as she seemed to have taken on board Fan's contention and agreed to discuss the issue with his father, even though his request for an increase in the amount was not accepted straight away. Fan's second argument is that his mother forgot to give him his pocket money on time. His mother had no way of proving that both of Fan's points were untenable, and even worse, she could not trust her own memory of whether she had given him the money. Although Fan was at a disadvantage with his mother at the outset, he managed to turn his negative position into a positive one for himself, and gradually took over the discussion. He seemed very clear about how the argument should go, how to engage his mother and how to persuade her to accept his ideas, using 'diplomatese' (the type of language used by diplomats) in different phases of the debate. As a result, Fan took on his mother and somewhat misled her into a solution favourable to himself. This suggests that children can play agentive roles in exerting their influence over situations.

Secondly, at a deeper level, this pocket money event seems to mediate a British perspective on the relationships between parents and children. In Chinese families, the traditional role of children is one that expresses obedience, proper conduct, impulse control and the acceptance of social obligations (Wu, 1996). Children are supposed to be subordinate to their parents and follow their wishes, rather than arguing back. Arguing with parents is thought of as disrespectful, and allowing children to argue with their parents in traditional Chinese culture is regarded as spoiling them. However, Fan seems not only to take a strong initiative in trying to persuade his mother but he also does it in quite a powerful and aggressive way. Although this would not be allowed in a traditional Chinese upbringing, parents in this new society may have to accustom themselves to a different kind of relationship with their children, one that has to acknowledge a child's right to stand up for himself/herself, to argue strongly for his/her own interests and to take positions that may be quite different from those that his/her parents would expect or want.

Another dimension here is that parents are confronted by the British expectation that children can and should have an allowance that is for them to manage, that children should be given early responsibility for some areas of their lives and that learning to make decisions for themselves needs to begin early in a child's life. This is quite a contrast with the child's role in Chinese families, where there is relatively less emphasis on independence and responsibility given to children at a young age (Wu, 1996). From the perspective of the parent–child relationship, the pocket money event seems to generate a different kind of power relationship between parents and children than in traditional Chinese families. Fan's behaviour seems to be presenting fairly conventional Chinese parents with the freedom and liberty of a Western society, rather than reinforcing traditional Chinese values. The arguments between Fan and his mother seem to suggest more of an equal relationship between child and adult, thus mediation occurring in the argument over pocket money creates a less authoritative parental status and a more liberal acceptance of the child's autonomy in the family.

Finally, it is clear that Fan's parents had appropriated some new elements of English culture into their everyday practices. On request, they had provided pocket money. By choosing a particular telephone contract, they had handed Fan some responsibility for managing his life and his right and willingness to argue his position. While it may not have been a comfortable experience for Fan's mother, it was acknowledged as her decision to join in and extend the debate between them. She might not have done this willingly, but she was learning to live with some important elements of British child–parent relationships.

Eating and food choices

Generally speaking, people of different backgrounds eat very differently, for food is culturally constructed and one's eating habits are socially determined (Meigs, 1997). Food choices can be influenced by one's traditions, one's upbringing, one's eating partners and one's beliefs in the nutrition of the food that one eats and its relations to health. Differences arise in the ingredients considered appropriate for each meal, the ways in which they should be prepared and cooked, the amount and variety at each meal, the taste preferences, the eating and cooking utensils, how foods are served, what is seen as appropriate eating etiquette and so on. Second, human beings' dietary habits originate from the natural supply in their living places and their eating habits are formed at a young age (Li, 2001). Therefore, even people from the same background may vary in their individual food preferences because of where they were born and brought up; even within families, children may have very different beliefs about food from those of their parents. Third, food habits and food preferences seem to construct one's identity and reflect one's self-concepts (Rappoport, 2003). For example, a vegetarian does not believe that meat is good for their health. Finally, just as the role and content of meals change with the times (Mäkelä, 2000), so people's eating habits change with the places they relocate to, although they may still retain most of their existing habits. Kannan (1978) found that the food practices in Asian immigrant families evolve into a mixed variety, but they retain their original food habits. As a result of child mediation, this seems true of the families here.

Traditional Chinese diet

Chinese food, similar to many other cuisines in the world, is well known for its diversity and sophistication in preparation and in having several dishes in one meal. Like people in other countries, the Chinese also pay attention to a balanced diet and seek to eat food that is healthy and delicious at the same time (Chang, 1977). Chinese people generally believe that the kind and the amount of food that one consumes are intimately related to one's health, and that health is promoted through eating (Newman, 2004). To promote health, food should be consumed at the right time to match one's physical condition, to maintain the body's energy and to keep it balanced and in harmony (Newman, 2000). Overindulging in food and drink is bad for one's health and should be avoided. To enjoy a healthy and tasty meal that combines colour, taste and flavour in each dish, Chinese people tend to spend a long time preparing their food. As in many countries around the world, cooking Chinese food is an art in itself. For a balanced meal, one needs to cook *fan* (grains and other starch foods) and *cai* (vegetable and meat dishes) separately. In consuming a meal, appropriate amounts of both *fan* and *cai* should be eaten, but in fact, *fan* is the more fundamental and indispensable food. Different utensils are used for cooking *fan* and *cai*, called *fan guo* (rice cooker) and *cai guo* (wok), respectively, and people eat with chopsticks along with spoons. Traditionally, there is a certain order to serving courses for feasts, which start with cold dishes such as different kinds of salad, followed by hot dishes and the main dish. During these courses, wine and liquor are consumed, after which rice or other starch foods are served. The whole meal is finished with a light soup or a slightly sweet fruit.

Most of the parents of the families here retained their old eating and cooking habits even after they moved to the new country. They mainly ate Chinese food and cooked in the Chinese style at least for their supper, in that it normally contained a few vegetables and meat or fish dishes, together with rice or noodles followed by a light vegetable soup and fruit. Although aware of many Western foods such as cheese, pizza, sandwiches, different dressings and sauces, most of the parents did not like them. Before the children started school in England, their eating habits were mainly of the Chinese style, although changes had taken place in their food choices since then.

Children's impacts on families' food choices

Most of the children's experiences of British food came from school or party meals. As far as the three daily meals were concerned, all of the children had school dinners at lunchtime, and had a Chinese supper almost every evening at home. Many of them came to like eating sausages, fish fingers, fried potato 'smiley faces' with ketchup and various kinds of cakes and ice creams became their favourite desserts. Virtually all the children in these families loved crisps, sweets and chocolates. Some of them even developed a dislike of fruits and vegetables. In the Shi family, what worried Mrs Shi was that Gang, after he had been in England for about three years, sometimes refused to eat a Chinese supper; instead, he preferred pasta, pizza and chips. During one of my visits to the Yang family on a half-term holiday, I was surprised to notice at the lunch table that all the adults had Chinese noodles while all the children had Western food such as cheese and bacon quiche and chicken lasagne.

In almost all the families, although they have primarily retained their Chinese style of cooking for most of their meals, their food practices have become more varied and mixed with some Western flavours. They have adapted themselves to the food habits of their children as a result of their children's requests or just for the sake of change. I will take the example of food-related activities to explore how children influence family food choices and, in doing so, once again mediate British culture for their parents.

From the children's verbal information, the parents came to know the names of many British foods and utensils. For example, in a conversation between the Tang family members on 9 May 2004, the children Ming and Liang managed to get across to their parents what gravy (a traditional British sauce made from meat juices, liquid and flour and served with vegetables and meat) tastes like, how to use it in a meal and that a container called a 'gravy boat' should be used. Also from her children, Mrs Tang heard other food names such as jacket potatoes, fish fingers, potato 'smiley faces' and so on. Mrs Tang had never heard of jacket potatoes until Ming told her about them. This prompted her to try this food during one of their weekend outings. She found it very tasty and quite healthy, and she tried it in her cooking at home. However, she then decided not to cook it too often because she thought that it was a waste of electricity and that Chinese food still seemed quicker and cheaper to cook than jacket potatoes. At the Yangs, whenever Fan or Hai wanted particular foods, they put the names of the food on the family's shopping list, which was placed on the work surface in the kitchen. Their father could then look for them when shopping at a supermarket, for he often did not know what these foods looked like.

Secondly, the children tended to exert some influence over how foods were prepared at home. Interestingly, the families had added forks for their children to use, since almost all of the children were used to using forks rather than chopsticks to eat their meals and a few of them had found chopsticks difficult to use. A similar scenario was reported by Kannan (1978), in which immigrant Indian children not only insisted that their parents cook English food for them at home, but they also started to use spoons instead of their hands when eating meals. At the Yangs', the Western food stored in their fridge became part of their cuisine, though mostly only for Fan and Hai's appetites. At the Shis' house, because of Gang's preference, his mother had to have a constant supply of tomato sauce in her fridge and she also tried to learn how to make sauce for pasta. During my initial visits to the Tangs (Feburary 2004), four-year-old Liang told his mother how to cook chips, as they were one of his favourite foods. He even wrote down instructions for his mother. Although the instructions included only key words such as potato, his attempts to persuade his mother to prepare chips and other Western foods for the family appeared to be effective. In their family, Mrs Tang tried to prepare just chips, pizza or lasagne during weekends. Another thing that the Tangs changed in their daily meal was that they added a dessert to the end of their dinner. Mrs Tang said,

> the children always have reasons for having some dessert every day, such as for being brilliant at school. I would buy and keep some frozen

desserts in the freezer whenever TESCO has a special offer, such as buy one get one free. The children like them, and we adults also eat them. (Translated fieldnotes)

This suggests that child mediation diversified the parents' food intake, so they came to eat food that they would not normally have consumed. Their food arrangements became more inclusive of various kinds of Western foods rather than exclusively Chinese foods.

Thirdly, parents kept adjusting their food varieties not just to cope with their own children's 'Westernized' appetites, but also to tackle the confrontational occasions when their children's English friends came over. Lin's mother learned to bake cakes and make fruit jelly as desserts and Hong's mother kept ice cream in the freezer. In the Yang family, the parents worried about food preparation when Fan or Hai invited their friends to play and eat at their house. Usually, because of their uncertainty, they ended up preparing both Western and Chinese foods. At the Tangs' house, Mrs Tang had experienced embarrassment and disappointment over the Chinese food she had spent a long time preparing for their children's friends because very few of them had tried it. She was so disappointed and embarrassed by this reaction to her food that she did not know what to do in later similar events. Therefore, on another occasion when preparing for her children's friends to come for tea and play, Mrs Tang depended entirely on eight-year-old Ming to tell her what games they should play and what food to cook for the other children. Figure 6.1 shows the food she prepared for the children on one of these occasions.

The food on their table was very similar to that of a typical school dinner: fish fingers, potato 'smiley faces', cocktail sausages and fruit juice, along with forks, plates and teacups. All this was prepared to cater for the

Figure 6.1 Serving English food for children is much easier

children's appetites so that they could eat happily. Being guided by her daughter, from then on Mrs Tang came to know what food to provide when British children visited – just heat ready-made food in the oven. Parents' changes in their food choices will be further demonstrated in their decisions about birthday party food in Chapter 7.

Mediation of foods

The parents have been the receivers of cultural mediation in a number of ways. The aforementioned incidents in the families suggest that children contribute to the family's adaptation to the cuisine style of the new society. The Chinese parents made adjustments in their food arrangements at home according to their children's requests; as Chang (1977) says, the Chinese way of eating is characterised by a notable flexibility and adaptability. Although most of the parents may have maintained their original beliefs about food nutrition and concepts of health, they were tentatively trying Western food, as suggested or imposed by their children. According to Meigs (1997), parents' self-embodiment in their eating preferences is shaken by their children's mediation. These parents gave in to their children in integrating varieties of English food into their daily life and began sampling these new foods.

In addition to the impact on their daily lives, parents seem to have learned several concepts about the new society through their children's mediation around food. First, the industrial society has freed people from spending a long time preparing meals. Almost everything can be bought from a supermarket to cater for various meal times, from morning cereals to supper desserts, from staples to snacks. It is now unnecessary to cook anything for oneself in order just to fill one's stomach during a busy life. Therefore, eating without holding on to the traditional Chinese way of cooking in the new society can definitely save time in preparation, and thus complex cooking may become optional (Marshall, 2000) rather than a chore for people. Second, many British people eat meals containing foods from many different countries, e.g. Italian spaghetti. One could even say that the British do not eat much British food, and one of the most popular foods in Britain is curry, albeit a rather anglicised version. The parents here have opportunities to eat food from all over the world, rather than just traditional British food. Third, food in the modern world has been commodified to attract children as an essential part of the consumer market. From the emphasis on food varieties designed particularly for children, it seems that mediation happens not just between Chinese and Western foods, but also between adult and children's foods in contemporary society.

Although the parents were not affected by mediation to the extent that they completely changed their own diet and food preferences, child mediation tended to impact on their food arrangements within the families. Throughout this section on food arrangements, the children's mediation not only taught their parents the names of many new foods (an assimilative level of mediation), but it also made parents adjust the dietary structures of the families' food, adopt some new foods, provide different utensils and sequence meals differently. More importantly, when the family had to face communication with the wider society, e.g. inviting children over to play and for tea, the mother appropriated new food-related elements into what she provided for the children. In this sense, mediation not only causes changes in the family's internal practices but it also has a positive effect on the family's external communication. This can be taken as an example of how mediating events at the appropriative level may extend towards the accommodative level of mediation, the details of which are in Chapter 7.

From the mediating events at the appropriative level examined above, there emerge several issues about child cultural mediation. Firstly, it seems clear that children's knowledge comes mostly from their schools and peers. While their peers may have been told stories by their parents or grandparents, Chinese children may depend only on school for such knowledge as the significance of the poppy and of Poppy Day. This suggests that English children and Chinese children operate in 'different directions' in the transmission of cultural knowledge. The former tend to receive knowledge and information from their parents, whereas Chinese children appear to provide knowledge for their parents. This dependence on their children may apply to many immigrant families. Therefore, knowledge transmission in immigrant families contrasts with that in indigenous families where, following the conventional socialisation procedure, parents instil knowledge and experience in their children and help them to become physically and mentally mature adults (see Chapter 2).

Secondly, child cultural mediation inevitably depends on how much knowledge and information the mediators have gained from their sources, and how well they themselves understand a certain cultural activity. It should be admitted that child cultural brokers might not always mediate an event to the fullest extent, due to their limited level of knowledge and life experiences in certain areas. This is supported by similar accounts in Vasquez *et al.* (1994) that children's cultural brokering or linguistic brokering may not always be satisfactory in situations associated with specialist knowledge such as in medicine, because of their lack of experience. However, children's competency should be understood as situated within certain circumstances (see Chapter 2), i.e. children still tend to have more knowledge than their parents in a particular circumstance, and have more opportunities than their parents to experience many cultural practices of the majority society. In other words, a child's role as a mediator between his/her parents and the mainstream culture is still important, although the information provided may not always be accurate.

Thirdly, as discussed in Chapter 3, child cultural mediation is a collaboration between parents and children. In the case of the discussion about raffle tickets between Gang and his mother, although it is hard to say how much the child helped her understand that fundraising activity, Gang's mother seemed to have brought into play her experiences from her own schooling in China. She did her bit according to what she had understood and bought two tickets as an indication of positively answering the school's call for action, although she could not figure out the exact purpose of the hamper. Under certain circumstances, parents may attempt to understand the cultural activity in their own ways, and take their own initiative to act accordingly.

Throughout this chapter, it has been suggested that mediating events at the appropriative level can be situated between the assimilative and accommodative levels, but often overlap them. Although these events mainly affect families' daily life arrangements and internal relations, mediating events at the appropriative level present features of the other two levels. The transference of factual knowledge at the appropriative level enables it to be closely adjacent to the assimilative level of mediation. In the event of Poppy Day, which is particular to the mainstream national culture, the children informed their parents about a British annual event. In fundraising activities, parents tend to learn various fundraising ideas along with many items of vocabulary. By being introduced to popular culture and rearranging family food routines, parents have learned cultural knowledge relating to their daily life and work situations, as well as the names of British foods. However, the impact of child mediation can be observed from more perspectives than just factual knowledge. Unlike those events that are spontaneous and ephemeral at the assimilative level, mediating events at the appropriative level are repeated. For example, Remembrance Day occurs annually in the UK, fundraising activities are ongoing at school. Thus, mediation through these events may linger with parents, impinging more profoundly on them. Their identity as Chinese migrants living in England might be confronted. Mrs Yang commented that even though she knew about the significance of Poppy Day, she had never bought or worn a poppy. Child mediation has affected their parents' practices in their daily life, from what kind of television programmes to watch, what food to buy and how to prepare meals, to how much pocket money to give their children and how to entertain their children's friends at home.

Meanwhile, with such mediating events, parents may come to know more about the mainstream society, English schooling and even parent–child relations in Britain; in other words, parents are increasing their knowledge and understanding of some of the deeper levels of British values, beliefs and practices. The children's mediation constantly confronts or challenges their parents' lack of knowledge in certain areas and even their lack of identification with the new society. In spite of the disparities between what is brokered and parents' existing belief systems and cultural practices, parents still tend to retain their own identity and preferences and make partial changes within their homes for their children's sake.

Further, it seems possible that parents may accept some practices after carrying them out and understanding their significance. For example, parents who initially felt that they should give their children money, now accept the practice of pocket money. In this sense, mediation at the appropriative level lays a path to the accommodative level of mediation, which I will explore in the next chapter.

7 The Accommodative Level of Child Cultural Mediation

As we have already seen, child cultural mediation can be perceived as happening within a continuum of practices. In other words, it may well be the case that they have features that can be carried across all three levels, although one mediating event is placed for analytical purposes in a particular phase of the continuum. Events described at this accommodative level, then, may also contain elements which, taken individually, incorporate elements associated with the other two levels. The concept of accommodation originates from Piaget and refers to qualitative changes in one's schema. The accommodative level of child cultural mediation can be characterised by three main attributes.

First, at this level, parents eventually tend to take an accepting attitude towards what is being mediated. Unlike those events that cause disagreements with and ambivalences towards cultural practices at the appropriative level, parents tend to endorse what is being mediated in these events. Although there may still be confrontations, tensions and challenges, the events involve parents in active participation; parents comprehend the cultural knowledge that is being passed from their children, and make voluntary and noticeable changes to their practices.

Second, parents' accommodation through mediating events tends to happen gradually over a period of time, in a process that may start with their appropriation of certain practices. In carrying out these practices initially to meet the demands of their children, parents may come to understand something of the underpinning values and issues. Thus, a variety of instances occurring within related events may lead to parents incorporating the purposes or values of the practices.

Third, events at this level tend to have a greater impact on families than those at the other two levels; they may affect how families act in their external relations with the main culture. Events can influence how parents want to present themselves to the new environment and how they want their families to be presented to others in the mainstream society. Thus, parents tend to take these events more seriously than those at the other two levels. They also greatly depend on their children for knowledge of how to carry out related practices. Thus, children's mediation, whether deliberate or incidental, seems indispensable to their parents' successful management of important situations that bring them into direct contact with the majority society. Without their children's facilitation, there could be a failure of communication with the host society, which might impinge on how their children identify themselves with their peer culture.

In the rest of this chapter, a number of instances connected with two major experiences, greeting cards and birthday parties, will be analysed in order to show how child cultural mediation at the accommodative level operates in the families.

Greeting Cards

Among the procedures or etiquette that the parents came to know, greeting cards were an important component. In addition to birthday cards, invitation cards and thank-you cards involved in birthday celebration rituals, other cards are associated with the modern Western world, many aspects of which were also mediated by the children for their parents. In this section, we shall see how card-related rituals are mediated for parents by their children and how, through this process, the parents not only increased their knowledge of how to deal with greeting cards in their daily life in the new culture, but also their understanding of the roles of greeting cards in human relationships and interpersonal communication in the new society.

Meanings of greeting cards

Greeting cards, as a form of expressing regard, concern and affection, are used in many parts of the world on occasions ranging from national to personal, from New Year, Christmas, Valentine's Day and Easter to birthdays, weddings, a newborn baby, job promotion, getting well, moving house and so on. Cards have penetrated into most official events and the most intimate relationships conceivable in contemporary daily life (Stern, 1988). The increasing types of cards on display in any card shop indicate that cards are used in almost every aspect of daily life. Nowadays, each year, billions of cards are sent around the world to families and friends, to commemorate various types of occasions and to mark various rituals in everyday life. It seems that even the most personal and intimate human relationships can be mediated by sending greeting cards (McGee, 1980).

Previous research on greeting cards suggests that the meanings of greeting cards can be understood from different perspectives. First, greeting cards signal a positive politeness and may sustain existing relationships and extend one's social connections (Erbaugh, 2000). Cards allow people who are physically apart from each other to keep in contact in a quick and cost-effective way. Thus, cards can be used as a replacement for face-to-face interaction. Secondly, cards can achieve better interpersonal functions than other verbal forms of interactions. Different from face-to-face interactions between interlocutors, greeting cards can 'provide an unobtrusive measure of culturally approved interpersonal communication' (Brabant & Mooney, 1989: 480). Similarly, possible conflicts in other verbal communication, for example, telephone calls, can be avoided. More importantly, cards can help express emotions and sentiments, which the senders are not sure how best to express in person. Thus, cards help to avoid the abruptness and inappropriateness of direct verbal formulation; consequently, cards can be used to propose relationships and present identities to new acquaintances.

During the course of selecting and buying cards, individual consumers personalise and create ownership of them. Whenever the sender picks out a card in a store, she/he is implicitly (and maybe explicitly) asking himself/ herself questions such as 'Does this card display what I want to express? How will the receiver like the card? What will it say about my identity?'. Similar questioning and decision making may be repeated many times before the card is eventually sent. Thus, purchasing cards is a subjective, rather than a neutral and objective process. The choice of cards is subject to social judgements of their appropriateness for specific contexts, particular functions and purposes and different social relationships. As Carrier (1990) argues, cards, as objects or commodities in a social space create and recreate personal social identities and relationships.

In the West, billions of greeting cards are sent every year, and everyone recognises the appropriateness of sending cards for particular occasions. Knowledge of card sending and receiving is part of the cultural capital. Given the fact that the parents in my study lived in mainland China or Taiwan before they came to England, it is worth considering whether this is true for them. On the whole it seems that while greeting cards have been developing in the West for the last 200 years, the history of greeting cards in a modern sense in China only emerged in the late 1970s (Erbaugh, 2000) and greeting cards in the Chinese language are named literally *heka* or 'congratulating cards'. Maybe because of the literal meaning of the Chinese word, cards in China only celebrate happy events such as New Year and people's birthdays. According to Erbaugh (2000), up to 1997, congratulation cards for a promotion, a newborn baby or moving house were rarely seen, at least in Nanjing, China – not to mention get-well cards and sympathy cards. Due to the paucity of literature on greeting cards in China and in order to get a more up-to-date picture of greeting cards in today's China, I carried out small-scale interviews using a short questionnaire with 15 respondents in China.

My small-scale interviews revealed that, in comparison with an average of 30 cards sent by each person in the USA every year (Cacioppo & Anderson, 1981), my respondents sent and received an average of five cards to and from their friends and business partners in 2005. It appears that the number of cards that are sent and received is related to the respondent's workplace and social networks. For example, those who work in schools tend to receive and send more cards than do those in other workplaces such as banks, joint venture firms and governmental departments. It also appears that the cards sent in China are used to maintain business relationships more than personal relationships. For instance, some of the respondents did not receive any cards from their friends, but they did receive a few cards from their children's kindergarten managers or photographers whose services they had used. Some respondents' employers sent cards to their clients with the company's logo as advertising. The majority of my respondents did not see cards as an important way of expressing care and concern, partly due to the fact that the advances in telecommunications and electronic networks allowed them to use what they considered more economical and quicker ways of communicating, such as phoning and texting. More importantly, my respondents tended to believe that cards are not sufficient to express their emotions in sincere friendships or for those relationships that are important to their career development.

For the families here, the card becomes a salient topic because the phenomenon tends to clash with the Chinese immigrants' previous knowledge and to go beyond their social experiences in their home culture. It is the underlying norms or meanings associated with cards that become problematic for the parents. Their further knowledge about and understanding of card-related rituals tends to come from their children as the main, if not the only, mediating channel. But where do children's knowledge and experiences of greeting cards come from? Do they have different experiences of greeting cards from adults?

Mediating the card-related rituals in the Chinese families

In this section, we shall see what happened in the Tang family on four occasions over a period of two years or so, and how Mrs Tang progressed in her accommodation of card-related rituals through her children's mediation.

Making cards for their father

In England, children's experiences in relation to greeting cards develop through a kind of apprenticeship system. Young children often come to discover the use of greeting cards through receiving them from adults, and perhaps participating in some ways when their parents send cards to other people, for instance, at Christmas. However, their subordinate financial status often determines that they do not buy, or seldom buy, cards themselves, although they may participate in the adult selection process. As a result, as well as often through encouragement from their parents, they may practise making their own greeting cards. When they start school, such card making is often incorporated into daily activities at certain times of the year; for example, whenever there is a festival, secular or religious, children are encouraged to make cards in class, which are then given to their parents.

The children here most probably started their experiences of sending cards after they had arrived in the new country. Unlike native children, their experiences of cards were derived not from their families, but almost entirely from their British schooling and peer interaction. After picking up the practice, however, these children tended to influence their parents' card-related experiences.

In one of my visits in January 2004, Mrs Tang showed me two cards that her children had made on their own for their father who was away on business in other countries. The children themselves called them 'missing-you' cards and 'welcome-back' cards, demonstrating that by now they fully understood that the principle of greeting cards could be adapted for almost any occasion. The making of the cards may well have been an expression of their own personal emotions, but the idea to make the cards by hand might have been because it was a quick decision and they had to use the resources available to them rather than search for a commercially made card. Therefore, they just chose ordinary paper that they easily found around their house.

As shown in Figure 7.1, five-year-old Liang made a 'missing-you' card using his own drawings and writing, which he wanted to hand to his father when he came home from his business trip.

Figure 7.1   Liang's 'missing you' card for his father

The card was a piece of A4 paper folded down the middle, shaped like a normal greeting card. On this piece of paper, Liang drew three smiling figures on the left side of the card. The figure on the far left looks like his mother, Mrs Tang and it looks as if she is preparing their dinner in the kitchen. The two people beside Mrs Tang most probably represent Liang himself and his sister Ming. The top figure looks like short-haired, five-year-old Liang and the person underneath appears to be eight-year-old Ming. This figure seems unfinished but is still drawn sufficiently well to convey the information; Kress (2003) notes that children make good use of core criteria in what they want to represent. This suggests that Liang considers the smiling face and the long hair as sufficient to represent his sister. Of the four members of the family, Liang only drew three of them, his father was not in the picture. The figures are awaiting the return of the absent father, in keeping with the child's notion of the 'missing-you' card. It might also be the case that the term has a double meaning, that Mr Tang is away from home and that Liang misses him. As Pahl (1999) argues, children bring their own life and cultural experiences and emotions into their representation and meaning making. In addition to the drawing, Liang also used written messages. On the right-hand side of the card, Liang wrote with a ballpoint pen the message 'Dear Daddy, Best Wishes for ever, Love from...' with proper spacing between the three lines of the message. The whole card looks brief, concrete and sincere. However, although the message covers the whole page, it is a simple address and closure. While a normal greeting card may start with 'To...', Liang borrows a feature of letter writing and starts off with 'Dear...'. Although Liang himself called the card a 'missing-you' card, no words were written to express this meaning. It seems that Liang was just beginning to explore what writing can do and what to write, in addition to his drawings. In other words, he might have been wondering what he should write or if the writing was necessary since his drawings could not have made his meaning any clearer.

Almost at the same time, eight-year-old Ming made her welcome-back card at home (see Figures 7.2 and 7.3) to give to her father on his return from a business trip.

Figures 7.2 and 7.3 show, respectively, the front cover of the card and one inside page of the message. On the front cover, Ming drew 10 heart shapes on the top edge and another 10 on the bottom, with a star in the middle symmetrically separating the heart shapes into two groups of five by using the colours yellow, light grey, green, pink and red for both the top and the bottom. These different colours seem to reflect Ming's cheerful mood in making the card for her father. Between the two lines of hearts,

Figure 7.2 The cover of Ming's 'welcome back' card for her father

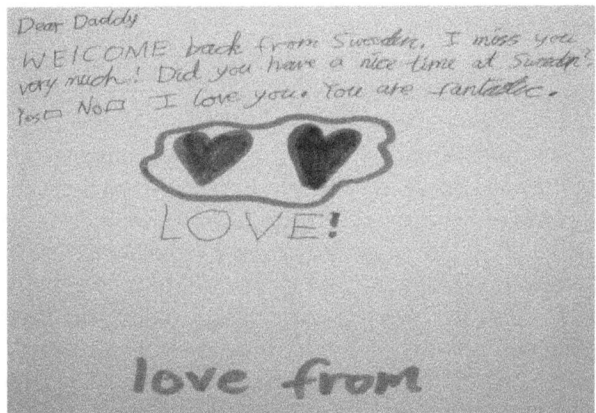

Figure 7.3 Inside Ming's 'welcome back' card for her father

Ming drew a big heart shape, with two smaller heart shapes inside it. In the space between the top small hearts and the middle big heart, Ming wrote 'welcome back' with an exclamation mark, in capital letters and in different colours. Around the big heart shape, the words *I love you* and another exclamation mark are evenly laid out at the left, right and lower parts of the big heart. The whole front cover looks neat and bright. She used expressive punctuation, various bright colours as well as 13 heart shapes in various sizes to show her love, delight and happiness at her father's return. Her emotions were further illustrated in one of the inside pages (Figure 7.3). Ming started this page with her message 'Dear Daddy, WELCOME back from Sweden. I miss you very much! Did you have a nice time at Sweden?

Yes ☐ No ☐ I love you. You are fantastic'. She closed her card with 'love from'. Ming made good use of the space between the main longer messages and the closure by circling two heart shapes together and inserting a boldfaced capitalised *love* with another exclamation mark outside the circle. Altogether, there are 4 exclamation marks and 15 heart shapes of various sizes on the whole card; and the two boldfaced capitalised *welcomes* on both parts made clear the theme of the card. Both her love for her father and her enthusiasm over making the card emerge on the card itself. In spite of eight-year-old Ming's clear indication of the card's theme, the messages in her card still look unusual in that she seems to put in writing what she might be able to say on seeing her father in person. This might suggest that she perceives writing as adding more weight to her meaning, i.e. more than the power of just spoken words to her father. Also, Ming set up an interactive situation by borrowing what she had learned from letter writing for her particular purpose.

Both Liang and Ming have demonstrated their capacity to add value to both the spoken word and hugs. They both may have recognised the permanent nature of writing as opposed to speaking, as their father might keep these cards with their words and drawings. In addition, it might also be the case that the children were using newly learned knowledge from school and, in a sense, extending their new knowledge by trying out a new tool of combining both writing and drawing.

From a social semiotic perspective, both Ming and Liang's drawing and writing are meaningful in a number of ways. First of all, as active meaning makers, they used the modes of writing and drawing and the resources available at the time to communicate the meaning they wanted to convey (Kress & Mavers, 2005). From the resources available at home, they chose those that they felt would best enable them to make their meanings clear. Secondly, due to their learning at school, they also used correct spellings and some of the conventional rules of writing letters in English. Their experiences of schooling can also be seen from the differences between the two children's messages. Ming wrote more than her younger brother and showed a better command of English and a more consolidated use of her literacy skills. Her creative design did not include any images of people, but used symbols, signs and words to express her emotions. Thirdly, they both appear to use spacing in the cards very well so that the layout of both cards is clear. Fourthly, their phrasing suggests that they both seem to have a clear awareness of their audience/receiver when constructing their cards. Ming's card is also more interactive and more considerate than her brother's, with a question, the choice of answers and the two tick boxes for a written response. In brief, it seems that Liang and Ming created their own images and messages and authored their cards to convey their current emotional state via the cards.

Mrs Tang commented that she did not find it hard to accept the practice that her children made many of their own cards, although card sending between friends was not a traditional practice in Chinese culture; however, she was a bit surprised that they wanted to give the cards to their father, which is not usual in Chinese culture.However, she did not stop them from making these cards, and she showed them to me with delight. She also said that her children made many cards at school, e.g. Christmas cards, which looked very similar to the cards in Figures 7.2 and 7.3, including the opening, the closing as well as the symbols and spacing used. It seems that their mother has learned how to write an English card and how children are taught to convey meanings in English schooling. In her schooling experience, it was mostly words rather than images that were generally encouraged in Chinese literacy development. Like other parents in mediating events at the appropriative level, she just accepted the card-sending practice, as long as that suited her children. She also told me that she found it acceptable that the children started the cards with *dear...* and ended them with *love from ...* in those to their father, although it was a bit strange to see such intimate phrasing as *dear* and *love* written so explicitly in a card. In Chinese culture, the equivalents of *dear* and *love* are normally used for romantic relationships between couples and lovers, but are seldom used to describe relations outside a family.

While unusual within the Chinese cultural tradition, making these cards as a within-family activity was easily appropriated by Mrs Tang and did not challenge her, nor move forward her understanding of the significance of card sending within British culture. At this point, card making was not an accommodative activity. However, in the next example some cultural conflict was generated when Liang began to send cards to friends and classmates.

'Is it good to write in this way?'

One day during the Easter holidays of 2004, I chatted with Mrs Tang in her house. She told me that about two weeks earlier she had had an argument with her son, five-year-old Liang, over what he wrote in a birthday card to one of his female classmates. I later found their conversation in the tapes that they had recorded at home. The following extract is their discussion.

M: the mother (Mrs Tang); **B**: the boy (Liang). Note: the text in italics is translated from Chinese.

Turn/Interlocutor/Transcript

1   **M**: *Liang, is it good to write in this way?* (she means the beginning *dear...* and ending of the card *lots of love from...*)
2   **B**: *Yes, right.* Everybody did it this way.
3   **M**: Everybody did this way, Ah? *Then, what about this, you don't need to write* 'your special, special friend' *at the end, do you?*
4   **B**: This is **my** card, Mum.
5   **M**: *I am just suggesting, there is the word* 'special' *already at the cover of the card, you don't need to write it again inside.*
6   **B**: *But that is what the person* who made the card *wrote, not what I wrote* (a bit annoyed)
7   **M**: All right, all right.

This discussion focuses on the appropriateness of the text in the card, which worries and perplexes Mrs Tang. In particular, she seems to disapprove that her son should write intimate words such as *dear, love* and *special* in a card to a female classmate. In her traditional Chinese value system, these words should only be used in families and very close relationships. In her opinion, her son's way of writing might incur serious consequences. In a later conversation, she told me that if this instance had happened in her home country, the girl's parents might have had bad feelings towards her son and his parents who might be thought of as not educating him properly. Even worse, the girl's parents might come round to ask for an explanation. Living in an unfamiliar society, Mrs Tang really did not want to get into this kind of trouble. The conversation being a moment of moral dilemma for Mrs Tang, she felt it her responsibility to ensure that her son's behaviour was appropriate. Mrs Tang said to me, 'I am a bit scared that the girl's parents may think, how on earth this Chinese mother educates her son, are all Chinese parents like this?' (translated fieldnotes). Transferring her own cultural experiences to the new cultural situation, Mrs Tang could not help but question her son, hence the conversation above. However, he offers an impressive defence of his actions.

In the first three turns, Liang argues that *everybody* writes cards this way. Although he did not clearly indicate his reference group of 'everybody', there seems to be an assumption that 'they' means his peer group. Generally, he seems to be telling his mother that his way was common and appropriate and that there was nothing to worry about. In other words, it seems that he was using the logic that the collective experiences of his peers should be a good model for him and he certainly did not want to be different or strange. Mrs Tang did not know if Liang's reasoning was right or wrong. Although she had seen that their cards to their father ended with *love*, she was not sure whether this ending could appear on cards to other people, as based on her home cultural background, this manner of closing a card was inappropriate and unacceptable. Since she could not find sufficient reasons to argue against her son, Mrs Tang seemed to accept her son's statement that this way was acceptable in the new culture.

It seems that both Mrs Tang and Liang have different perceptions about the word 'special' being written and repeated. Mrs Liang was worried both about the repetition and the relational implication of the word. Liang's writing may cause 'social risks associated with choosing the wrong words' (Jaffe, 1999: 124). It seemed to her that messages on ready-made cards may be formulaic and not personalised, but her son's addition may create an illocutionary force in the phrase and antipathy from the receiver's end. According to her, Liang's addition of the word is redundant in terms of its appropriateness in this social interaction. However, Liang's argument is a very interesting one, that the word 'special' on the cover was written by someone else and that by putting his own word 'special' in the card he was personalising it; it seems that he was moving the card from a commercial gift commodity to a personal object (Jaffe, 1999). This is quite an important conceptual move for the five-year-old. It goes right to the heart of many debates about the role of cards, and is a position that rejects his card as being a straightforward, depersonalised object that is identical to the thousands of other printed examples. He wants to make this card a personal gift from him to a particular receiver and his view of the way to do this is to inscribe it with what seems to him unique sentiments.

The above example demonstrates a situation that is disturbing to Mrs Tang. She cannot simply assimilate these behaviours into her notions of acceptable social practices. She did allow Liang to leave what he had written in the card but she was uncomfortable about it. It was difficult for her to object explicitly when Liang was able to argue that this is what everybody does, for to object might make Liang an outsider rather than an insider in his peer group. By allowing Liang to keep his personal message, she is making the first moves towards a shift in understanding how in England certain social relationships can be manifested through word choices that are different from those within her own cultural background.

'Just write love..., it doesn't matter'

About a year later, Ming was writing thank-you cards to people who had attended her birthday party and/or who had sent her presents. From their audio-recording at home, I heard the conversation between Ming and her mother.

M: the mother (Mrs Tang); **G**: the girl (Ming). Note: the text in italics is translated from Chinese.

G: *Do we need to write* 'we all enjoy your presents?'
M: *Good.*
G: Lots of, *it is all right if we don't write* 'lots of . from'
M: *Just write* love *underneath, it doesn't matter.*

This short transaction illustrates how Mrs Tang and her daughter cooperated to write this thank-you card. Comparing this conversation with the earlier one between Mrs Tang and her son, there appears to be a sharp contrast in Mrs Tang's attitudes towards how to finish a card. In the previous conversation, Mrs Tang seems to be full of uncertainty and anxiety about the personal messages, in particular those that express a close relationship between two people; here she seems to have become used to this manner of card closure.

Under her ostensible insouciance, there may be complex connotations. It might be the case that Mrs Tang did not take writing intimate words in a card as seriously as she had before, as she may have realised that this is how people in the new culture express their emotions. Since it would not incur any further problems for the family, as had been proved by the instance of her son writing 'special' on his card, she did not need to fuss about it anymore. When I talked with her about the above extract, Mrs Tang said 'that's the Western manner of writing a card. They just write it in that way, and do not mean it as seriously as what we think' (translated fieldnotes). Here, it seems that Mrs Tang had accepted her daughter's way, or the 'English' way, of writing a card, although they were only talking about how to position the words at the end of the card.

This accommodative shift was also evident in a later conversation during Christmas 2005. I went to see the family, and happened to chat with Mrs Tang about their writing of Christmas cards. Mrs Tang told me that 'they do not write love to everybody they send cards to, only to some people. You can ask Ming, she told me this the other day' (*originally spoken in Chinese, except the word love*). Ming was close by, and said affirmatively 'yes' 'I wrote best wishes to some of them, but love only to my best friends' (*originally spoken in English*). 'How about Liang?' I continued to ask Ming. 'He doesn't really understand, he just wrote love to everybody' (*originally spoken in English*), she said solemnly.

Thus, it seems that parents' perception and understanding of certain cultural practices tend to change with their children's. When children learn more about the distinctions of closing cards, probably from their peer communication, they pass these differences on to their parents. In other words, children's mediation for parents seems to vary with the development of their knowledge of the world. The parents may not feel comfortable, but they have accommodated to the fact that in the UK, the ways in which relationships between people are manifested through words have different connotations and meanings, and do not represent the same values and meanings as they would in their own country. They now accept that it is appropriate for their children to use these different formulations and that in reality these do not imply very much more than general expressions of friendship.

The Tang family accepted card sending as a common practice in the new society, and they took positive actions towards it, changing their own behaviour. Mrs Tang told me that she realised that there is an almost inevitable expenditure on cards, which are more expensive in the new country, and that she had bought some blank cards and Christmas cards from Taiwan when they went back after their first year in England, so that both the parents and the children could write messages on the cards to send to their friends, instead of purchasing cards locally. The children seem to have made the difference between writing cards in English and in Chinese clearer to their parents. The tradition that Chinese parents were familiar with was that the card is written in a similar way to a short letter, with a Chinese manner of addressing, closure and signature.

One of the great differences in writing cards in the two cultures is the use of the words *dear* and *love*, whose equivalents in Chinese are only appropriate for close or romantic relationships. This is why Mrs Tang felt so uncomfortable when she saw her son use such intimate words when writing the card to his female classmate. However, the difference is not just in the writing style but also in the way that people from the two cultures perceive the connotations of the words 'dear' and 'love'. As Wilkins and Gareis (2006) also find, first-generation immigrants from non-English-speaking cultures seldom use verbal 'love' expressions to their friends or families, and that non-native speakers of English and bilingual speakers of English find it easier and less embarrassing to say the words 'I love you' in English than in their native or another language.

Finally, it is important to consider that the children's insistence and assertion demonstrate their agency over their social life in the new society. If something similar to the first instance between Liang and his mother happened in their original society, Mrs Tang would be confident in assuming an authoritative manner and make Liang follow her advice because of her familiarity with that cultural code. However, in this new culture, her uncertainty tends to attenuate her authoritative guiding role for her children.

Although parents usually take responsibility for their children's culturally approved behaviour, in immigrant families what is culturally appropriate or inappropriate may have to be decided either by the children themselves or by negotiation between parents and children.

Birthday Celebrations

In the next example, we shall see how Chinese children who are new to British culture celebrate their birthdays, how they influence their parents' decisions and practices in carrying out Western-style rituals of celebrating birthdays and how these experiences broker not only their parents' knowledge about British birthday parties, but also their wider understanding of British culture.

Ever since human beings have been able to keep time and understand the pattern of cycles, they have marked or celebrated special or important days in their lives. Numerous rites of passage occur in the human lifetime and our lives are full of ritualised behaviours (Rook, 1985). The celebration of birthdays is one of the most common age-related rituals, although they occur in many different forms across the world. Historically, it is said that birthday celebrations are an ancient European tradition that dates back to the pagan cultures before the rise of Christianity and came about as an attempt to ward off evil spirits that made people more vulnerable on their birthday (Rinkoff, 1967); hence the traditions of gift-giving and well-wishing. The fact that there are few records of early birthday celebrations might suggest that only kings and other high-ranking nobles were wealthy enough to celebrate their birthday, and this may explain some countries' custom of wearing a birthday crown when celebrating birthdays. As time went on, common people, rich or poor, came to have their own birthday celebrated in various ways. Factors such as social and economic status, traditions and customs specific to families in different countries and people of various religions determine how birthdays are celebrated. This suggests that the marking of birthdays is a deeply-rooted social, cultural and historical phenomenon (Grime, 2000), and thus while people new to a country may well understand the notion of celebrating birthdays, the particular customs and practices of the new country may be very unfamiliar.

Celebrating birthdays in the Western world

The concept of birthday is 'complex, multidimensional and integrative' and not 'as simple as it seems' (Klavir & Leiser, 2002: 252). First of all, birthday celebrations appear to be a time to exhibit one's individuation. Generally, a birthday involves a party centred on the celebrant. The birthday party can be perceived as a symbolic action that is 'essential to the development of self-hood' (Horowitz, 1993: 261) and identity. The procedural activities such as having a cake with candles on it, receiving gifts and being sung the birthday song seem to dramatise social relationships between the individual and other members of his/her group. It may also act as a convenient way of bringing together families and friends and thus cement and reinforce the social relationships of individuals. The modern Western birthday party for a child derives from Germany, with the word *Kinderfest* (children's festival) (Pleck, 2000). Around the 1920s, with the introduction of party-planning books, children in most Western countries came to associate birthday parties with cakes, songs, gifts and games (Rinkoff, 1967). According to Pleck (2000: 141), 'birthday parties are seen as such an essential part of childhood that the lack of one proves parental indifference, if not outright neglect'. For children themselves, the social aspects of birthdays appear visible and dominant in their lives, and children value their parties. Some young children (aged between four and six) assume that their birthdays are synonymous with celebrating parties (Klavir & Leiser, 2002; Shamgar-Handelman & Handelman, 1991).

Secondly, birthday celebrations are concerned with the concept of time and time-related aspects of life. Similar to a wedding ceremony, a birthday party reinforces the universal emphasis on human maturation (Pleck, 2000), and indicates a change in the person's social status. Older children (aged between seven and nine) understand that a party celebrates something more than a social occasion; rather, it includes the irreversibility of biological ageing and a cultural construction of time (Shamgar-Handelman & Handelman, 1991). Celebrating their birthdays suggests how children conceptualise the cyclical, linear and episodic nature of time (Klavir & Leiser, 2002). As a public occasion, the party marks a stage of biological growth, makes salient a child's personal growth in socialisation and acknowledges a child's movement towards adulthood.

Thirdly, the complexity of the birthday concept resides in its relevance to that of age. Shamgar-Handelman and Handelman (1991) claim that a birthday party is actually a celebration of age. Age is the index of time, social status and even one's potential and capabilities. Generally speaking, chronological age is still an important criterion of social demarcation and a 'conceptual apparatus' to create social order (Musgrove & Middleton, 1981: 53). People of different age categories are ranked and assigned different social roles in 'relatively enduring ways' (Foner, 1975: 147, cited in Shamgar-Handelman & Handelman, 1991: 295). Age determines the criteria of numerous obligations and rights, e.g. at certain ages, one can enter into formal education, have an identity card, marry legally, be recruited into the armed forces and so on. For children themselves, age appears significant since it determines their daily activities such as school and recreation. On one day in every year, a child bids farewell to his/her membership of one age category, and includes himself/herself in another. They are individuated and reclassified into the new category of social norms. This inclusion–exclusion or discard–recast process for children seems to be the point when they are supposed to get ready for different moral and social expectations and normative practices bestowed on them by society. In other words, birthday parties tend to indicate a transition and a movement from childhood to adulthood.

Research on birthday parties suggests that only very limited attention has been paid to this 'deceptively simple' yet prevalent concept in human life. Feng (1994) reports that children from non-Western cultural origins do not have birthday celebration practices and that some Asian-American children do not have a tradition of celebrating their birthdays with their peers. However, other studies find that birthday parties in many countries tend to be Westernised. Hendry (1986) mentions that in recent years, Japanese children's birthday celebrations have followed Western principles such as having a cake with candles and a gathering of friends who dress up and bring gifts. Baumann (1992) explored a joint birthday celebration for two children (aged 11 and 8 years, respectively) in a Punjabi family that took place in a seemingly 'English' way, despite the Punjabi tradition that a child's birthday is not celebrated. The parents invited guests, most of whom were from Punjabi backgrounds. During the party, although there were some special preparations such as folk dancing and the elder feeding the celebrants the cake rather than the celebrants offering cakes to the guests, the celebration included what Nesbitt (1995) calls typical Western rituals such as cutting the cake and singing the birthday song. Baumann suggests that the parents had incorporated the Western ideas of tracing time and acknowledging individuality into their particular way of demonstrating their parental affection for their children. However, the study did not mention how the children participated in the planning of the party or to what extent their views were taken into account.

Otnes and McGrath (1994) explored how American preschool children are socialised to participate in such a modern ritual. They investigated gender differences in ritual socialisation and found that boys focus more on aggressive activities and games, while girls appear to prefer more sedate activities and pay more attention to tangible ritual artefacts than boys do. Otnes et al. (1995) further emphasise the process by which mothers socialise their children through ritual artefacts, scripts, performance roles and ritual audience involvement in the birthday party, while at the same time the children are actively involved in the different steps. Their study also finds that British parents endeavour to make their children's birthday parties distinct from those of their peers. This finds support in Pleck's (2000) historical report that children's demands, together with parents' desire for novelty and the sense of competition have been driving birthday parties outside the home since the 1980s. Current studies on birthday parties tend to disregard how children lead any change in the family birthday celebrations, and how they influence their parents' decisions about parties.

In traditional Chinese culture, people can add a year to their age at Chinese New Year. Many Chinese people paid little attention to their birthdays and even did not remember them at all until the early 1980s (Watson 2005). Conventionally, in some areas of China, only elderly people are regarded as qualified or respectable enough to have their birthdays celebrated as big events. Most adults' birthdays were not celebrated or they were only marked with treats such as eating noodles and eggs that symbolise a long life and good luck.This was also the case with most children's birthdays. The other reason for not celebrating a child's birthday was that a child's birthday marks a mother's physical 'pain day', which should be tempered and attenuated as much as possible. However, the custom of a 'full month' birthday prevails in many areas of China and in immigrant Chinese communities (Pleck, 2000). This is a celebration held within families a month after an infant's birth, since it was traditionally regarded as the child becoming one year old (Newman, 2004). A celebration is also held on the first anniversary of a child's birth (when a child is one year old according to the Western reckoning of ages) when the child is regarded as two years old. This celebration traditionally involves displaying a variety of objects in front of the baby. An ancient belief is that what the baby picks up may predict his/her future career. Another custom from the past was that family members would bring the child special food and gifts of clothing or toys decorated with tigers, which were believed to protect the child from harm and danger.

My small-scale survey of parents in China suggests that if a child's birthday is celebrated, it is primarily done so by families and relatives. In recent years, some families have started to celebrate the first birthday of a child by inviting close relatives and/or the parents' friends to a get-together at a restaurant. My brother emailed me family photos taken at a dinner for my nephew's first birthday. In the survey, one 11-year-old girl had invited five of her classmates to her birthday celebration. This is consistent with Yan's (2005) finding that some children now have their birthday parties, with a few guests, in local McDonald's fast-food restaurants in Beijing, and with Watson's (2005) report that a party package including food, cake and gifts tends to attract faddish youngsters in Hong Kong, Beijing and Shanghai. However, most parents still think it unimportant to have birthdays celebrated because they themselves never had any birthday celebration; a few of them, however, agree that a child's birthday should be celebrated in order to show the child attention and affection, and to inform the child that he or she has grown a year older. The survey points to a Western influence on children's birthday celebrations in China. The traditional point of view that a child's birthday should not be celebrated appears to be shifting to the new perspective that children's birthdays are worth celebrating. However, in spite of Western influence on procedures, most children's celebrations are still limited to within families.

Against this background, we shall see below how in the families in the study, children affect parental understanding, planning and decisions related to birthday parties, i.e. how children act as agents to impart knowledge of birthday celebrations to their parents, shape their parents' ritualistic practices and socialise their parents to participate in a range of birthday party procedures.

The birthday party becomes a salient topic from the data for three reasons. Firstly, disparity in children's birthday celebrations between cultures leads to a large amount of birthday-related conversation and activity within the families. Secondly, birthday parties are such a popular social activity in children's lives in England that it seems that no family with children can actually escape from attending or throwing a party every now and then in any one year, although not all English families have the finances for expensive birthday parties for their children. The third reason is that, underpinning birthday celebrations in Britain, there are a number of broader cultural beliefs, attitudes and assumptions that are not necessarily familiar to parents in immigrant families.

Mediating rituals of birthday celebration

The Chinese parents were very surprised to find that in the UK most children's birthdays are celebrated not just within families but also with the child's friends by, for example, holding a party. A party with friends is important in the British child's life and Chinese children new to Britain may easily spot the different practices in terms of birthday celebrations and may, unconsciously, pass on these differences to their parents. The parents initially had no knowledge of the procedures of birthday rituals in Britain, let alone their significance in children's lives and in the new culture. They learned how to deal with the relevant procedures through their children's growing awareness of how British children celebrate their birthdays. These are instances of events or incidents happening initially in the children's lives, which impact on the parents' understanding and knowledge.

This knowledge starts with noticing what children do and how they act in their school life. In the Yang family, during the first months after their arrival in the UK, Ming and Liang sometimes brought home some chocolate and sweets from school, which they usually showed their mother as they left the school, in order to get permission to eat one or two on their way home (access to sweets is often restricted in some Chinese families). In these cases, Mrs Yang was told that the sweets came from a child in the class who had had a birthday. In one of my first conversations, Mrs Yang asked me if I knew that children in the UK brought something into school for their classmates to eat on their birthday. She was not really able to attach any significant meaning to these events. I could not answer her until I noticed my own daughter had the same experience with her friends at school.

Parents wanted some confirmation of what they had concluded from their children's behaviour about aspects of the new culture. They wanted to know if a similar phenomenon happened in other schools in the UK. The parents were also seeking more understanding of this ritualistic phenomenon, which contradicts their own belief about children eating sweets. At this moment, child cultural mediation draws the parents' attention to a different practice. Despite the incidents of getting sweets from classmates, the parents still had no real awareness of other ways of celebrating a child's birthday, not even an idea of the underlying principles of parties. Although the relevant norms or rituals may have been assumed and become unreflective to British parents and children, the Chinese parents built up their knowledge base about birthday parties when their children started to attend their peers' birthday parties, or rather, when they received their first invitations to parties.

To parents who are new to the ritual, the idea of children attending parties may seem more complicated than it looks to a native. Although for the children it is an opportunity to just go and enjoy themselves, for the parents it is an occasion for learning. Their children's attendance at parties offers the parents opportunities to learn about the ritual, and there may not be any other channels of learning. Children mediate the rituals to their parents through every step in the process of attending a party.

A party invitation

An invitation to a child's birthday party means the possibility of attending a party. In July 2003, the second month after the Tang family's arrival in the UK, seven-year-old Ming was invited to a birthday party at a Wacky Warehouse (an indoor play area). She was very excited and desperately wanted to go. The parents could not but agree because, after all, this was the first party that Ming was going to attend in the new country. At that moment, neither Ming nor her parents knew what the party would be like, nor what the children would do. Through Ming attending, her parents were able to gain a general picture about a child's birthday party, and Ming's attendance satisfied both the parents' and the child's curiosity and needs.

Something similar occurred in the Zhao family when four-year-old Lin received his first invitation from one of his friends in his reception class to a birthday party at a Wacky Warehouse. His mother told me,

Of course Lin must go, as neither he nor I have ever seen what a birthday party looks like. We had been looking forward to being invited since I had only heard of the parties from other parents. (Translated fieldnotes)

Lin's mother is keen to learn about the birthday ritual. There seems to have been no disagreement or hesitation before the decision was made to attend this party.

From their children receiving invitations, the Chinese parents will have learned how far in advance the invitations should be sent out and what a party invitation looks like. Through their children's descriptions, the parents may have a general picture of a birthday party in the new country. However, acceptance of a birthday party invitation only provides the possibility of learning. Although almost none of the children refused a party invitation, acceptance of the invitation posed some dilemmas for the parents. It means more details for the parents to consider, such as what presents are proper to buy and what clothes they and their children should wear to the party. The process of preparing for the child's attending a party is another trial-and-error process in understanding party etiquette.

What presents to buy

Gift-giving is a very important component of British children's birthday parties. In the Tang family, as Ming was being allowed to go to her first party, by now her mother had realised that gift-giving was important and she had to start thinking about what present to buy. For Mrs Tang, a number of problems now existed. How much should she spend? What kind of present would be socially and personally acceptable? Mrs Tang's strategy for solving these problems was to go to Tesco and ask staff there what would be appropriate. On their recommendation, she bought a Barbie doll without consulting her daughter. However, on showing this to Ming, Mrs Tang was told that the girl for whom the present was bought did not like Barbie dolls. Having learned a lesson from this, from then on Mrs Tang always took her daughter along with her when she needed to buy birthday presents for children. She said, 'I have to take Ming to buy presents because she can help me to choose' (translated fieldnotes). Ming told me that usually she and her brother chose the presents and then they would negotiate with their mother, mostly in terms of their cost.

In the Zhao family, Lin did not go with his mother to buy a present for his friend's birthday. This is not because his mother could manage on her own but because, according to Lin's mother, her son did not seem to care about what present to take to the party. He cared very much about what games he would be playing. However, Mrs Zhao admitted that although the present she bought was appropriate for a girl (since it was a girl's party), she did not realise that the present was still inappropriate in terms of cost until Lin got an expensive birthday present from the little girl, who later attended his birthday party. Though a bit embarrassing, this helped Mrs Zhao to adjust her later expenditure on birthday presents for other children.

Thus, the mothers adopted different strategies, either depending on their children to make choices in the purchase or being taught lessons for future purchases through trial and error. Unlike the mothers in Otnes et al.'s (1995) study who deliberately planned themes and bought artefacts together with their children, Mrs Tang had to take her children with her to the shops and even discuss the theme with her children due to her own lack of background knowledge on this ritual practice. She needed guidance from her children, whereas in Otnes et al.'s study, it is the parents who guide their children. The situation in Lin's family was different. His mother had her own plan and budget to buy a present without Lin accompanying her. Although this is just one case, it is consistent with Otnes and McGrath's (1994) finding that girls tend to be more involved than boys in birthday present buying and pay more attention to tangible items in ritual activities while boys focus more on the games.

What to wear to a party

After the parents and the children had made the decision about attending the parties and had bought the presents, the children were able just to look forward to the day. However, the mothers' minds were still working on the next consideration of what to wear on the party day. They were perhaps wondering 'What should I, or my child wear, in order not to show any inappropriateness', and even 'Do I have to stay there and watch my child?'. The answer to the second question could be solved on the day, but an imminent decision had to be made on what to wear.

Lin's mother expressed this kind of perplexity before her son went to his first party. She said that her son did not care too much about what to wear at that age and wore a T-shirt in his favourite colour. But as for her own dress code, it took her quite a while to make a compromise between a dress and jeans. Eventually she chose an informal dress. On the party day, everything seemed all right, but the mother admitted that she should not have bothered too much about what to wear. She said,

I saw that some other parents just wore what they usually wear, just like when they pick up their children from school. Then I understood that the main characters in the party are the children not the parents. Why was I bothered? Also, most of the parents did not stay and only turned up at the moments of leaving and collecting their children. The boys in the party did not look very unusual in what they wore, but there were some little girls wearing their pretty dresses. (Translated fieldnotes)

Thus, from careful observation, parents gain some idea of the dress code for different participants on this ritualistic occasion.

A party bag

A party bag, also called a 'goody bag' is a plastic bag, usually printed with popular cultural images such as Winnie-the-Pooh, Snow White or Shrek. In the bag, the party organiser puts a slice of birthday cake, snacks and small toys for the participants to take home after the party finishes. Since the party bag requires presents to be bought by the organising side for the participating children, it becomes a big issue for parents when they find themselves organising their own child's party. The Chinese parents learned about the contents of the bag from their own children attending parties.

While I was observing one Saturday in September 2003, Liang came back from a birthday party. In his party bag, there was a small portion of birthday cake, several chocolate bars, a few balloons of different colours and a whistle shaped like a football. His mother said to me 'that is what they brought back from a birthday party, the cake and the chocolates are all too too sweet' (translated fieldnotes). At his mother's suggestion, Liang agreed to share the sweet cake with his sister, though he looked reluctant. Liang's response to sharing the cake was the same as that of the children in Otnes and McGrath's (1994) study, for whom cakes were an everyday taboo or forbidden food. Liang's mother said, 'it is interesting that children do not eat their cake at the party, but bring it back. And the children are treated with a meal at the party' (translated fieldnotes).

A special birthday party

On 8 June 2004, I went with Mrs Tang to collect Ming and Liang from school at the end of the school day. Before the children came out of their classrooms, Mrs Tang said to me, 'The first thing that Liang will tell me must be that he got some sweets from somebody's birthday, and he will ask if he can eat one now'. We both laughed when Liang came up to her, since Liang did get some sweets that day and did ask exactly that question. When Ming came out of the junior area of the school, she showed her mother an invitation card. The following is an extract from the conversation between Ming and her mother.

M: Mrs Tang (the mother); **G**: Ming (the nine-year-old girl). Note: the text in italics is translated from Chinese.

G: Mum, look, this is, Molly, 8th, 8th horse-riding birthday party on Sunday 8th of August, you look, this is her horse.
M: *Ah, is this her family's horse? How beautiful!*
G: *It is 4, 4 to 6 o'clock,* then it is in Glade Jade Riding School, East Lane Road, Wallfoton.
M: *Where is the place?*
G: Wallfoton
M: *Where is Wallfoton?*
G: *There is a Glade Jade Riding School, she said it is near someone...* *
(inaudible).
M: *Oh, does everyone get this, or just* girls?
G: *No. Only some*
M: *Ah, only some.*
G: *I was the* first one to get the invitation.
M: Why?
G: *Because as soon as* Molly *took that, she took my name.*
M: *Really! She only invited girls, right?*
G: *I don't know.*
M: *8th of August, the Father's Day in Taiwan. Ah, here attached a map. Look,*
(Then she turned to me, with a smile) *how thoughtful is the organizer! I seem to have never been to this place, I will have to look for it first. I become familiar with many places just because I need to send the children to different party venues.*

The above extract shows that receiving the card acted as the start of this mediating instance. Although the parents may have known about birthday parties from preparing their children for them, Mrs Tang and her daughter were puzzled as to what a horse-riding party really looked like. It is clear that Ming was very glad that she had been invited. It seems that Mrs Tang was also impressed with the idea of a horse-riding party and the thoughtfulness of the party organiser. However, her attention was very quickly diverted to the practicality of dealing with the party: the venue and how to get there. Mrs Tang said that attending parties also enriched her daily experiences by just getting to know the locations and the themes of the parties.

When Ming got the party invitation, the discussion around it became one of the central topics in the household. On 17 June 2004, while the two children were telling their mother about their day at school, Ming asked her mother about attending the party. The following extract is from a transcript of the family's own recording.

M: Mrs Tang (the mother); **G**: Ming (the nine-year-old girl). Note: the text in italics is translated from Chinese.

G: *Can I go to* Molly's *horse-riding party?*
M: *OK.*
G: Yeah! *Can we buy a, some small* horses *for her since she* loves horses?
M: *What small horses?*
G: I just looked at the lucky shop to *see if there are* the gifts, little horses *because she* loves horses, *her* favourite thing in the world is horses
M: *Then in her house she must have lots of horses, doesn't she?*
G: *Mm. Everybody must buy many* horses *for her,* even boys.

As Otnes and McGrath (1994) suggest, girls are more interested in the tangible items involved in a birthday party, and this extract shows eight-year-old Ming offering advice to her mother on the choice of a present, not only what present to buy but also where to buy it. In later chats between Ming and her mother, I discovered that Ming's advice was quite useful in making the purchase.

On the party day, Mrs Tang got Ming to the party on time and she rode on a horse for the first time in her life. Ming told her parents that children were entertained by riding on well-trained horses that performed different acts according to instructions and music. She also commented that this horse-riding party was unique and was the most enjoyable party she had yet attended. Ming said more to her mother in the next extract,

M: the mother (Mrs Tang), **G**: the girl (Ming). Note: the text in italics is translated from Chinese.

G: *It was a great fun, and my* horse *was called* Pickie. *It was a boy.* We had a race and played musical statues. *It is just to go straight, straight, and straight and then* block the horse.
M: *What is block?*
G: It is just walk around a circle, make a block, a stop.

This extract illustrates a typical cultural brokering episode in which Ming excitedly told her parents about what she had been doing at the party. As usual, her parents did not know all the words and had to stop her to ask. In addition, Ming was conscious of some words she thought she had taught her parents. Figure 7.4 is an extract from Ming's notebook.

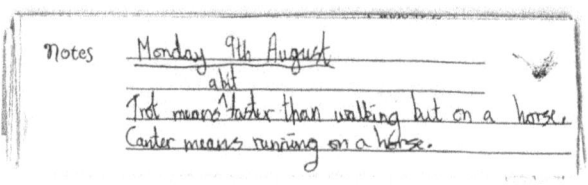

Figure 7.4   A word entry in Ming's notebook

Like all the other words, sentences, rhymes and doggerels that Ming wrote in her notebook, 'trot' and 'canter' were two words that she thought she had taught her mother. Although it is not clear if the girl had learned the words from the party or from her schoolwork, her teaching them to her parents took place after the party.

The horse-riding party was also most surprising to her parents. After the party, although he was very tired but glad that Ming had enjoyed the party so much on the day, her father said,

I've never heard of having a party in a horse-riding ring, but children do enjoy it very much. I've never thought of anything like that. This is how children in the Western countries are brought up. They feel themselves special, making fun and becoming socialized. (Translated fieldnotes)

Up to this point, the parents seemed to have some knowledge and understanding of the procedures for a child's birthday party through preparing their children to attend a party and noticing what their children brought home from a party. However, all this experience did not fully prepare them for that inevitable moment when it was their child's birthday and they had to organise the party.

Organising birthday parties

There are quite a lot of issues to consider in organising a party. The first is the venue: where should the party be? This venue may determine the theme, how well the party appeals to the children coming to it and what the children will play when they are there. The venue also affects what the children are going to eat during the party. The second is timing: when is it best to reserve the party venue? What day is appropriate to hold a party particularly when the actual birthday is not on a weekend? When is the best time to send out invitations? The third is participants: how many and which children should be invited? How should the invitations be passed to the other children? Is it the child or the parent who sends out the invitations? Fourth is the question of presents or the contents of the party bags: what presents should be put in the party bags for the participants to take home and where can a birthday cake be bought and what kind of birthday cake is appropriate? Lastly, on the party day, how should the host or hostess cater for the children – and perhaps their parents as well – and what behaviour is appropriate as party organisers? What games or prizes are appropriate? What timing or sequence is appropriate for each of the procedures or programmes such as games, cake presentation, blowing out the candles, eating the party tea and sending the guests off with the party bags? To parents who have only been in the new country for a short period of time, these seemed to be massive hurdles to cross one after the other, for none of the parents wanted their child to be embarrassed or humiliated because the parent had got something wrong. Even though some parents tried to find excuses for not having a birthday party, ultimately they could not escape. This day came in the Tang family when Liang had his fifth birthday, his first birthday in the UK.

Liang's first birthday party

When Liang was about to turn five years old, his parents agreed to host a party and invite his friends as he requested. Mrs Tang said that although it was their first experience of hosting a party, she felt more confident than before as Liang and Ming had attended several parties so she had a better grasp of what was required.

After discussing the issues together, they decided on an indoor play area in a local pub; Liang had attended a classmate's party in the same place.

Mrs Tang told me that she had chosen that venue for several reasons. First, the appropriateness of the arena was guaranteed as some of the participants had been there before. Second, in addition to an indoor play area, the location serves Western meals for children such as chicken nuggets and pizza and deals with the invitation cards and the party bags as well as a birthday cake. The staff take care of the timing for each step of the programme on the day. The whole package makes Mrs Tang's life much easier since many of the problems mentioned in the previous section are immediately solved. All she needed to do was to book the place, send out the invitations, look after the children and entertain their parents as necessary on the day. Interestingly, it was the similarity to other children's birthday parties that made her feel secure. This appears distinct from Otnes *et al.*'s (1994) study where the parents' emphasis was on trying to make their children's birthday parties unique.

Mrs Tang emphasised to me that unlike children in Taiwan, Liang made his own decisions about who would be invited to the party; she did not intervene, but just paid for the party. Although there was a member of staff in the party arena, I saw both Mr and Mrs Tang busy keeping an eye on the timing, and entertaining all the children and one or two parents who had stayed for the party. They looked very relieved when the parents came to collect their children who had been eating and playing for about two hours.

When chatting about the birthday party, Mrs Tang told me, 'It is quite expensive for us and I have taken time and trouble coping with the different procedures. But what else can I do, children in the UK always have their birthday parties in this way' (translated fieldnotes). Mr Tang said 'I think this is good for children. This is how children in the UK have fun and make friends from when they are very young' (translated fieldnotes). For Liang, these issues seemed secondary to his concerns about his presents, as most children enjoy unwrapping presents (Otnes & McGrath, 1994). Probably for the reason that children's burning interest in unwrapping birthday presents worries some parents in terms of how their children might respond to these presents (Otnes & McGrath, 1994), Liang was only allowed to open his presents when they were all back at home from the party venue. The first thing he asked when they got back home was 'Can I open my presents now?'. The boy's amazed and joyous 'Wow's made Mrs Tang keep coming back into the living room to look at the presents. She found there were different kinds of toys and toy cars, and even a five-pound note in an envelope, 'Ah, cash can be sent as a present as well?!', she exclaimed. This suggests that parents did not just apply what they had learned to the organisation of parties, but they had also got more ideas and more references as to what sort of birthday presents to send. Whether parents realised it or not, as time went on, their knowledge of birthday parties was being enriched.

We can see then that a child's birthday party is an alien practice for the parents. They themselves have not been equipped with sufficient knowledge about parties and are not sure about how appropriate it is to have other kinds of parties. However, they have to take action in order to meet their children's needs. They would rather follow the pattern of other parties than to risk embarrassing their children and themselves.

Deciding a theme for Ming's ninth birthday party

About a month after the horse-riding party, it was Ming's ninth birthday. Ming had asked if she could have a horse-riding party as well so that she could ride a horse again. This request was declined, and Ming accepted it. She said 'my mum said it is a bit expensive, and I don't want to be a copy cat anyway'. This last remark is interesting in that it shows Ming diverging from the strategy of following the pattern of other parties that parents use as a safe approach to organising a party. Eventually, they decided to have a swimming party. Ming said, 'That is Dad's idea, and it turned out to be good'. Mr Tang explained:

from the parties the children have attended, it is just that to invite other children to play a sport or an activity that most children like, or at least it should be what your child likes doing. Ming likes swimming, and I have asked a leisure centre where children above eight years old can go to the pool themselves. (Translated fieldnotes)

Since the leisure centre did not provide food for the party children, both Ming and her parents agreed to book dinner at a nearby McDonald's for which the mother had already saved some vouchers. As to the contents of the party bag, Mrs Tang had taken advantage of their short trip back to Taiwan in August of that year, and brought some stationery from Taiwan, as she explained:

Ming went to the shop in Taiwan together with me, and she said buying stationery is a good idea. It is not expensive for me as well. The children coming to the party also liked it. (Translated fieldnotes)

Having been in the UK for two and a half years, Ming and Liang had attended about 30 parties with different attractive names such as a strawberry-picking party, a bowling party and a Wacky Warehouse play party. Almost half of their weekends each term were occupied with attending a party. After so many parties, their mother seemed very confident in dealing with presents.

I can just go to Tesco on my own now to buy presents for their classmates, most often I can pick up the right things. I am very experienced now, so to speak. (Translated fieldnote)

For the Tang family, the swimming party was a success and it shows that the parents had adjusted to the birthday party ritual quite well. Mr Tang had learned how to decide on the theme of the birthday party, and Mrs Tang had grasped the norms of arranging the birthday meal and filling the party bags. Mr Tang commented, 'If I go back to Taiwan, I would start having birthday parties for my children. It is a good thing for children' (translated fieldnotes). In comparison with the first birthday celebration organised for their son, they had made great progress, from depending on a packaged birthday party service for many of the steps in the procedure, to designing almost every step on their own initiative. With Ming actively participating in the planning of the theme, the food and the contents of the party bags, the parents arranged everything appropriately. The parents had thus appropriated the practice into their daily life since they had bought things for the party when they went back to their home country for a short stay. More importantly, it seems that the parents had come to appreciate the underpinning value of birthday parties.

Accommodating to the ritual of birthday celebration

None of the families excluded themselves from this birthday-celebrating cultural practice. Parties for children's friends' birthdays were very popular and took up many weekends and much leisure time. The families' daily lives were involved in buying presents, getting ready for the parties, delivering and collecting the children and other related activities. Since birthday parties were not customary for the parents, they tended to pay extra attention to each step of the procedure for attending and organising birthday parties, to make sure they conformed with the norm of the majority. They did not want their children to feel different from their peer community.

The process of accommodation to the relevant principles, codes of behaviours and even the underpinning values is gradual. Similar to learning about the card-related ritual, parents' accommodation started with their appropriation of the relevant procedures in preparing and observing their children attending other parties. They learned how to be a good participant in attending parties, what presents were appropriate to buy for the birthday child, and if there was any particular dress code for a party attendee, or for his/her parents. As for organising parties, they learned how to be a sensible party organiser, when to send a party invitation, what to do before a party and what to put in a party bag, as an important component of party planning.

After attending a few parties, the parents had to apply this knowledge to their own organisation of parties, due to their children's request for their own party. Pleck (2000) describes a similar situation where children begged their parents for a Western-style birthday party. Although the parents had acquired some knowledge, they had to depend on their children's active participation in the party planning. The process of organising Liang's first birthday party and Ming's swimming party suggests how indispensable children's participation is in carrying out the procedures appropriately. It also suggests that Mrs Tang seems to have appropriated the codes for the birthday food, which is not the traditional Chinese food she thought best for children, but purely Western-style food. Moreover, both parents seem to have successfully applied the knowledge of how to invent a party theme, how the location of the party should be decided, as well as other detailed procedures such as what presents to buy to fill the party bags. Attending and organising birthday parties allowed ample opportunity for parents to appreciate the birthday party ritual. They came to understand the values beneath it. Mr Tang's comment in particular, that he would have parties in Taiwan because they help children to make friends, suggests that parents have accommodated to the cultural practice of celebrating a child's birthday and the underlying purposes and values.

In comparison with the process of accommodating to the card-related ritual, there seems less resistance or conflict in the discussion between parents and children on the birthday celebration procedures. This may be because parents realise the importance of parties in externally presenting their families to others. Furthermore, birthday parties are not just experiences for the children, but also a source of fun for the parents. In a sense, the parties also enriched the daily recreational activities of these families new to the mainstream society.

In spite of the parents' ultimate endorsement of the practice, the learning process caused tension, unease and stress for the parents. Liang's mother realised that the child himself decided whom to invite while the parents' direct role was just to provide financial assistance wherever necessary. In order to alleviate the stress in coping with the procedures, some parents still tried to find an excuse to avoid parties either for financial reasons or social reasons or both. Moreoover, none of the parents organised their children's parties at home on their own. Instead, they relied on packaged birthday party services, which suggests that even though the parents have been exposed to and informed of the customs and practices, it may still take time for them to internalise their learning and apply their knowledge confidently and autonomously. In other words, birthday parties can involve rich ceremony (Klavir & Leiser, 2002) and parents need practice, as is the case with any other ritual implementation (Grime, 2000).

Processes of Accommodation

Engaging with cultural differences in parenting

Celebrating a child's birthday seems to suggest that the social position of children or their status as individuals has been perceived differently in China and Britain, as well as highlighting different parenting practices and perspectives.

In Western countries such as the UK, a birthday party enables children to be conscious of their own status as an individual in relation to other children, e.g. in the presentation of a birthday cake and the receiving of gifts (Hendry, 1986; Otnes & McGrath, 1994; Otnes *et al.*, 1995; Shamgar-Handelman & Handelman, 1991; Weil, 1986). However, as argued in Chapter 1, the collectivism embedded within Chinese culture may imply that being an individual and special might not be as important as attaching oneself to a collective group that has more similarities than differences. In other words, specialness seems to be synonymous with difference, which is not evocative of collectivism. Thus, while Western parents are more likely to develop a child's self and uniqueness (Jose *et al.*, 2000), Chinese parents tend to encourage their children to be attuned to their families, communities and society without stressing their differences from others (Markus & Kitayama, 1991). Additionally, feeling special may strengthen a self-conceited and arrogant personality, which is against the Confucian idea that children should be cultivated to be modest. In the Tang family, this traditional notion of bringing up a child has shifted so much that Mr Tang seems to embrace the value that children should feel special even at a young age.

Secondly, independence seems to be viewed differently by parents in the two cultures. English parents perceive independence as a very important quality for children to have in order to survive on their own in society and react to the outside world in their own ways. As Klein (1965: 547) claims, 'independence is highly valued in almost all strata of English society, traditional or mobile, working class or middle class'. Children are supposed to thinking independently and have their own social contacts. In order to foster independence, children need to develop the relevant skills and abilities in all aspects of life from a young age. To English parents, choosing their own friends to play with can be part of independence training (Klein, 1965). They may take advantage of schooling and other social activities such as parties to develop their children's social skills. In China, independence seems to have been conceptualised differently. Xiao (2000: 468) claims, 'historically, Chinese education did not emphasise independent thinking'. Independence is synonymous with self-sufficiency in terms of materialistic resources (Xiao, 1999). Therefore, parents expect their children to achieve educational success, leading to career success in order to support themselves financially. As Francis and Archer (2005) find, Chinese people, irrespective of their social and economic class, tend to value education in a child's development. Davis and Sensenbrenner (2000) also reported that generally the success of a Chinese child is measured by his/her educational achievements in China. Comparatively speaking, Chinese parents pay more attention to their children's academic achievement (Lin & Fu, 1990; Smith, 1989) and tend to think that children's social skills are less important than their academic skills and that their social skills can be developed later in life.

Thirdly, English parents tend to think that children, as well as adults, should enjoy life as much as possible by relaxing more and working less: childhood should be a period free of worry and full of happiness. In order to achieve this, parents expect to make a great effort both mentally and financially in order to enrich their children's cultural experiences from a young age. In China, bringing up a child is more concerned with developing self-control and discipline (*guan jiao*) via parental training rather than indulging the child, as is also the case in other traditional east and south-east Asian cultures (Chao, 1994; Feng, 1994; Jose *et al.*, 2000; Lin & Fu, 1990). Thus, Chinese parents are likely to exert more influence and control over their children's development than English parents do. Furthermore, Confucianism tells parents that in order to attain economic achievements, children are supposed to work hard and play less when they are young. Along with obedience and hard work, thrift and saving are also valued in Confucian doctrines in order to bring prosperity to families (Ho, 1994; Xiao, 2000). This is another reason for not offering children luxurious materialistic resources (holding a birthday party may be counted in this category) to encourage lavish habits. Therefore, it is not the case that parents do not want to enrich their children's experiences, but they would rather prioritise their resources in educational activities or training (Francis & Archer, 2005; Huntsinger *et al.*, 1997). At a time of limited resources, celebrating children's birthdays can be put off until later in life.

The process of ritual socialisation

The generally accepted sequence of socialisation assumes that parents have been socialised much earlier than their children, and thus, in turn, socialise their children. Conventionally, this seems true for ritual socialisation in a given society. Otnes and McGrath (1994) have defined ritual socialisation as:

the processes by which individuals acquire the abilities, interests and information necessary for them to participate in rituals, and to master the use and understanding of specific goods and services used by themselves and others in a ritual setting. (Otnes & McGrath, 1994: 44–75)

This definition suggests that there is no fixed order of ritual socialisation and that it depends on practices and situations in different sociocultural contexts. Otnes *et al.* (1995) describe how mothers in mainstream American society take advantage of various moments and opportunities related to birthday parties to instil in their children ritual knowledge of mainstream culture in the USA. However, what we have seen here is that the parents' understanding tends to happen subsequent to that of their children. The children knew better and earlier than their parents, and thus informed or influenced their parents' behaviour. The socialisation of the birthday celebration ritual in the families is a reversed sequence. While the mothers in Otnes *et al.*'s (1995) study are conscious of their particular roles as a socialising agent and the intended outcomes, the children here may not, or may only slightly, realise their own mediating and teaching roles to their parents.

In addition, the above definition of ritual socialisation seems to stress the learning of information and the use and understanding of certain goods and services. It suggests that here, children facilitated their parents' learning about how to organise birthday parties, which made them feel quite confident in dealing with the presents, the packaged services and other aspects of the ritual. The parents have obtained, from their children and through their children, basic knowledge related to the skill that enables them to practise more at later opportunities.

Ritual studies (e.g. Baumann, 1992; Harris, 1997) suggest that ritual practices involve the performance of different participants, creating and constructing social dimensions (De Coppet, 1992). As Parkin (1992: 14) claims, rituals 'are not just expressive of abstract ideas but do things, have effects on the world, and are work that is carried out – that they are indeed performances'. In addition to its explicit meaning, i.e. the rules or customs to follow, the ritual still has implicit symbolic meanings that may form a basis for social identities (Horowitz, 1993) and transmit a value or a complex set of values for a particular group (Harris, 1997). English parents, in organising parties for their children or themselves, are actually relating their actions to their systems of beliefs and values about the child, childhood and individuals. Harris (1997: 39) argues that the participants of a ritual may 'regularly participate in and actively utilise highly meaningful symbolic systems uncomprehendingly'. To some English parents, the birthday ritual has been present throughout their lives and they are so accustomed to it that they may just carry out the procedures without reflection, and maybe without much comprehension either. However, the Chinese parents, in the process of carrying out the ritual, led by their children's involvement in the peer culture, use it to comprehend and appreciate the value system about children and childhood in the mainstream culture. Although the parents seem to be concerned mostly with the procedural rules or customs of a birthday party, their elaborate preparations for the party suggest that they are actually seeking to share, whether ostensibly or unconsciously, the underlying values that the ritual represents.

Further, the birthday party can be viewed as a collective ritual carried out among the peers of a mainstream school, and as an opportunity for the Chinese children to integrate with that cultural group. As Durkheim (1976) argues, a collective ritual may provide integration into the social group. A ritual can be a special occasion to reflect the participants' common beliefs and knowledge foundation, and may also offer a sense of sharing them (Parkin, 1992). Attending and organising birthday parties help to build friendships and negotiate differing social relationships with the Chinese children's peers and the peers' parents in the mainstream society. Children as well as their parents, through the Western-styled birthday party, display a conformity to or integration into the ritual practice of the mainstream society.

Implicit child cultural mediation in the birthday ritual

Birthday celebrations also show how child cultural mediation happens in daily life without children's consciousness or volition. Unlike football terminologies, children do not tell their parents directly what a certain thing means, but unconsciously guide their parents in how to carry out each step. Although the children tell their mothers directly what the parents should do, the parents seem to realise the subtle codes underlying birthday rituals. Some of the codes, such as what to wear for a party, are codes that they have already acquired in past social experiences in their home country, but whether they still apply in the new society needs to be confirmed. Meanwhile, they learn other codes through their children communicating with mainstream practice. Although if you type 'how to organise a birthday party' into Google there is lots of help, a 'how-to' book on English birthday parties is not available. What is more, as part of the informal culture of the new society discussed in Chapter 1, many of the party-related norms may have been assumed and are not in any book. What might inform mainstream English parents might not meet the needs of parents new to England. For the parents, what they learn from and through their children may have been thought as sufficient to prepare their children for the parties and to organise one when necessary.

Although parents are responsible for nurturing, caring and socialising their children into communities and have the financial power to make the final purchase (Clarke, 2003), the Chinese children here exerted their own influence over their parents, and actively participated in the family's decision-making process. In other words, the Chinese parents have the power to control financial resources, but are not sure how to distribute these resources appropriately in the new society; they have to resort to their children. From the perspective of the economy, children, like adults, become consumers and they influence their family purchases (Pecora, 1998). This has been shown particularly in the families purchasing gifts to attend parties. Children participate in the preparation of parties, guiding and impacting the procedures, though indirectly in some cases. Children have served as cultural agents to Westernise their own birthday celebrations.

Earlier, we saw similar processes when buying greeting cards. In leading their parents to conduct the ritualistic practices of these two common cultural phenomena in the new society, children have introduced and consolidated their parents to an unfamiliar landscape. In spite of tensions and challenges in the process, parents appear to be accepting the embedded norms and values. We have seen that accommodative mediation happens as a gradual process. The process of carrying out the ritual also highlights different cultural orientations between collectivism and individualism, and reveals distinct attitudes towards children and childhood in the two cultures, in how parents enrich children's experiences and develop their independence and social skills. Although it takes time for parents to absorb all the principles, norms, values and beliefs underlying birthday parties, the children's impact on their parents is essential in responding to the mainstream ritual. In short, with their children's mediation and guidance, parents have enacted the new practices and managed their communication with the outside society more appropriately; and in doing so, some of them at least have changed their ideas about childhood and have accommodated to the values of the new environment.

8 Demystifying Child Cultural Mediation

Working with children in Mandarin-speaking Chinese families, this book has explored the role of children in developing their parents' knowledge and understanding of the new country they have moved to and, in particular, the book has been aimed at providing insights into the nature of child cultural mediation, including what knowledge children pass to their parents, how child cultural mediation occurs and what impact children's mediation has on their parents' participation in the new society. In this final chapter, we shall draw some principles and characteristics of child cultural mediation from the particular cases and examples in the book.

Chapter 3 identifies a substantial number of studies in which cultural mediation was taking place; however, most of these studies were concerned with what has become known as language brokering. These studies are examples of 'explicit cultural mediation' because they had a number of distinctive features, some of which related to what I call 'visibility'. In explicit cultural mediation, the mediating events take place in particular spaces, which are often marked with clear boundaries. Thus, they are often, in effect, quite self-contained events. These events covered a wide range of domains such as education, health, commerce, law, finance, everyday living and entertainment. However, in Chapter 3, I also raised issues about those areas of life in which child cultural mediation takes place but which are not so clearly marked. While there are many examples of explicit mediation, there are hardly any that would represent what I term 'implicit' mediation. Thus, in the absence of previous research, I have analysed cases that show implicit mediation at work. The exploration has revealed the following characteristics of implicit child cultural mediation.

(1) While implicit cultural mediation was widespread and extensive, its processes were not easily visible to the observer, nor were they to the parents, who were often unaware that their children had culturally mediated their lives.

This relative invisibility derives from a number of factors. Firstly, implicit cultural mediation was intrinsically bound in the ongoing everyday lives of the families and one of the things that made this study difficult was how to explain to parents what I was looking for, and another was how I could identify it when it happened. Although I used a wide and extensive range of data collection techniques – see Appendix – seeking to extract evidence from the everydayness of family life was very hard. Secondly, these events were seldom marked by clear boundaries or locations, and it was therefore often difficult to call them events. They could occur almost anywhere, be minutely short or run across several weeks. Thirdly, unlike many language brokering events, they did not have rules, rituals and procedures, nor could they be forecasted in advance, especially those phenomena that belonged to the assimilative level. These were often spontaneous, sometimes very short, mostly language or factually based, and they happened so often that they were not distinctive in any way; it was simply how everyday life proceeded within the families.

Even when events became more complex, such as those that were defined as appropriative and accommodative, they were not easily identified by family members as being about cultural mediation. They were mostly understood as content interactions. Thus, the level at which they were understood was to do with arguing about pocket money and whether a card should be signed 'with love' or discussing what kinds of clothes were appropriate for birthday parties. Unlike explicit cultural mediation where the procedures and roles for mediation were often very obvious, implicit mediation was mostly invisible, and if it became visible at all, it was often only after a period of time that the parents realised something had changed, such as when Mrs Tang said she felt 'experienced' and Mr Tang said he would have parties in Taiwan for his children.

In short, while implicit cultural mediation was largely invisible as a process, the evidence of Chapters 5 through 7 shows that it was widespread in the lives of the families and that the children's mediation did impact on parental relationships with the new culture.

(2) Children were generally unaware of any role they had in being cultural mediators in implicit mediation.

A second point to make about implicit mediation is the matter of children's own awareness. As indicated in Chapter 3, children tend to be very conscious of their position as intermediaries in explicit cultural mediating events that occur in language brokering, and of the consequences of their behaviour for their parents and their families. However, implicit mediating events tend to be unreflective and incidental. Children are simply living their lives as children, wanting to be like their peers and learning about the world from their schooling. Cultural mediation is often unintentional as children simply report on their daily lives or seek to reflect their own integration into the society in which they are growing up. For the children, everyday life is about being embedded in the popular culture that surrounds them; they are simply absorbing Western clothes, Western food, Western music, English television programmes and many other cultural practices in England. The children are living these things, not seeking to educate their parents or broker the new culture for their parents; cultural mediation is a by-product of them expressing their values, attitudes and knowledge that either simply adds to their parents' experience of their English environment, or causes tension or disputes with their parents so that their parents are forced to take note of things in the new situation.

It tends to be the simpler areas of knowledge, 'assimilative mediation', that add in general ways to parental understanding of the new culture. Even in appropriative and accommodative examples, children's intent is much more to do with getting their own way than in seeking to explicitly mediate British culture. They are coercing their parents to meet their own interests and the sometimes quite significant changes in parental cultural knowledge that emerge are simply unintended consequences of the children's actions.

Among the distinctive features of cultural mediation discussed in Chapter 3, are the challenges for child mediators. A number of language brokering studies have shown that explicit cultural mediation poses a variety of challenges for children. The children encounter linguistic, knowledge and social difficulties in any task of interpretation or translation as they are probably still learning the new language and are unfamiliar with some of the social settings in which explicit cultural brokering occurs. Despite the fact that some children enjoy their brokering experiences, other children find these situations intense, embarrassing and highly demanding due to their lack of experience in dealing with complex social occasions that usually involve adults. While language brokering events can illustrate challenges in explicit mediation, the paucity of literature on implicit mediation means that the challenges for children in the analysis here are noticed for the first time and need to be investigated further.

(3) Cultural mediation did not involve the children in as much complexity and complex challenges as are experienced by children involved in language brokering events.

Unlike many language brokering events, implicit mediation by the Chinese children here was usually carried out at or around the home, and largely involved only their parents. Thus, the children did not work with strangers and did not work with other adults. Secondly, as discussed in the previous section, the children were largely unaware of their own cultural mediation for their parents. So it is not the children but their parents who feel challenged. Drawing on the knowledge and experiences they have gained from school and their peer group, the child mediators take their own initiative to offer linguistic and factual knowledge and to request certain cultural practices. They picked up the topics for discussion or argument familiar to them, for example, pocket money and birthday parties. The child mediators knew more than their parents in those subject matters they debated about. As the knowledge holders and experts on certain procedures, they challenged their parents, rather than vice versa. For example, Mrs Yang did not know how much pocket money she should give to her son Fan, so she had to listen to his suggestions based on his peer experience.

As with other situations when they relied on their children as a resource, the parents were challenged and did not seem to have other reference points to help with a decision and therefore had to be guided by their children.

Thirdly, even if more complex events occurred, the child mediators did not have to deal with things immediately. In explicit cultural mediating, such as language brokering, events often demand instant responses and solutions. These children did not face these challenges, as they often had plenty of time to discuss and work out the solutions together with their parents. In the discussion about a school fundraising activity in the Shi family, the child did not correctly inform his mother about the school activity and the Marks & Spencer hamper. Despite this, and the fact that his mother found it hard to understand and respond to the school letter, the mediation did not end up having a negative outcome for the family, unlike the high-stake results of some explicit cultural mediating events.

Finally, more often than not, implicit mediation occurred in situations that originated with something the children wanted to do, or were connected with solving everyday practical problems, such as what food to cook and what games to play when inviting the children's English friends. Hence, implicit mediation appears less goal oriented and less challenging to the children. This does not mean that children do not face challenges, but the challenges arise out of the contention between parents and children when their desires or behaviours make their parents uncomfortable. These challenges are experienced by all children as they negotiate their freedom to wear or do what they want. Thus, contestations within the family tend to reflect children's growing willingness to express their opinions, demand things and generally seek greater independence in their development.

(4) Implicit cultural mediation changes parent–child relationships differently to changes associated with explicit mediation.

Studies of language brokering suggest explicit mediation extensively shifts parental relationships with children. In language brokering events, parents often become dependent on their children's competence and willingness to operate effectively and honestly on their behalf. Acting as a filter and holder of different kinds of knowledge about the new social systems, children may take over responsibility and make decisions for their parents, deliberately or unconsciously, especially in situations that require an immediate response. Consequently, the traditional roles of parents and children tend to be altered and even reversed in explicit child cultural mediation.

On the other hand, as implicit cultural mediation tends to be disguised in almost all normal family situations and more conventional parent/child power relationships are maintained, the power shift in implicit mediation is much less than that in explicit mediation. However, parents do not have unquestioned authority as they did before migrating to the new society. They are no longer sure about how to act on certain social occasions, such as what they [the parents] should wear when delivering their children to a birthday party, what their children should wear to birthday parties, or what is the appropriate way to write a greeting card. Facing new knowledge, customs and practices, parents have to follow their children's advice, partly because parents may not know 'what to do' and 'how to do it' on such social occasions and partly because parents, without any previous authoritative experiences, worry about acting inappropriately in certain social circumstances and having a bad impact on their children's peer relations. They feel unable to judge the validity of their children's remarks, but often have to act on them, e.g. in raising the amount of a child's pocket money, even when they have their doubts.

The decreased level of parental authority leads to a more reciprocal or interdependent relationship between parents and children. This special relationship becomes part of the family interaction pattern, in which parents and children work together to present their family to the new society. Eight-year-old Ming and her parents collaborated on what to buy as presents for the special horse-riding birthday party of one of her friends. Their cooperation worked very well towards the success of Ming's swimming party for her ninth birthday. This suggests that child mediators tend to have more freedom to express their opinions, rather than being fully obedient to their parents as in traditional Chinese families.

Thus, while implicit cultural mediation does not result in the same level of parental dependency as explicit cultural mediation, parental control over their children tends to loosen. The parents in this study are not as reliant on their children to contact schoolteachers or other interlocutors in public events as those in language brokering studies. However, they still lose their power to their children, especially when they are confronted by new values and norms through their children. Mrs Tang had to give in to her five-year-old son when he insisted on writing his own word 'special' several times on a birthday card to a female classmate, even though her own codes of behaviour told her of its inappropriateness. Although the young boy's boldness in arguing with his mother would have been unacceptable in her original cultural model, Mrs Tang submitted to the new mode of relationship with her child. While similar arguments happen in all families, parents in immigrant families perhaps find such events more confrontational than parents in mainstream families. This cultural conflict derives from the fact that children quickly adopt the beliefs and values, such as individualism, freedom seeking and equality, of a Western society. Although the Chinese parents are not comfortable with and are even anxious about these disputes and confrontations, they tend to have no choice but to live with them.

(5) In implicit child cultural mediation it is the children's agency in seeking to become members of the new culture that impacts on parents' understanding of that culture.
    In Chapter 2, I discussed how the new childhood studies perceive childhood as a social and cultural construction, and children themselves as active social actors and agents. In Chapter 3, I showed how language brokering studies provide strong evidence of children's agency in brokering events as they take responsibility in negotiating and making decisions for parents. From my observations in the families, it was very unusual for children to exert agency in a direct way in cultural mediation. As discussed above, the mediation was generally invisible, lacked some challenges for the children and did not impact on power relationships within the families to the same level as in language brokering. The children did not set out to take responsibility for their parents' lives, they did not seek to speak their words for them and they did not undertake responsibilities beyond what would normally be expected of children of a particular chronological age.
    However, the acculturation of the parents ultimately does owe quite a lot to other ways in which the children exerted agency in their general everyday lives. Firstly, the children were active within their family's life. In these Mandarin-speaking Chinese families, the children participated in events such as shopping, food choices, holiday planning and social activities. When Fan and Hai in the Yang family wrote down the names of foods for their father, they were participating in the family's shopping. In the Tang family, although Ming and Liang's food choices did not change their parents' tastes, their contribution to the variety of family's food was

considerable. In the birthday celebrations, the children took an active and central part in informing their parents about how to attend and organise parties appropriately.

Secondly, Chapters 5 through 7 show that child cultural mediation is based on children being negotiators within their everyday social lives. In these families, there were continual compromises and negotiations between the parents and children and many of these discussions raised issues for parents about cultural choices. Fan negotiated with his mother in a discussion that started with an argument over his mobile phone bill, but ended up with Fan achieving his own goals. One of the youngest mediators, Liang also demonstrated his negotiating skill in writing a greeting card in his own way. His reasoning was so powerful that his mother eventually gave in, despite her strong reservations. All these instances suggest that children, as negotiators of their family life, can be good at manipulating their parents to follow their lead or accept their ways of implementing certain practices and rituals, as is argued in general in the new childhood studies. What is different here is that, as in the above two examples, this often involves issues that draw parents' attention to values and ideas associated with the new environment.

Thirdly, children can also be viewed as decision-makers seeking to shape their daily lives, social relations and identities. Ming decided for her mother what food to prepare and what games to play when her and her brother's English friends came to play in their house. Mrs Tang had to follow her daughter's advice, since she herself had learned a lesson in an incident when her well-prepared Chinese food had been declined by English children. Liang made his own decision on whom to invite to his first birthday party. This surprised his mother, and she compared his behaviour with most children in her home country, where parents would make their decisions for them under similar circumstances. Again, the consequences of the children's agency raise issues for the parents about the new culture.

Finally, child cultural mediation can be viewed as work, given our discussion in Chapter 2 that work can be reconceptualised to include production and conversion of resources and values, the process of which may not result in immediate economic and financial benefits, but emotionally significant contributions to personal and family well-being. Although the children in this book were not employed by their parents, they communicated the mainstream cultural practices and values implicitly to their parents, which facilitated their parents' everyday living and functioning in the new society. The exertion of their agency in becoming members of the new culture was essential in making their parents' experiences in the new land less disturbing and much richer.

(6) Implicit child cultural mediation is a multimodal activity.
Whatever language they use, children tend to pass linguistic and cultural knowledge on to their parents. Liang pointed out the standard pronunciation of certain English sounds to his mother; Fan taught his mother historical knowledge mainly in Chinese, but code-switched to English when he had difficulty expressing himself in Chinese; Ming taught her mother different football terminologies, and she also wrote down the spelling of the words that she taught her mother.

However, children do not simply rely on oral language for mediation, and the Chinese children used a wider range of modalities to make their meanings. As demonstrated in Chapter 7, children are very good at symbolic representation and they tend to use different types of tools, consciously or not, in their mediation for their parents, although the verbal means tends to be used most frequently. The children also deployed visual means such as drawings or pictures in transferring the cultural message for their parents. Through making their own cards for their father, Liang and Ming drew on the knowledge that they had just learned from their English schooling, to mediate for their mother that cards can be a proper and widely accepted way of expressing greetings and wishes to various interpersonal relationships ranging from acquaintances to friends and from distant to close relatives.

Kress and Mavers (2005) argue that as active meaning makers, children employ whatever resources and ways that they think are meaningful and powerful at the moment of communication, whether they are images, symbols, signs or words. Liang and Ming supported this view when they made good use of their drawings and writing as well as their literacy skills that they had just developed at school. Just as the children in Farrell *et al.* (2010) adopted visual means to create meaning about their immigrant experiences, Liang and Ming used their own drawings and words to convey messages and to express their emotions. Not only did Liang and Ming create their own images and messages, but they also authored their cards to communicate their current emotional states via the cards. With this multimodal activity, they also revealed to their mother the practice of using cards for different occasions in the mainstream society, although they themselves may not have realised this mediation at all. Similarly in the Zhou family, Hong brought to Mrs Zhou a sheet of paper from school on which she had scribbled the rhyme 'Remember, Remember, the 5th of November'. On the same page, she had sketched a human figure, beside which she had written 'Guy'. She told her mother that Bonfire Night was related to a man who attempted to burn down the Houses of Parliament. Although Mrs Zhou was not clear what exactly it was about, through Hong's words and drawing, she knew a little more about the relation between Guy Fawkes and the bonfire tradition in English history.

(7) Child mediators derive their own knowledge about the new culture mainly from school and their peer community.
Children seem to acquire their knowledge from two main sources, which then influences their parents' acculturation to the new society. Firstly, school seems to be a very important source for child cultural mediation. Newly arrived children pick up the English language very quickly from both the school curriculum and native speakers. They also simultaneously learn different kinds of social and cultural knowledge.Influenced by what they constantly see and hear in school, children tune themselves into a variety of mainstream practices. Thus, school becomes an essential component in the children's own socialisation.

Moving from school to home, the children inevitably exerted a subtle influence on their parents about the new language and new practices. In particular, the conversations that tended to occur just after the children had arrived home from school provided a wealth of material that, while simply accepted by the children, offered many new insights about the new environment. The willingness of the parents to support their children's development meant that their own factual knowledge of the new culture grew alongside that of their children. When the Yang family took their children to visit the site of the Battle of Hastings, it was as a result of knowledge that the children had learned at school. It was also as a result of the children's schooling that the families became aware of many significant events in British life, for instance, memorial events such as Poppy Day and charitable events such as disaster relief collections. Alongside the factual elements of these events came deeper-level meanings about beliefs and values associated with significant elements of British culture.

Secondly, in all children's lives, peer culture is important and it was no different for these children. Most children want to be accepted by their peer community. The peer community has very powerful relationships with popular culture, whether it is television programmes, music, fashion, choice of mobile phones, etc. Many of the examples we have seen in earlier chapters reflect the influence of the peer community on the children. Fan initiated his family's watching *Dr Who* on Saturdays so that he could participate in the peer discussion about it and enjoy sharing something in common with his classmates. The same Fan asked for pocket money because he saw his peers spend their weekly or monthly allowance at their own discretion. Wanting to 'fit in' led to many discussions when going to and organising birthday parties, and informed discussions about what to wear at parties and at special occasions at schools. It is clear that child peer culture and popular culture carry multiple meanings that are puzzling not only to immigrant families but also to many indigenous families. Thus, they are powerful sites for contestation as parents question the underlying values, and it is this confrontation that forced the parents of the Chinese families to pay attention to many areas of life around them that would have remained mostly invisible to them if they had not had children.

(8) The process of child cultural mediation operates through a continuum containing three levels, assimilation, appropriation and accommodation, and the children mediate implicitly rather than explicitly.

The analysis of the data resulted in being able to describe the process of child cultural mediation as taking place in the families at the three levels. These levels had many similarities with the three elements of the concept of culture developed by Hall (1959, 1990): the technical, formal and informal. The 'technical' culture can be found in dictionaries or manuals, can be explained or transmitted explicitly in oral or written communication and can be taught or learned in certain formulaic manner. The 'formal' culture refers to the accepted ways of behaving, doing or acting and includes customs, rules, rituals and practices. Though being more subjective than the 'technical' culture, the 'formal' culture can still be articulated and learned by the newcomer. The 'informal' culture refers to the individually interpreted cultural meaning, the personal way of doing and behaving, but most importantly the values and orientations that are invisible and implicit to outsiders and are often not even explainable and overt to the insiders of a culture.

While Hall's tripartite analysis is important, it does not seek to describe or explain how these elements of culture are absorbed, especially by those who are not brought up on the inside of a particular culture and thus acquire their cultural capital differently. The analysis of the data from the perspective of how knowledge is absorbed led to the postulation of a continuum, ranging from the 'assimilative' through the 'appropriative' to the 'accommodative'. The choice of these terms is meant to do what Hall did not do, which is to indicate how parents in immigrant groups develop an understanding of the new culture through their children.

The technical, formal and informal cultures do not have a clear-cut, one-to-one correspondence with the assimilative, appropriative and accommodative levels of mediation. In other words, although what is mediated at the assimilative level falls into Hall's 'technical' category, this does not mean that mediation of the appropriative and accommodative levels does not include any element of the technical culture. On the contrary, the technical cultural element was mediated across the assimilative, appropriative and accommodative levels. For example, the name of the tree *conifer* was imparted to the parents at the assimilative level, the Western food choices at the appropriative level and the procedures for throwing a birthday party at the accommodative level. All these details included in the three levels of mediation could be found in a dictionary, brochure or encyclopaedia if they were not mediated by the children. They can be explained in a linguistic form or learned in a formulaic manner, and are hence 'technical'.

However, although the technical elements can be noticed in the appropriative and accommodative levels, what was mediated at the appropriative level falls mostly into Hall's formal culture, and what was mediated at the accommodative level falls mostly into Hall's informal culture. At the appropriative level, both technical and formal cultural elements were mediated to the parents, and Hall's three levels also emerged within the accommodative level. For instance, the episodes of pocket money at the appropriative level and of the greeting card and the birthday party at the accommodative level can be explained as part of the accepted ways of behaviours in the mainstream society and can be learned quite explicitly. Yet, the deeper meaning beneath these practices and rituals cannot be overtly explained to outsiders by insiders and may not even be visible to them. These are the values and orientations acquired automatically in everyday life, which belong to informal culture. They are what the Chinese child mediators divulged to their parents unconsciously.

The assimilative level tends to relate primarily to acquiring cultural knowledge that is easily understood because it can be assimilated to existing schemas held by the adults. There is no obvious conceptual change, but more a quantitative accumulation of knowledge, such as new words and new facts about elements of the new culture. Thus, the children offer vocabulary items, comment on parents' pronunciation and offer simple facts and explanations. These things do not demand new ways of thinking; they involve elements that are already familiar to adults because of their own existing general knowledge. Chapter 5 included many examples of these, such as Liang correcting his mother's pronunciation of the word *poem*, Ming teaching her mother about the football terminology of *foul* and Fan clarifying a piece of historical knowledge for his mother. It is clear from these descriptions that assimilative mediation involves straightforward transmission of factual knowledge which may be found in dictionaries or books, and that it happens in everyday life spontaneously, ephemerally and frequently within the families.

The appropriative level indicates what happens as parents in immigrant families acquire an understanding of more significant aspects of the new culture. The effects on parents tend to be more complicated than at the assimilative level; they may begin to change some of their everyday practices and they may have to consider aspects of their own identity. However, at this level, even though parents may modify some aspects of their behaviour and incorporate certain practices into their everyday routines, they may not accept that there is some underlying cultural validity to them. They may change their behaviour for the sake of their children's desire to be accepted by peer groups, such as serving English food to them and their friends, but the parents do not change their attitudes about the acceptability of English food or start to eat it themselves. It is a matter of saving face for the children rather than because of any deeper-level liking of the food. Thus, although they make some changes for their children's sake within the home, they may not appreciate the underpinning values, attitudes or principles. However, the instances at this level tend to be recurrent and allow parents constant access to their embedded meanings. Although this level of mediation may confront or challenge parents and cause tensions and ambivalence, it has the potential to become parents' accommodation of practices and related values. In the instance of giving children pocket money, the parents may accept it as a right thing to do and understand its significance after carrying it out for a while, though they were unwilling to do that initially.

The accommodative level tends to result in deeper-level changes of understanding of the new culture and may lead to significant changes in parental behaviour and beliefs. The issues being mediated at this level touch something particular to the mainstream culture, something that parents may have never experienced in their home culture, in their childhood or in their education. The mediating process at this level often appears gradual, multifaceted and complex. These mediating events equip the parents not just with new ritual and cultural practices, but also new values and beliefs. While taking certain actions as a result of child initiation, parents may eventually accept the meanings or significance of new practices and take their own initiative in applying the norms or principles learned from their children in their own daily social interaction. At this level, although parents often met the new practices in a reluctant way, they tended eventually to accept what was being mediated. The Tang family understood that card sending is such a prevalent practice in the new society that they bought cards from Taiwan when they went back for a holiday, in order to conform to this practice within their manageable family budget. Even the father appreciated the values of birthday parties for children to such an extent that he said he intended to move this practice back to his home country. Therefore, the effects on parents at the accommodative level seem to be more significant than at any of the other levels.

Having identified these three levels in the data, it is critical to revisit the fact that they are not independent levels but are part of a continuum. As explained in previous chapters, although mediating events are largely discrete for analytical purposes, they do not represent clear-cut sequential stages or levels of cultural mediation, but overlap with each other in the continuum of child cultural mediation. In the example of the children mediating the practices of writing and sending greeting cards, they are in one way simply operating at the assimilative level; in other words, they are simply adding to what the parents already knew about greeting card practices. However, underneath this, the children are also mediating things relating to the value orientation of interpersonal relationships in England and this results in the parents appropriating the activity as an acceptable one within family life, and ultimately accommodating the ways in which children in England have greater freedoms and choices than would have been common back in their home countries. The role of the children is critical at each of these three levels, for they are acquiring this new cultural capital by being immersed in it through their schooling and peer culture. The evidence about how parents accommodate practices such as celebrating birthday parties or sending greeting cards, demonstrates that children do not teach their parents in a formal sense, but in a more implicit manner, which even so, is very powerful.

(9) Child cultural mediation challenges and changes parental values and behaviours.
    Migrants rely on many different kinds of resources, formal and informal, social and personal, to survive and thrive in the new society. In their adaptation, they may get support from governmental departments, local authorities or higher educational institutions, as well as their existing ethnic community. They may resort to media, and their daily tacit observations in their social interaction with local people. However, in many families it is the children who tend to become the most significant resource in their acculturation. The way that child cultural mediation influences the parental relationship to the new culture can be examined from the aspects of values and behaviours.
    Firstly, in the families studied, child cultural mediation influenced the parents' beliefs about and attitudes towards many aspects of children and childhood and towards parental relationships to their children. In traditional Chinese culture, children are expected to attune themselves to the families or groups they belong to, rather than expressing their own individualism and specialness; and their personal goals are expected to conform to those of the family and community. As a consequence of this collectivistic orientation, children's individuality is perceived as relatively unimportant. Furthermore,

independence appears to be synonymous with self-sufficiency in terms of materialistic resources, rather than being associated with independent thinking and personal social contacts, and children's educational success is emphasised in order to secure their life financially. In terms of child–parent relationships, parents are at a higher level in the hierarchy, and children are expected to respect their parents as the authority, show obedience and follow their advice and guidance without questioning.

In the families described here, these traditional views were being constantly challenged by the children's behaviour. In many respects, everyday living was like living on a frontier between Chinese notions of child–parent relationships and British children's autonomy and freedom. Many things the children said or did, things that they had absorbed unquestioningly from their school and peer communities, created dissonance and discomfort for their parents. However, the parents were sensitive to their children's need to fit in to the school and peer community, and the result was that initially there was considerable compromise on the part of the parents. Without understanding, they nevertheless adjusted their behaviour to help their child's social participation, even though the results were actually sometimes embarrassing for the children and themselves (as when Ming and Liang performed traditional Chinese songs at a school 'Pop Idol' activity, instead of singing the latest pop songs, as did all the other children).

However, as a result of the children's implicit mediation, many parents not only accepted that while in England it was appropriate to allow their own children the same rights and freedoms as other children, but they also began to believe that positive values could emerge from these new relationships with their children. They began to appreciate that while in their own culture children have a very subordinate role, it might actually be good for children to experience taking responsibility for their lives. Having pocket money, for example, helps them begin to manage the economics of their lives, and they can have a role in choosing their own clothes. Contributing to decisions about organising parties was something to which children were entitled since they should be stakeholders in their own lives. Therefore, to some extent, parents alter their value orientation from collectivism to individualism. When their children challenged them and argued with them, as in Liang's case of writing a greeting card in his own way, the parents showed a degree of submission to their children and came to have a different attitude to allowing more equal parent–child relationships being cultivated in their families.

Secondly, parents' behaviour as well as their attitudes changed as a result of child cultural mediation. The changes in behaviour occurred when their values were altered, as shown in the mediating instances of birthday party practices. The parents embraced the values embedded in birthday rituals and came to choose themes and organise parties for their children appropriately. The instances of greeting cards impacted on the parents of one family so much that they changed the way that they dealt with interpersonal relationships. They took it into consideration in planning their family budgets and seriously accepted this practice. It is clear that they started changing their social interaction patterns and intended to establish or sustain friendly relationships and social contacts by using greeting cards.

In addition, even when parents did not accept new values, they nevertheless still changed their behaviour. They carried out certain cultural practices, such as participating in fundraising activities at children's school, giving pocket money to children, adding more varieties in their daily food arrangements, even when they were not sure of their underpinning values. Although we cannot be sure if Mrs Yang altered her beliefs about giving children pocket money, it is clear, nevertheless, that she adopted the practice of giving pocket money to her sons. This was also the case in the Tang family where English foods are served at home for their own families as well as for their children's English friends; however, parents' beliefs about food culture may be intact. That is, they changed their behavior neither out of their willingness nor their full understanding of them, but just as a result of being coerced by and succumb to their children.

Therefore, in implicit child cultural mediation, it is not just language, but more importantly, cultural codes or the 'hidden agenda' of the English environment that has been passed on to parents. Implicit child cultural mediation offers more channels for parents to get in touch with the majority population, to get to know the society they have just moved into and to evaluate their relocating experiences. With children's mediation, parents may feel more intimately related to, rather than isolated from the new culture. Being positioned as the intermediary between parents and mainstream society, children create links between the two cultures, help parents understand cultural phenomena and cultural practices in the new society, appreciate hidden agendas about living in the new country and improve migrant families' social and emotional well-being in the new world.

Conclusion

Given that mobility and globalisation are increasingly impacting on the current world, it becomes increasingly important for researchers, practitioners and parents to learn about the issues that arise. The nine characteristics of implicit child cultural mediation explored above can be contextualised by readers from various professions concerned with the interaction between children and parents, and in different disciplines such as the sociology of families and childhood studies, ethnography/anthropology, cultural studies, education and intercultural communication. In addition to academic audiences, it would be useful for international or immigrant families in both the UK and other parts of the world to become aware of these characteristics. The real-life vignettes related to each characteristic could raise the awareness of parents adjusting to a new community and appreciating the support their own children can provide. They could also improve family relationships and emotional well-being.

Similarly, schools and education authorities would find these characteristics useful in order to establish links between home and school, learning about international families and the literacy practice in their homes, so that educationists can adjust their own support systems more appropriately. Finally, agencies preparing families for living overseas would also find the knowledge of these characteristics useful as they underpin the unique role of children in their parents' acculturation.

The study recorded by this book represents only a partial examination of what now seems to be a very important and largely neglected area. Nevertheless, it can point to a number of future research directions and draw implications for areas relating to immigrant and refugee groups. The case studies of the six families provide a snapshot of how child cultural mediation operates in the dynamic of Mandarin-speaking Chinese families. The families presented in this book are not representative of all Chinese immigrant families and equally it is only a small number of English families that they have taken as reference for their cultural learning, and the discussion of contrast between Chinese and English cultures throughout the book has been in general terms as a matter of style and convenience and does not imply generalisation. A longitudinal study of more families may reveal the long-term effects of mediation on parents and children to a wider extent. As has been shown in Chapter 7, child cultural mediation may change parents' existing values, and further and wider empirical studies could follow up how these changes occur and take effect.

In conclusion, I hope that the book enriches the area of child cultural mediation because it shows mediation exists not just in families where parents do not speak English, but in families where parents' proficiency of English is good. Secondly, the book has demonstrated that child cultural mediation can be carried out both explicitly and tacitly, both intentionally and incidentally, both by means of language and other forms of communication. Having a clearer picture of cultural mediation at home, local school authorities, government departments and social services can have a better understanding of the life and needs of immigrant groups. They might ask, for example, if education and language policy should move towards facilitating child cultural mediation by placing more importance on bicultural and bilingual development, rather than overemphasising the role of the mainstream language and culture. As the influx of immigrants continues in many countries, many more children of immigrants will inevitably become intercultural mediators between the mainstream society and their parents. The issues raised in the book can be applied beyond the Chinese community in England to migrant communities around the world. If the policymaking and other services provided for immigrants and their children can be improved and their quality of life in the new society can be enhanced, then the overall living standard of the country will be raised. It is my hope that this book will be a timely contribution to such tasks.

Appendix

Methodological Issues in Ethnographic Studies

For me, conducting this study has been a journey of learning: learning how to conduct qualitative research; how to search exhaustively and read critically the literature about one topic; and how to make seamless transferences from fieldwork to text and from participants to readers, between whom I have tried to be a neutral mediator. As a neophyte who observed and implemented each step of the research procedures, I have been baptised into how an interpretive inquiry should work. It derives from everyday life, records authentic interaction and distils the new knowledge from the most mundane, the most secular and the most taken for granted. The research process is iterative, painstaking, but enriching and rewarding. A good researcher has faith in it, carries it out tirelessly and constantly refines his/her overall skills. The difference between my study and any other previous studies on the topic of child mediation lies in the approach to the research. While most previous studies adopted questionnaire and retrospective interviews with various numbers of participants made up of adolescents or young adults, I conducted an ethnographic study with young children and their parents, based on their everyday lives in untutored 'natural' surroundings. This has proved more suitable to access private territory such as family homes. How I conducted this ethnographic research within the families will be explained in this Appendix.

My study explored this social phenomenon by looking into its nature, and at experiences and interactions in the process of child cultural mediation within families. What I wanted to investigate were the microlevel, day-to-day instances of mediation in family situations. I needed, therefore, to get close to the families in order to gain finely grained insights into this aspect of their lives, and to understand individuals' perceptions, motivations and responses in relation to what the new culture brings them.

Negotiating, gaining and sustaining access

Working with families tends to present more challenges to fieldwork because the researcher enters a 'privatized social space' (James, 2001: 254).

There are boundaries for the researcher to cross between the public and the private, since most people deal with their own family issues, retreating from their social interaction with outsiders. My access to families in the study was facilitated in three main ways.

While I am fairly fluent in English, I am Chinese and a native speaker of Mandarin. I am also a sojourner, having come to the UK in 2001 in order to develop my education, although I am now working in the UK. Thus, I share many aspects of the cultural lives of these families. Secondly, I also have a daughter, born in China, but who was attending a British primary school at the time of the research. She came to the UK from China when she was four and a half, and like the children in my study, within a year she was fairly fluent in English, even speaking it with a Manchester accent. This was particularly important for my relationships with the parents as there was a lot that we did not understand about the English education system. It was also the case that having a daughter around the same age as some of the children in my study, and that she sometimes accompanied me to the families' homes, social relationships were often very relaxed and comfortable.

I gained access to my first group of families by initially contacting gatekeepers such as head teachers and parents. When I voluntarily observed classes of younger children in a complementary Chinese school, I was aware of the potential for these children and families to participate in the study; therefore, my Director of Studies and I went to meet the head teacher of the school for his support. It was then agreed that I send letters via the children when they attended sessions on Sunday, to gain their parents' permission to approach their children. I got more responses from younger children's parents than from those of older children, maybe because most of the younger children's parents had already matched my name with my face, having met me in the classroom. Not having extensive feedback, I sent another letter three weeks later via the mailing list of the website of the Chinese Students and Scholars Association, to remind some parents and also to let more parents know about my research, as the previous letter may not have reached them for various reasons. I got more participants after this letter.

I then went to talk in more detail with all the interested parents about my research interest and got to know more about their backgrounds and their interests in their children's academic and bilingual development. This is how I established my first group of parents. At this stage, the parents' rather than the children's views were elicited about participating in the research. Although the children passed the letter to their parents, they might not have known what it was about.

I established my second group of contacts via casual talk with established friends to whom I had not previously mentioned my research. However, during some informal conversations, I was told quite a few narratives related to my topic. I got immediate and positive responses from another two families in one social gathering with some friends. After I talked with their children and the parents at the same time, they agreed to participate in my research. The most important reason for the ease in entering these two families appears to be my established friendship with them. Access may be more easily gained and relationships more quickly established with the existing participants as guides who may pass both trust and credits to possible new contacts.

Thirdly, I made gaining, negotiating and maintaining access a continuous process. Although in some ways I was an insider in the community, it took me quite a while to let the participants know me before I actually went into the families' homes. I did not request full access to all areas of data sites but left space for both the subjects and the researcher's later negotiation. In the later stage of my fieldwork, I found it necessary to observe the children in their classrooms. I therefore obtained a letter of support from my supervisor, wrote letters to the head teachers and compiled consent forms for the parents for further permission to go into their children's classrooms. To my surprise, however, although they had allowed me to visit their homes, not all parents agreed, for the reason that they worried that their children might feel pressurised by me being in their classrooms. Given that one of the families raised this concern, my classroom observations did not cover the two children of this family, nor did their head teacher see my and my supervisor's letters. However, although this family raised objections to this access, my observation in another school was facilitated by the parents, who offered to introduce me to the head teacher.

Sustaining access demanded that I always fitted in with the plans and feeling of the families, especially the children. My visits relied largely on how the parents arranged and thought of their children's timetable, interests and activities. For most of my visits, I phoned the families in advance. According to my relationships with them, some families allowed me to sleep over to see the occurrences of mediating activities in the morning and evening routines. Generally speaking, I had to be very flexible in the choice of days and times to stay with the families. I needed to focus more on their agenda in naturally occurring activities rather than imposing my agenda on them.

Data collection at family homes

Participant observation

Although participant observation is time consuming, it is important to carry out a proper observation in the right place at the right time (Bell,

2005; Walsh, 2004). During the first few visits to the field, observation tends to be descriptive (Spradley, 1980), that is, entering into the field with only general questions in mind, such as 'what's going on here?'. The answers to these questions may help the researcher decide the targets of focused observation in which he/she may look for answers to particular questions. After a couple of general observations in each family, I started focusing on different families over a few hours after school and before dinner, as well as some weekends and holidays. This allowed me to see how certain mediating events happened and what their impacts possibly were. I concentrated on parent–child chats before and during dinner in some families, on doing homework together, reading schoolbooks together or playing games together in others. In visiting the families, I also played games with the children, including football. I obtained permission to sleep over in three of the families' home and go on day trips with them in order to witness the possible occurrences of mediating in wider family contexts. I also chose to observe a few classrooms, followed by immediate home visits on the same day to see how the children integrated themselves with their school peers and to have a general idea of how events or incidents at school were or were not mediated to parents.

Ethnographic interviewing

Participant observation laid a sound foundation for my ethnographic interviewing with the children as well as their parents. The relationship of trust between us enabled my ethnographic interviewing to be informal, friendly and similar to casual conversations. Ethnographic interviewing at the participants' home setting may be accompanied by or interrupted by other activities at home. Although this is not a normal interview setting that most researchers are used to, it was spontaneous and unobtrusive in my fieldwork. Most of what I learned about the families, such as their personal details and history of their previous occupations, came from short conversations with them. My interviewing was usually done through chatting while parents were doing something else, for example, cooking or ironing, washing up, and while the children were playing with their games and toys, or having snacks.

Collaborative techniques

Being aware of the elusive nature of data in child cultural mediation, I found it necessary to seek the families' collaboration with data capturing. After having established a rapport with the families, I provided a diary notebook for every adult and child, and a cassette recorder for each family and for one child who particularly requested it. I invited them to keep their diary notes and audio record their conversations at home, and encouraged them to draw pictures about their mediating experiences.

At the time of collecting the data, digital recorders were very expensive, but low-cost cassette recorders still existed, so I gave each family a cassette recorder. Having been given a cassette recorder, each family could switch it on to record whatever they thought was related to the topic, or simply switch it on whenever the parents and the children spoke to each other, from sitting at the dinner table to commuting in their car. Five-year-old Liang was given an extra recorder for himself as he requested. During one of my visits, I found he had put 'his own' recorder in a drawer within easy reach. I also found that the recorders were put close to dinner tables or desks in the dining room or the rooms (including bedrooms) where the parents and the children read books together.

Eventually, I got 11 tapes in total from the families, 6 from the Tangs, 3 from the Yangs and 1 each from the Zhous and the Shis. The Li and the Zhao families did not seem to like recording very much and did not return any tapes. I tried to transcribe verbatim these tapes, and got in touch with the families when I could not figure out words in their conversations. In most cases, the children's voices were too soft to capture, which was the most difficult part of my transcription. Every time I brought the tapes back to the families, it was the children who helped me to understand what they had said.

In some families, both the parents and the children took audio-recording seriously and the children's voices became different from their normal voices because they knew that they were being recorded and the parents sometimes used very soft voices when they said something that they thought unrelated to the topic; when there was no utterance from anybody, the mother sometimes switched off the machine, and turned it on again when somebody spoke. In this regard, the parents found controlling the machine quite a burden. I also kept adjusting the use of the recorder according to the families' feedback, for example, I told them not to worry too much about stopping the cassette recorder even if nobody was talking, and just to leave it on until they finished one activity. In this way, conversations sounded more relaxed and more encompassing.

Keeping diaries

I supplied each parent and child with notebooks of various sizes and with child-friendly designs and invited them to keep a diary of any teaching and learning incidents that happened between them. I did not make other requirements than having each entry dated, as I thought that in my ethnographic study, I had better not intervene too much but leave the parents and the children to record whatever they felt appropriate to the topic. The parents used the notebooks in two ways. Some of them wrote whatever they thought they had learned from their children, together with the contexts in which the learning happened; some wrote down the linguistic items, how mediating incidents had happened and how they thought or felt at that moment. The parents wrote their diaries in both English and Chinese. The topics ranged from English words to the events that had happened between them and their children, where they had learned about the English language, the mainstream society and even a child's peer culture. In their diaries, the children listed in English what they had taught their parents under dates and days, including English words, phrases and their explanations, funny doggerels that they picked up from playing as well as games they played with their friends at school; others used pictures here and there in their notes of the objects that they thought they had taught their parents. They also kept their diaries of their school days and daily life. The notes I eventually got looked very different in terms of writing styles between the parents and the children.

Artefact collection

Cultural artefacts as 'material traces' (Hodder, 2003: 159) are another informative technique that ethnographers use nowadays. It is particularly useful in gathering data from children with more creativity and novelty. In my study, artefact collection allowed me to answer my research questions from more perspectives as visual data can be traces of the lives and meaningful constituents of the families' everyday behaviours (Mason, 1996). I collected children's unsolicited drawings and pictures, their homework or art crafts, schoolwork or diary notes, school letters and parents' diary notes. I encouraged the children to draw their experience of teaching and helping their parents. I found it useful and creative to inform young children about the abstract research topic and involve them in the activities (Punch, 2002a; Thomas & O'Kane, 1998). Also, it offered children a more direct voice and a chance to document their actions and perspectives (Prout, 2002). I used this method several times in each family and stopped when they got bored. The method confirmed the data from other sources, for example, children drew pictures of the objects whose English names they taught their parents. It should be noted that confidentiality is worth considering, for example, personal details and photographs should not be identifiable.

Transcribing and sharing writing

I started indexing the tapes when I got the first one from the families, and then transcribed verbatim the sections that appeared relevant to the study. It was particularly difficult to transcribe the first few tapes from some families, since often there were background noises of people playing on computers, watching television or eating their meals, and sometimes the voices were inaudible because of the softness of the children's voices and the distance from the equipment. Some children were involved in the transcribing process when I could not figure out their talk at home. In my pilot study, I also gave my translated interview transcripts to one of the mothers, who commented on the informality in my translation of her Chinese version. After I drafted the chapter introducing them, I then invited each family to read the pertinent sections, in order to get their reaction to the writing. I told them that I was interested in what they thought of my presentation of their family.

Working with the children

Working with children in their homes tends to complicate ethical issues, not just because the researcher enters private territory but also because children are conventionally in a subordinate position in the domestic arena (James, 2001). Since my research was aimed at child–parent interaction primarily in the home context, working with children is an important dimension of my fieldwork, that is, conventional power relationships and child–adult difference must be considered. In my study, this imbalance had to be addressed in two directions, one was the extent to which this imbalance affected the children participating in my study, for example, when children's voices could not be heard much, to what extent did I ameliorate this situation? The other is whether or how much this imbalance impacted on the relationship between me as an adult researcher and the child participants in my fieldwork.

I take the position that children are competent social actors and I respected their views, requests and competences in my fieldwork but, at the same time, it is also important to recognise the difference between adults and children and address the difference properly (Mayall, 2000). To increase the likelihood that children were more heard than just seen in their home settings, during my stay with the families I tended to demonstrate my interest in their opinions and my openness to learning from them, even sometimes focusing more on the children's talk than that of their parents. I also encouraged the children to control the cassette recorder whenever they liked and respected a child's request, for example, to provide a tape recorder for Liang when he required it.

In real life, children are seldom the gatekeepers to their family and do not usually occupy a position of power within their home (James, 2001).

There was a danger of this type in my study when I had to seek the parents' permission prior to seeking the children's permission. I made sure that I got the children's consent at different stages. For instance, I encouraged the parents to ask their children if I did not speak to children directly, then I would confirm face-to-face with the children the next time I saw them, either in their home or in a community activity, about their willingness to participate in the research activities. By so doing, I at least let the children know about the study and express their opinions, respecting their competencies (Morrow & Richards, 1996; Thomas & O'Kane, 1998). The collaborative techniques I used also sought to address this issue. On the informed consent form relating to classroom observations, I left space for the signatures of not only the parents but also the children. For children, consent seems not just about accepting or rejecting research activities but also 'about making an informed choice and becoming emotionally committed to it' (Thomas & O'Kane, 1998: 345). I found some children took their participation seriously because when I met them in my writing-up stage, they asked me if I had finished my study of them.

In my study, I found myself attempting to be involved with children's activities, such as playing football or other games with them. This involvement was a great help to me in building up a rapport with the children. Due to my special way of getting to know the families, almost automatically the children may have equated me with their parents' generation. This kind of classification seems to have been alleviated when I brought my daughter to the visits during weekends or school holidays. Her presence seemed to decrease my intrusiveness as a researcher since it looked like a situation where a few children played together, with their parents getting together at the same time.

A researcher's positioning

A researcher is often likely to have both outsider and insider experiences (Spradley, 1979), but my dual researcher position was not unproblematic. In terms of the language spoken and the cultural tradition, I had the insider perspective to research these families: this offered me a privilege that wrought its influence over gaining access to these families. For every single subtle step in the fieldwork, from choosing the time and date of visits to dealing with tensions within the families, my insider insights seemed to lead me accurately to the limits, both as a researcher and as a friend. Different from the majority of professional researchers, I was a full participant observer going through the same experiences as the parents. For example, helping my daughter attend her first birthday party in England solved some of my uncertainties as to what to wear and what presents to buy for similar occasions. Interestingly, my general knowledge of English culture from my schooling in China did not provide me with answers to all the subtle cultural questions associated with English social practices.

Being an insider seems to have helped me cope with the tensions in the families. An important dimension in maintaining relationships with families is how a researcher should cope with any tension in families during his/her visits. Generally speaking, the researcher needs to step back whenever there is any tension in families. In other words, there always seems a moment when the researcher may need to pause or withdraw from communication with the families, for example, when tensions arise. However, it appears necessary to analyse the different causes of the tensions within the families. The researcher should have a sense of the causes of a particular tension, make judgements accordingly, and adopt different approaches in order not to lose any contact just because of a tension that has nothing to do with him or her.

Despite having an advantageous position in being an insider of the Mandarin-speaking community, I was an outsider to each individual family, since there is always a microcosm of subculture within a household. This requires me to take a learner's attitude, or an accepting attitude, towards each discrepancy between my own subculture and that of the families. To achieve this, I needed to immerse myself in the mundane and routine of everyday life. I accommodated my needs to their ways of doing things, meshed my own agenda with the families' routine activities and children's interests, without imposing any meaning or activities on them (Brewer, 2000). I also fixed my visits to the families' schedules. During my *limited* and *precious* time with the families, I kept an open mind about the issues, which seemed to minimize my obstruction to the families.

Data presentation

A major source of data was always the scrupulous writing of fieldnotes for 'if it's not written down, it never happened' (Taylor & Bogdan, 1998: 67). Fieldnotes were collected throughout the whole of the research time. As a companion to the fieldnotes, I almost always audio tape-recorded participant interviews and observations. It should be noted that due to the busy schedules of the families, talking over the telephone was helpful in the data generation of my study. Hence, my fieldnotes included those taken during telephone calls.

One issue for me was how to deal with the two languages involved and whether a researcher should translate one language into another in fieldnotes. In most cases of data gathering, the children spoke more English than Mandarin, whereas the parents did the opposite. In order to depict the events or the situations as accurately as possible, I tried to write my notes in the language spoken by the subjects. I found myself writing down virtually anything that happened during my stay with the families and almost everything that may have crossed my mind then. Key words, phrases, fragment sentences and paraphrasing were also helpful (Arthur & Nazroo, 2003; Spradley, 1980) when time was not sufficient in the field. I used the dialogue form and quotation marks to record the remarks as accurately as possible, for example, for the conversations between the parent, the children and myself. By using square brackets, I differentiated the original talk of the participants from the commentary I made during and after the scenes. As Hammersley and Atkinson (1983) suggest, distinctions should be made between the subjects' direct quotations from the researcher's summaries (Spradley's 'native terms' and 'observer terms'). These were useful in later record construction and interpretation and triggered my further questions.

Researchers have to make decisions as to which language to use in the whole process of research, as it is not uncommon that more than one language is necessarily involved. Depending on the nature of the inquiry and the researchers' linguistic background, it is often the case that the fieldwork is carried out using a language other than English. Attia (2011) used Arabic in her fieldwork, which was situated in the Arabic Language Institute (ALI) in Cairo, Egypt, to explore teachers' pedagogical beliefs about using information and communication technology (ICT) in teaching Arabic as a foreign language. In their writing up of the report, most researchers used English for practical considerations such as English being a medium of supervision and dissemination of research findings, and resource limitations, for example, data analysis software being more often than not incompatible with only English.

In data presentation, researchers may adopt various approaches. In my study, I transcribed the data verbatim in line with the language used, that is, transcriptions were made in the language originally spoken on the tapes: English and Chinese. Then I translated the Chinese parts into English, but I inserted English translations in italics in order to differentiate them from those originally spoken in English. To some extent, my translation is visible to readers. As mentioned previously, when I brought my transcription back to each family for their reading and feedback, they were welcome to point out any inappropriate translations of the extracts.

The use of my verbatim fieldnotes and avoiding the tendency of translation also helped avoid amalgamated language, which Spradley (1980: 66) defined as 'ethnographer's language with unidentified mixture of usages from others [*the subjects*]... taking the things spoken by others and rephrasing them into a composite picture of the cultural scene'. Although amalgamated language can simplify complicated situations in fieldwork, it runs the risk of distorting the cultural meaning. In order to minimize this distortion, I used audio recording (see Silverman, 2001) in both participant observation and ethnographic interviewing, which helped expand my fieldnotes later.

References

Abreu, G. and Hale, H. (2011) Trajectories of cultural identity development of young immigrant people: The impact of family practices. *Psychology Studies* 56 (1), 53–61. doi 10.1007/s12646-011-0061-6.

Acoach, C.L. and Webb, L.M. (2004) The influence of language brokering on Hispanic teenagers' acculturation, academic performance, and nonverbal decoding skills: A preliminary study. *The Howard Journal of Communication* 15, 1–19.

Alanen, L. (1998) Children and the family order. In I. Hutchby and J. Moran-Ellis (eds) *Children and Social Competence: Arenas of Action* (pp. 29–45). London: Falmer Press.

Alderson, P. (1993) *Children's Consent to Surgery*. Milton Keynes: Open University Press.

Alderson, P. (1995) *Listening to Children: Children, Ethics and Social Research*. London: Barnardo's.

Alred, G. and Byram, M. (2002) Becoming an intercultural mediator: A longitudinal study of residence abroad. *Journal of Multilingual and Multicultural Development* 23 (5), 339–352.

Altheide, D. and Johnson, J. (1998) Criteria for assessing interpretive validity in qualitative research. In N. Denzin and Y. Lincoln (eds) *Collecting and Interpreting Qualitative Materials* (pp. 283–312). London: Sage.

Aries, P. (1982) The discovery of childhood. In C. Jenks (ed.) *The Sociology of Childhood: Essential Readings* (pp. 27–41). Aldershot: Batsford Academic and Educational Ltd.

Arthur, J.A. (2000) *Invisible Sojourners: African Immigrant Diaspora in the United States*. Westport, CT: Praeger.

Arthur, S. and Nazroo, J. (2003) Designing fieldwork strategies and materials. In J. Ritchie and J. Lewis (eds) *Qualitative Research Practice: A Guide for Social Science Students and Researchers* (pp. 109–137). London: Sage.

Asher, R.E. (ed.) (1994) *The Encyclopaedia of Language and Linguistics*. Oxford: Pergamon.

Atkinson, P. (1992) *Understanding Ethnographic Texts*. Newbury Park, CA: Sage.

Attia, M. (2011) *Reflective Practice in Research Undertaken Multilingually*. Presentation at the BAAL Annual Conference.

Au, K.H. (1993) *Literacy Instruction in Multicultural Settings*. London and Tokyo: Harcourt Brace College Publishers.

Banks, J.A. (2002) *An Introduction to Multicultural Education* (3rd edn). Boston, MA: Allyn and Bacon.

Baptiste, D.A. (1993) Immigrant families, adolescents and acculturation: Insights for therapists. *Marriage and Family Review* 19 (3–4), 341–363.

Barry, B. (2001) *Culture and Equality: An Egalitarian Critique of Multiculturalism*. Oxford: Blackwell Publishing.

Bateson, G. (1972) *Steps to an Ecology of Mind*. San Francisco, CA: Chandler.

Baumann, G. (1992) Ritual implicates 'Others': Rereading Durkheim in a plural society. In D. de Coppet (ed.) *Understanding Rituals* (pp. 97–116). London and New York: Routledge.

Baynham, M. (1993) Code switching and mode switching: Community interpreters and mediators of literacy. In B. Street (ed.) *Cross-cultural Approaches to Literacy* (pp. 294–314). Cambridge: Cambridge University Press.

Baynham, M. and Masing, H.L. (2000) Mediators and mediation in multilingual literacy events. In M. Martin-Jones and K. Jones (eds) *Multilingual Literacies* (pp. 189–207). Amsterdam/Philadelphia: John Benjamins.

Bell, J. (2005) *Doing Your Research Project: A Guide for First-Time Researchers in Education, Health, and Social Science* (4th edn). Maidenhead: Open University Press.

Berry, J.W. (1988) Acculturation and psychological adaptation: A conceptual overview. In J.W. Berry and R.C. Annis (eds) *Ethnic Psychology: Research and Practice With Immigrants, Native People, Ethnic Groups And Sojourners* (pp. 41–52). Amsterdam: Swets and Zeitlinger.

Berry, J.W. (1995) Psychology of acculturation. In N. Goldberger and J. Veroff (eds) *The Culture and Psychology Reader* (pp. 457–488). New York: New York University Press.

Berry, J.W. (2003) Conceptual approaches to acculturation. In K.M. Chun, P.B. Organista and G. Marin (eds) *Acculturation: Advances in Theory, Measurement, and Applied Research* (pp. 17–38). Washington, DC: American Psychological Association.

Bickley, V.C. (1982) Language as the Bridge. In S. Bochner (ed.) *Cultures in Contact: Studies in Cross-Cultural Interaction* (pp. 99–125). Oxford: Pergamon Press.

Birman, D. (2005) Ethical issues in research with immigrants and refugees. In J.E. Trimble and C. Fisher (eds) *The Handbook of Ethical Research with Ethnocultural Populations and Communities* (pp. 155–178). Thousand Oaks, CA: Sage.

Birman, D. and Trickett, E. (2001) The process of acculturation in first-generation Immigrants: A study of Soviet Jewish refugee adolescents and parents. *Journal of Cross-Cultural Psychology* 32 (4), 456–477.

Blaxter, L., Hughes, C. and Tight, M. (2001) *How to Research* (2nd edn). Buckingham: Open University Press.

Bloch, A. (2002) *The Migration and Settlement of Refugees in Britain*. New York: Palgrave Macmillan.

Bochner, S. (ed.) (1981) *The Mediating Person: Bridges between Cultures*. Cambridge, MA: Schenkman Publishing Company.

Bochner, S. (1981) The social psychology of cultural mediation. In S. Bochner (ed.) *The Mediating Person: Bridges between Cultures* (pp. 6–36). Cambridge: Schenkman Publishing Company.

Bochner, S. (ed.) (1982) *Cultures in Contact: Studies in Cross-Cultural Interaction*. Oxford: Pergamon Press.

Bowling, A. (2002) *Research Methods in Health: Investigating Health and Health Services* (2nd edn). Maidenhead: Open University Press.

Boyden, J. (1997) Childhood and the policy makers: A comparative perspective on the globalization of childhood. In A. James and A. Prout (eds) *Constructing and Reconstructing Childhood: Contemporary Issues in the Sociological Study of Childhood* (pp. 190–215). London: Routledge.

Boyden, J., Ling, B. and Myer, W. (1998) *What Works for Working Children*. Stockholm: Radda Barnen/UNICEF.

Brabant, S. and Mooney, L.A. (1989) When 'critters' act like people: Anthropomorphism in greeting cards. *Sociological Spectrum* 9, 477–494.

Brake, T., Medina-Walker, D. and Walker, T. (1995) *Doing Business Internationally: The Guide to Cross-Cultural Success*. Burr Ridge, IL: Irwin.

Brewer, J.D. (2000) *Ethnography*. Buckingham: Open University Press.

Brislin, R., Cushner, K., Cherrie, C. and Yong, M. (1986) *Intercultural Interaction: A Practical Guide*. London: Sage.

Brown, N. (1992) Beachboys as culture brokers in Bakau Town, The Gambia. *Community Development Journal* 27 (4), 361–370.

Bruner, J. (1997) Celebrating divergence: Piaget and Vygotsky. *Human Development* 40, 63–73.

Bryman, A. (1989) *Research Methods and Organization Studies*. London: Urwin Hyman.

Burgess, R.G. (ed.) (1989) *The Ethics of Educational Research*. London: Falmer Press.

Buriel, R. and De Ment, T. (1997) Immigration and sociocultural change in Mexican, Chinese and Vietnamese American families. In A. Booth, A.C. Crouter and N. Landale (eds) *Immigration and the Family: Research and Policy on U.S. Immigrants* (pp. 91–131). Mahwah, NJ: Lawrence Erlbaum.

Buriel, R., Perez, W., De Ment, T.L., Chavez, D.V. and Moran, V.R. (1998) The relationship of language brokering to academic performance, biculturalism, and self-efficacy among Latino adolescents. *Hispanic Journal of Behavioural Sciences* 20 (3), 283–297.

Byram, M. (1997) *Teaching and Assessing Intercultural Communicative Competence*. Clevedon: Multilingual Matters.

Cacioppo, J.T. and Anderson, B.L. (1981) Greeting cards as data on social processes. *Basic and Applied Social Psychology* 2 (2), 115–119.

Carrier, J. (1990) Reconciling commodities and personal relations in industrial society. *Theory and Society* 19, 579–598.

Castle, S. and Millier, M.J. (2003) *The Age of Migration*. New York: Palgrave Macmillan.

Chamberlain, M. (1999) The family as model and metaphor in Caribbean migration to Britain. *Journal of Ethnic and Migration Studies* 25, 251–266.

Chang, K.C. (1977) *Food in Chinese Culture: Anthropological and Historical Perspectives*. New Haven, CT: Yale University Press.

Chao, R.K. (1994) Beyond parental control and authoritarian parenting style: Understanding Chinese parenting through the cultural notion of training. *Child Development* 65, 1111–1119.

Chen, A. (2007) *Chinese in Britain*. BBC Radio 4: 3.45–4.15 pm, 30 April to 11 May 2007.

Cheng, W.K. (2002) Constructing Cathay: John Macgowan, cultural brokerage, and missionary knowledge of china. *Journal of Asian Pacific Communication* 12 (2), 269–290.

Christensen, P.H. (2004) Children's participation in ethnographic research: Issues of power and representation. *Children and Society* 18, 165–176.

Christensen, P. and James, A. (2001) What are schools for? The temporal experience of children's learning in northern England. In L. Alanen and B. Mayall (eds) *Conceptualizing Child–Adult Relations* (pp. 70–84). London: Falmer Press.

Chu, C.M. (1999) Immigrant children mediators (ICM): Bridging the literacy gap in immigrant communities. *The New Review of Children's Literature and Librarianship* 85–94.

Chun, K. and Akutsu, P. (2003) Acculturation among ethnic minority families. In K.M. Chun, P.B. Organista and G. Marin (eds) *Acculturation: Advances in Theory, Measurement, and Applied Research* (pp. 95–119). Washington, DC: American Psychological Association.

Clarke, P. (2003) Parental gift-giving behaviour at Christmas: An exploratory study. Unpublished PhD thesis, Griffith University Australia.

Cohen, S., Moran-Ellis, J. and Smaje, C. (1999) Children as informal interpreters in GP consultations: Pragmatics and ideology. *Sociology of Health and Illness* 21 (2), 163–186.

Cole, M. (1995) Culture and cognitive development: From cross-cultural research to creating systems of cultural mediation. *Culture and Psychology* 1, 25–54.

Cole, M. (1996) *Cultural Psychology: A Once and Future Discipline*. Cambridge, MA: Harvard University Press.

Collins, P.H. (2000) *Black Feminist Thought: Knowledge, Consciousness, and the Politics o Empowerment*. New York and London: Routledge.

Corona, R., Stevens, L.F., Halford, R.W., Shaffer, C.M., Reid-Quinones, K. and Gonzalez, T. (2012) A qualitative analysis of what Latino parents and adolescents think and feel about language brokering. *Journal of Child Family Studies* 21, 788–798.

Corsaro, W.A. (2011) *The Sociology of Childhood*. London: Sage.

Costigan, C.L. and Su. T.F. (2004) Orthogonal versus linear models of acculturation among immigrant Chinese Canadians: A comparison of mothers, fathers, and children. *International Journal of Behavioural Development* 28 (6), 518–527.

Coulthard, M. (1985) *An Introduction to Discourse Analysis*. London: Longman.

Davis, D.S. and Sensenbrenner, J.S. (2000) Commercialising childhood: Parental purchases for Shanghai's only child. In D.S. Davis (ed.) *The Consumer Revolution in Urban China* (pp. 54–79). Berkeley, CA: University of California Press.

Davis, J. (1998) Understanding the meanings of children: A reflexive process. *Children and Society* 12, 325–335.

De Coppet, D. (ed.) (1992) *Understanding Rituals*. London and New York: Routledge.

Delgado-Gaitan, C. (1994) Sociocultural change through literacy: Toward the empowerment of families. In B.M. Ferdman, R. Weber and A.G. Ramirez (eds) *Literacy Across Languages and Cultures* (pp. 143–169). Albany, NY: State University of New York Press.

Dennis, P.A. (1994) The life of a culture broker. *Human Organization* 53 (3), 303–308.

Denzin, N.K. and Lincoln, Y.S. (1994) Introduction: Entering the field of qualitative research. In N.K. Denzin and Y.S. Lincoln (eds) *Handbook of Qualitative Research* (pp. 1–17). Thousand Oaks, CA: Sage.

Denzin, N.K. and Lincoln, Y.S. (eds) (2000) *Handbook of Qualitative Research* (2nd edn). Thousand Oaks, CA: Sage.

Denzin, N.K. and Lincoln, Y.S. (eds) (2002) *The Qualitative Inquiry Reader*. Thousand Oaks, CA: Sage.

Derrida, J. (2001) *The Work of Mourning* (edited by P-A. Brault and M. Naess). Chicago, IL: University of Chicago Press.

Donaldson, M. (1978) *Children's Mind*. London: Collins.

Dorner, L.M., Orellena, M.F. and Li-Grining, C.P. (2007) "I helped my mom and it helped me: Translating the skills of language brokers into improved standardized test scores. *American Journal of Education* 113, 451–478.

Dorner, L., Orellena, M.F. and Jimenez, R. (2008) 'It's one of those things that you do to help the family': Language brokering and the development of immigrant adolescents. *Journal of Adolescent Research* 23, 515–543.

Du Bois-Raymond, M. (2001) Negotiating families. In M. Du Bois-Raymond, H. Suncker and H. Kruger (eds) *Childhood in Europe* (pp. 63–90). New York: Peter Lang.

Duran, P. (2003) Children as mediators for the second language learning of their migrant parents. *Language and Education* 17 (5), 311–331.

Durkheim, E. (1976) *The Elementary Forms of the Religious Life* (2nd edn) (trans. J.W. Swain). London: Allen & Unwin.

Erbaugh, M.S. (2000) Greeting cards in China. In D.S. Davis (ed.) *The Consumer Revolution in Urban China* (pp. 171–200). Berkeley, CA: University of California Press.

Fairclough, N. (2001) *Language and Power* (2nd edn). London: Longman.

Farrell, M., Arizpe, E. and McAdam, J. (2010) Journeys across visual borders: Annotated spreads of 'The Arrival' by Shaun Tan as a method of understanding pupils' creation of meaning through visual images. *Australian Journal of Language and Literacy* 33 (3), 198–210.

Felix-Ortiz, M. (1994) A multidimensional measure of cultural identity for Latino and Latina adolescents. *Hispanic Journal of Behavioural Sciences* 16, 99–116.

Feng, J. (1994) Asian-American children: What teachers should know. ERIC Clearinghouse on Elementary and Early Childhood Education, Urbana, IL. See www.ericdigests. org/1994/teachers.htm (accessed 12 October 2006).

Findlay, A., Hoy, C. and Stockdale, A. (2004) In what sense English? An exploration of English migrants and identification. *Journal of Ethnic and Migration Studies* 30 (1), pp. 59–79.

Fine, G. and Deegan, J. (1996) Three principles of Serendip: Insight, chance, and discovery in qualitative research. *International Journal of Qualitative Studies in Education* 9, 434–447.

Fine, M. (1994) Working the hyphens: Reinventing self and other in qualitative research. In N.K. Denzin and Y.S. Lincoln (eds) *Handbook of Qualitative Research* (pp. 70–82). Thousand Oaks, CA: Sage.

Fine, M. and Weis, L.(1998) Writing the 'wrongs' of fieldwork: Confronting our own research/writing dilemmas in urban ethnographies. In G. Shacklock and J. Smyth (eds) *Being Reflexive in Critical Educational and Social Research* (pp. 13–35). London and Bristol: Falmer Press.

Francis, B. and Archer, L. (2005) British-Chinese pupils' and parents' constructions of the value of education. *British Educational Research Journal* 31 (1), 89–108.

Furnham, A. and Thomas, P. (1984) Pocket money: A study of economic education. *British Journal of Developmental Psychology* 2, 205–212.

Furnham, A. and Bochner, S. (1986) *Culture Shock: Psychological Reactions To Unfamiliar Environment*. London and New York: Methuen.

Gabriel, N. (2004a) Being a child today. In J. Willan, R. Parker-Rees and J. Savage (eds) *Early Childhood Studies: An Introduction to the Studies of Children's Worlds and Children's Lives* (pp. 65–74). Exeter: Learning Matters.

Gabriel, N. (2004b) Adults' concepts of childhood. In J. Willan, R. Parker-Rees and J. Savage (eds) *Early Childhood Studies: An Introduction to the Studies of Children's Worlds and Children's Lives* (pp. 45–54). Exeter: Learning Matters.

Garcia, E. (1994) *Understanding and Meeting the Challenge of Student Cultural Diversity*. Boston, MA: Houghton Mifflin.

Garcia Coll, C. and Magnuson, K. (1997) The psychological experience of immigration: A developmental perspective. In A. Booth, A.C. Crouter and N. Landale (eds) *Immigration and the Family: Research and Policy on U.S. Immigrants* (pp. 91–131). Mahwah, NJ: Lawrence Erlbaum.

Gardner, H. (1998) Social and cognitive competencies in learning: Which is which? In I. Hutchby and J. Moran-Ellis (eds) *Children and Social Competence: Arenas of Action* (pp. 115–133). London: Falmer Press.

Garvey, A. and Jackson, B. (1975) Chinese Children: Research and Action Project into the Needs. Research Report, National Educational Research and Development Trust.

Gathercole, V., Sebastian, E. and Soto, P. (1999) The early acquisition of Spanish verbal morphology: Across-the-board or piecemeal knowledge? *International Journal of Bilingualism* 2 & 3, 133–182.

Geertz, C. (1960) The Javanese Kijaji: The changing role of a cultural broker. *Comparative Studies in Social History* 2, 228–249.

Geertz, C. (1973) *The Interpretation of Cultures: Selected Essays*. New York: Basic Books.

Gentemann, K.M. (1983) The cultural broker concept in bicultural education. *Journal of Negro Education* 52 (2), 118–129.

Giddens, A. (1979) *Central Problems in Social Theory*. London: Macmillan.

Gillen, J. (2000) Versions of Vygotsky. *British Journal of Educational Studies* 48 (2), 183–198.

Glaser, B.G. and Strauss, A.L. (1967) *The Discovery of Grounded Theory: Strategies for Qualitative Research*. Chicago, IL: Aldine de Gruyter.

Glenn, E.N. and Yap, S.G. (2004) Chinese American families. In R.L. Taylor (ed.) *Minority Families in the United States: A Multicultural Perspective* (pp. 134–163) (3rd edn). Upper Saddle River, NJ: Prentice Hall.

Goffman, E. (1959) *The Presentation of Self in Everyday Life*. New York: Doubleday.

Gopaul-McNicol, S. and Thomas-Presswood, T. (1998) *Working with Linguistically and Culturally Different Children: Innovative Clinical and Educational Approaches*. Boston and Singapore: Allyn and Bacon.

Greenberg, N. (2006) Overview of art and organism: A biological perspective on art and aesthetics. See www.notes.utk.edu/bio/greenberg.nsf (assessed 9 June 2006).

Gregory, E. (1998) Siblings as mediators of literacy in linguistic minority communities. *Language and Education* 12 (1), 33–54.

Gregory, E., Long, S. and Volk, D. (eds) (2004) *Many Pathways to Literacy: Young Children Learning with Siblings, Grandparents, Peers and Communities*. London: RoutledgeFalmer.

Greig, A. and Taylor, J. (1999) *Doing Research with Children*. London: Sage.

Grime, R. (2000) *Deeply Into the Bone: Re-inventing Rites of Passage*. Berkeley, CA: University of California Press.

Grimes, R. (1982) *Beginnings in Ritual Studies*. Lanham, MA: University Press of America.

Guo, Z. (2007) Young children as cultural mediators: A study of mandarin-speaking Chinese families in the UK. Unpublished PhD thesis. Manchester Metropolitan University.

HAC (Home Affairs Committee, House of Commons) (1985) *Chinese Community in Britain* (2nd Report). London: HMSO.

Hall, E.T. (1959, 1990) *The Silent Language*. New York: Doubleday.

Hall, N. (2004) The child in the middle: Agency and diplomacy in language brokering events. In G. Hansen, K. Malmkjaer and D. Gile (eds) *Claims, Changes and Challenges in Translation Studies* (pp. 285–297). Amsterdam: John Benjamins.

Hall, N. and Sham, S. (2007) Language brokering as young people's work: Evidence from Chinese adolescents in England. *Language and Education: An International Journal* 21 (1), 16–30.

Hall, N. and Guo, Z. (2012) Child language and cultural brokering. In A. Jiménez Ivars and J.B. Mayor (eds) *Recent Developments in Natural Translation and Interpreting Studies*. (pp. 51–75). Vienna: Peter Lang.

Halliday, M.A.K. (1975) *Learning How to Mean: Exploration in the Department of Language*. London: Edward Arnold.

Hammmersley, M. and Atkinson, P. (1983) *Ethnography: Principles in Practice*. London: Routledge.

Hammersley, M. and Atkinson, P. (1995) *Ethnography: Principles in Practice* (2nd edn). London: Routledge.

Harris, B. and Sherwood, B. (1978) Translation as an innate skill. In D. Gerver and H.W. Sinaiko (eds) *Language Interpretation and Communication* (pp. 155–170). New York: Plenum Press.

Harris, R. (2006) 'My language', 'my culture', 'my religion': Communities, practices and diasporas. *NALDIC Quarterly* 3 (3), 33–34.

Harris, S.N. (1997) Ritual: Communication and meaning. *Journal of Ritual Studies* 11 (1), 35–44.

Hendrick, H. (2008) The child as a social actor in historical sources: Problems of identification and interpretation. In P. Christensen and A. James (eds) *Research with Children: Perspectives and Practices* (2nd edn) (pp. 40–63). London: Routledge.

Hendry, J. (1986) *Becoming Japanese: The World of the Pre-School Child*. Honolulu, HI: University of Hawaii Press.

Henn, M., Weinstein, M. and Foard, N. (2006) *A Short Introduction to Social Research*. London: Sage.

Heyl, B.S. (2001) Ethnographic interviewing. In P. Atkinson, A. Coffey, S. Delamont, J. Lofland and L. Lofland (eds) *Handbook of Ethnography* (pp. 369–383). London: Sage.

Hinderaker, E. (2002.) Translation and cultural brokerage. In P.J. Deloria and N. Salisbury (eds) *A Companion to American Indian History* (pp. 357–375). Oxford: Blackwell Publishing.

Ho, D. (1994) Filial piety, authoritarian moralism, and cognitive conservatism in Chinese societies. *Genetic, Social and General Psychological Monographs* 120, 347–365.

Hodder, I. (2003) The interpretation of documents and material culture. In N.K. Denzin and Y.S. Lincoln (eds) *Collecting and Interpreting Qualitative Materials* (pp. 155–175). Thousand Oaks, CA: Sage.

Hoffman, E. (1989) *Lost in Translation*. London: Vintage.

Hofstede, G. (1991) *Culture and Organizations: Software of the Mind*. London: McGraw-Hill.

Hofstede, G. and Hofstede, G.J. (2005) *Culture and Organizations: Software of the Mind* (2nd edn). London: McGraw-Hill.

Horowitz, R. (1993) The power of ritual in a Chicano community: A young woman's status and expanding family ties. *Marriage and Family Review* 19 (3–4), 257–280.

Hua, J.M. and Costigan, C.L. (2012) The familial context of adolescent language brokering within immigrant Chinese families in Canada. *Journal of Youth and Adolescence* 41, 894–906.

Huntsinger, C.S., Jose, P.E., Liaw, F.R. and Ching, W. (1997) Cultural differences in early mathematics learning: A comparison of Euro-American, Chinese-American, and Taiwan Chinese families. *International Journal of Behavioural Development* 21, 371–388.

Hutchby, I. and Moran-Ellis, J. (eds) (1998) *Children and Social Competence: Arenas of Action*. London: Falmer Press.

Hyatt, J. and Simons, H. (1999) Cultural codes – Who hold the key?: The concept and conduct of evaluation in Central and Eastern Europe. *Evaluation* 5, 23–41.

Jaffe, A. (1999) Packaged sentiments: The social meanings of greeting cards. *Journal of Material Culture* 4 (2), 115–141.

James, A. (2001) Ethnography in the study of children and childhood. In P. Atkinson, A. Coffey, S. Delamont, J. Lofland and L. Lofland (eds) *Handbook of Ethnography* (pp. 246–257). London: Sage.

James, A. (2004) Understanding childhood from an interdisciplinary perspectives: Problems and potentials. In P.B. Pufall and R.P. Unsworth (eds) *Rethinking Childhood* (pp. 25–37). Piscataway, NJ: Rutgers University Press.

James, A. (2005) *The Future of Childhood*. London: Routledge.

James, A. and James, A. (2004) *Constructing Childhood: Theory, Policy and Social Practice*. Basingstoke: Palgrave Macmillan.

James, A. and James, A. (2008) *Key Concepts in Childhood Studies*. Los Angeles, CA: Sage.

James, A. and Prout, A. (1997) Re-presenting childhood: Time and transition in the study of childhood. In A. James and A. Prout (eds) *Constructing and Reconstructing Childhood: Contemporary Issues in the Sociological Study of Childhood* (pp. 230–250). London: Routledge.

James, A. and Prout, A. (eds) (1990) *Constructing and Reconstructing Childhood: Contemporary Issues in the Sociological Study of Childhood*. London: Routledge.

James, A., Jenks, C. and Prout, A. (1998) *Theorizing Childhood*. Cambridge: Polity Press.

Jenkins, P. (1993) *Children's Rights: A Participative Exercise for Learning about Children's Rights in England and Wales*. London: Longman.

Jenks, C. (1982, 1992) *The Sociology of Childhood: Essential Readings*. Aldershot: Batsford Academic and Educational Ltd.

Jenks, C. (1996) *Childhood*. London: Routledge.

Jenks, C. (2004) Constructing childhood sociologically. In M.J. Kehily (ed.) *An Introduction to Childhood Studies* (pp. 77–95). Maidenhead: Open University Press.

Jenks, C. (2005) *Culture*. London: Routledge.

Jones, C.J. and Trickett, E.J. (2005) Immigrant adolescents behaving as culture brokers: A study of families from the Former Soviet Union. *The Journal of Social Psychology* 145 (4), 405–427.

Jones, C.J., Trickett, E.J. and Birman, D. (2012) Determinants and consequences of child culture brokering in families from the Former Soviet Union. *American Journal of Community Psychology* 50, 182–196.

Jorgensen, D.L. (1989) *Participant Observation*. Newbury Park, CA: Sage.

Jose, P.E., Huntsinger, C.S., Huntsinger, P.R. and Liaw F.R. (2000) Parental values and practices relevant to young children's social development in Taiwan and the United States. *Journal of Cross-Cultural Psychology* 31 (6), 677–702.

Kalman, J. (1999) *Writing on the Plaza: Mediated Literacy Practices Among Scribes and Clients in Mexico City*. Cresskill, NJ: Hampton Press.

Kannan, C.T. (1978) *Cultural Adaptation of Asian Immigrants: First and Second Generation*. Middlesex.

Katan, D. (1999) *Translating Cultures: An Introduction for Translators, Interpreters and Mediators*. Manchester: St. Jerome Publishing.

Katan, D. (2004) *Translating Cultures: An Introduction for Translators, Interpreters and Mediators*. Manchester: St. Jerome Publishing.

Kaur, S. and Mills, R. (1993) Children as interpreters. In E. Mills and J. Mills (eds) *Bilingualism in the Primary School: A Handbook for Teachers* (pp. 113–125). London: Routledge.

Kelly, R. (2007, June 10) Translation 'should be cut'. BBC 10pm news, UK.

Kenner, C. (2004) *Becoming Biliterate: Young Children Learning Different Writing Systems*. Stoke-on-Trent: Trentham Books.

Kibria, N. (1993) *Family Tightrope: The Changing Lives of Vietnamese Americans*. Princeton, NJ: Princeton University Press.

Klavir, R. and Leiser, D. (2002) When astronomy, biology, and culture converge: Children's conceptions about birthdays. *Journal of Genet Psychology* 163 (22), 239–253.

Klein, J. (1965) *Samples from English Cultures, Vol. II*. London: Routledge and Kegan Paul Limited.

Knapp-Potthoff, A. and Knapp-Potthoff, K. (1986) Interweaving two discourses – The difficult task of the non-professional interpreter. In J. House and S. Blum-Kulk (eds) *Interlingual and Intercultural Communication: Discourse and Cognition in Translation and Second Language Acquisition Studies* (pp. 151–168). Tubingen: Narr.

Kress, G. (2003) Perspectives on making meaning: The differential principles and means of adults and children. In N. Hall, J. Larson and J. Marsh (eds) *Handbook of Early Childhood Literacy* (pp. 154–166). London: Sage.

Kress, G. and Mavers, D. (2005) Social semiotics and multimodal texts. In B. Somekh and C. Lewin (eds) *Research Methods in the Social Sciences* (pp. 172–179). London: Sage.

Kurin, R. (1997) *Reflections of a Culture Broker: A View from the Smithsonian.* Washington, DC: Smithsonian Institution Press.

Lansdown, G. (2005) *The Evolving Capacities of the Child.* Florence: UNICEF Innocenti Research Centre/Save the Children.

Lancaster, P. (2003) *Listening to Young Children.* Maidenhead: Open University Press.

Lattany, K.H. (1994) Off timing: Stepping to the different drummer. In G. Early (ed.) *Lure and Loathing* (pp. 164–175). New York: Penguin Press.

Leslie, L.A. (1992) The role of informal support networks in the adjustment of Central American immigrant families. *Journal of Community Psychology* 20, 243–256.

Levine, R.A. (2007) Ethnographic studies of childhood: A historical overview. *American Anthropologist* 109 (3), 247–260.

Lewis, J. and Ritchie, J. (2003) Generating from qualitative research. In J. Ritchie and J. Lewis (eds) *Qualitative Research Practice: A Guide for Social Science Students and Researchers* (pp. 263–286). London: Sage.

Li, G. (2002) *"East is East, West is West"? Home Literacy, Cultural, And Schooling.* New York: Peter Lang.

Li, W. (1994) *Three Generations, Two Languages, One Family: Language Choice and Language Shift in a Chinese Community in Britain.* Clevedon: Multilingual Matters.

Li, Z. (2001) (Trans.) *A Glimpse of the Chinese Culture.* Beijing: China Intercontinental Press.

Lin, C. and Fu, V.R. (1990) A comparison of child-rearing practices among Chinese, immigrant Chinese, and Caucasian-American parents. *Child Development* 68, 557–568.

Lincoln, Y.S. and Denzin, N.K. (2000) The seventh moment: Out of the past. In N.K. Denzin and Y.S. Lincoln (eds) *Handbook of Qualitative Research* (2nd edn) (pp. 1047–1065). Thousand Oaks, CA: Sage.

Lincoln, Y.S. and Guba, G.E. (1985) *Naturalistic Inquiry.* Beverley Hill, CA: Sage.

Lindsay, G. (2000) Researching children's perspectives: Ethical issues. In A. Lewis and G. Lindsay (eds) *Researching Children's Perspectives* (pp. 3–20). Buckingham: Open University Press.

Liu, S. (2006) An examination of the effects of print media exposure and contact on subjective social reality and acculturation attitudes. *International Journal of Intercultural Relations* 30 (3), 365–382.

Lloyd-Smith, M. and Tarr, J. (2000) Researching children's perspectives: A sociological dimension. In A. Lewis and G. Lindsay (eds) *Researching Children's Perspectives* (pp. 59–69). Buckingham: Open University Press.

Lofland, J. and Lofland, L.H. (1995) *Analyzing Social Settings* (3rd edn). Belmont, CA: Wadsworth.

Love, J.A. and Buriel, R. (2007) Language brokering, autonomy, parent-child bonding, biculturalism, and depression. *Hispanic Journal of Behavioral Sciences* 29, 472–491.

Lowe, R. (2004) Childhood through the ages. In T. Maynard and N. Thomas (eds) *An Introduction to Early Childhood Studies* (pp. 65–74). London: Sage.

Luk-Fong, Y.Y.P. (2005) A search for new ways of describing parent–child relationships: Voices from principals, teachers, guidance professionals, parents and pupils. *Childhood* 12 (1), 111–137.

Ma, J.Z. (2004) Reading the Word and the World: A child in the interplay of her contexts in the reading of dual-language books with her mother. Unpublished PhD Thesis. The University of Bristol.

Mäkelä, J. (2000) Cultural definitions of the meal. In H.L. Meiselman (ed.) *Dimensions of the Meal: The Science, Culture, Business and Art of Eating* (pp. 7–18). Gaithersburg, MD: Aspen Publications.

Malakoff, M. and Hakuta, K. (1991) Translation skill and metalinguistic awareness in bilinguals. In E. Bialystok (ed.) *Language Processing In Bilingual Children* (pp. 141–166). New York: Cambridge University Press.

Mandell, N. (1991) The least-adult role in studying children. In F. Waksler (ed.) *Studying the Social Worlds of Children* (pp. 38–60). London: Falmer Press.

Margalit, A. (2002) *The Ethics of Memory*. Cambridge, MA: Harvard University Press.

Marín, G. and Gamba, R. (2003) Acculturation and changes in cultural values. In K.M. Chun, P.B. Organista and G. Marín (eds) *Acculturation: Advances in Theory, Measurement, and Applied Research* (pp. 83–94). Washington, DC: American Psychological Association.

Markus, H.R. and Kitayama, S. (1991) Culture and the self: Implications for cognition, emotion, and motivation. *Psychological Review* 98, 224–253.

Marsh, J. (2004a) The techno-literacy practices of young children. *Journal of Early Childhood Research* 2 (1), 51–66.

Marsh, J. (2004b) *BBC Child of Our Time: Young Children's Use of Popular Culture, Media and New Technologies*. Sheffield: University of Sheffield.

Marshall, D.W. (2000) British meals and food choice. In H.L. Meiselman (ed.) *Dimensions of the Meal: The Science, Culture, Business and Art of Eating* (pp. 202–220). Gaithersburg, MD: Aspen Publications.

Martinez, C.R., McClure, H.H. and Eddy, J.M. (2009) Language brokering contexts and behavioral and emotional adjustment among Latino parents and adolescents. *Journal of Early Adolescence* 29 (1), 71–98.

Mason, J. (1996) *Qualitative Researching*. London: Sage.

Mason, J. (2002) *Qualitative Researching* (2nd edn). London: Sage.

Masson, J. (2000) Researching children's perspectives: Legal issues. In A. Lewis and G. Lindsay (eds) *Researching Children's Perspectives* (pp. 34–45). Buckingham: Open University Press.

Mayall, B. (1994) *Children's Childhoods: Observed and Experienced*. London: Falmer Press.

Mayall, B. (2000) Conversations with children: Working with generational issues. In P. Christensen and A. James (eds) *Research with Children* (pp. 120–36). London: Falmer Press.

Mayall, B. (2002) *Towards a Sociology of Childhood: Thinking from Children's Lives*. Buckingham: Open University Press.

McGee, M. (1980) Faith, fantasy, and flowers: A content analysis of the American sympathy card. *Omega* 11 (1), 25–35.

McKay, S.L. (1993) *Agendas for Second Language Literacy*. Cambridge: Cambridge University Press.

McLeod, B. (1981) The mediating person and cultural identity. In S. Bochner (ed.) *The Mediating Person: Bridges between Cultures* (pp. 37–52). Cambridge: Schenkman Publishing Company.

McQuillan, J. and Tse, L. (1995) Child language brokering in linguistic minority communities: Effects on culture, cognition, and literacy. *Language and Education* 9, 195–215.

Meigs, A. (1997) Food as cultural construction. In C. Counihan and P. Esterik (eds) *Food and Culture: A Reader* (pp. 95–106). New York: Routledge.

Menjivar, C. (2000) *Fragmented Ties: Salvadoran Immigrant Networks in America*. Berkeley, CA: University of California Press.

Metro News, Manchester, Friday February 11, 2005.

Mitchell, C. and Reid-Walsh, J. (2002) *Researching Children's Popular Culture: The Cultural Spaces of Childhood*. London: Routledge.

Mo, T. (1992) *Sour Sweet*. London: Vintage.

Morales, A. and Hanson, W.E. (2005) Language brokering: An integrative review of the literature. *Hispanic Journal of Behavioural Sciences* 27 (4), 471–503.

Morrison, M. (2002) Using diaries in research. In M. Coleman and A. Briggs (eds) *Research Methods in Educational Leadership and Management* (pp. 213–232). London: Paul Chapman Publishing.

Morrow, V. (1994) Responsible children?: Aspects of children's work and employment outside school in contemporary UK. In B. Mayall (ed.) *Children's Childhoods: Observed and Experienced* (pp. 128–143). London: Falmer Press.

Morrow, V. (1995) Invisible children?: Towards a reconceptualisation of childhood. *Sociological Studies of Children* 7, 207–230.

Morrow, V. (1999) "It's Cool, … Cos You Can't Give us Detentions and Things, Can You?!": Reflections on researching children. In P. Milner and B. Carolin (eds) *Time to Listen to Children* (pp. 203–215). London: Routledge.

Morrow, V. and Richards, M. (1996) The ethics of social research with children: An overview. *Children and Society* 10, 90–105.

Murphy, L.E. (2003) Public mothers: Native American and Metis women as Creole mediators in the nineteenth-century midwest. *Journal of Women's History* 14 (4), 142–166.

Musgrove, F. and Middleton, R. (1981) Rites of passage and the meaning of age in three contrasted social groups: Professional footballers, teachers and Methodist ministers. *British Journal of Sociology* 32 (1), 39–55.

Nauck, B. (2001) Intercultural contact and intergenerational transmission in immigrant families. *Journal of Cross-Cultural Psychology* 32 (2), 159–173.

Nazroo, J. and Karlsen, S. (2003) Patterns of identity among ethnic minority people: Diversity and commonality. *Ethnic and Racial Studies* 26 (5), 902–930.

Neale, B. and Smart, C. (1998) *Agents or Dependants?: Struggling to Listen to Children in Family Law and Family Research*. Working paper 3, Centre for Research on Family, Kinship and Childhood. University of Leeds.

Nesbitt, E. (1995) Many happy returns: Some British South African children's birthday parties. *Multicultural Teaching* 14 (1), 34–35, 40.

Newman, J.M. (2000) Chinese meals. In H.L. Meiselman (ed.) *Dimensions of the Meal: The Science, Culture, Business and Art of Eating* (pp. 163–177). Gaithersburg, MD: Aspen Publications.

Newman, J.M. (2004) *Food Culture in China*. London: Greenwood Press.

Nsamenang, A.B. (1992) *Human Development in Cultural Context: A Third-World Perspective*. Newbury Park, CA: Sage.

Okagaki, L. and Bojczyk, K.E. (2002) Perspectives on Asian American development. In G.C. Hall and S. Okazaki (eds) *Asian American Psychology: The Science of Lives in Context* (pp. 67–104). Washington, DC: American Psychological Association.

Orellana, M.F. (2001) The work kids do: Mexican and Central American immigrant children's contributions to household and schools in California. *Harvard Educational Review* 71 (3), 366–389.

Orellana, M.F. (2009) *Translating Childhoods: Immigrant Youth, Language, and Culture.* Piscataway, NJ: Rutgers University Press.

Orellana, M.F., Dorner, L. and Pulido, L. (2003b) Accessing assets: Immigrant youth's work as family translators or "para-phrasers". *Social Problems* 50 (4), 505–524.

Orellana, M.F., Reynolds, J., Dorner, L. and Meza, M. (2003a) In other words: Translating or "para-phrasing" as a family literacy practice in immigrant household. *Reading Research Quarterly* 38 (1), 12–34.

Otnes, C. and McGrath, M.A. (1994) Ritual socialization and the children's birthday party: The early emergence of gender differences. *Journal of Ritual Studies* 8, 73–93.

Otnes, C., Nelson, M. and McGrath, M.A. (1995) The children's birthday party: A study of mothers as socialization agents. *Advances in Consumer Research* 22, 622–627.

Pahl, K. (1999) *Transformations: Meaning Making In Nursery Education.* Stoke on Trent: Trentham Books.

Parke, R.D. and Ladd, G.W. (eds) (1992) *Family-Peer Relationships: Modes of Linkage.* London: Lawrence Erlbaum.

Parkin, D. (1992) Ritual as spatial direction and bodily division. In D. de Coppet (ed.) *Understanding Rituals* (pp. 11–25). London and New York: Routledge.

Partida, J. (1996) The effects of immigration on children in the Mexican-American community. *Child and Adolescent Social Work Journal* 13 (3), 241–254.

Pecora, N.O. (1998) *The Business of Children's Entertainment.* New York and London: The Guilford Press.

Perreira, K.M., Chapman, M.V. and Stein, G. (2006) Becoming an American Parent: Overcoming strength in a new immigrant Latino community. *Journal of Family Issues* 27 (10), 1383–1414.

Phinney, J.S. (1990) Ethnic identity in adolescents and adults: Review of research. *Psychological Bulletin* 108, 499–514.

Phinney, J.S. (2003) Ethnic identity and acculturation. In K.M. Chun, P.B. Organista and G. Marin (eds) *Acculturation: Advances in Theory, Measurement, and Applied Research* (pp. 63–82). Washington, DC: American Psychological Association.

Pleck, E.H. (2000) *Celebrating the Family: Ethnicity, Consumer Culture, and Family Rituals.* Cambridge, MA: Harvard University Press.

Pole, C. and Morrison, M. (2003) *Ethnography for Education.* Maidenhead: Open University Press.

Portes, A. and Rumbaut, R.G. (2001) *Legacies: The Story of the Immigrant Second Generation.* Berkeley and London: University of California Press.

Prout, A. (2002) Researching children as social actors: An introduction to the children 5–16 programme. *Children and Society* 16, 67–76.

Prout, A. and James, A. (1997) A new paradigm for the sociology of childhood? Provenance, promise and problems. In A. James and A. Prout (eds) *Constructing and Reconstructing Childhood: Contemporary Issues in the Sociological Study of Childhood* (pp. 7–33). London: Routledge.

Puig, M.E. (2002) The adultification of refugee children: Implications for cross-cultural social work practice. *Journal of Human Behavior in the Social Environment* 5 (3/4), 85–95.

Punch, S. (2002a) Interviewing strategies with young people: The 'Secret Box', stimulus material and task-based activities. *Children & Society* 16, 45–56.

Punch, S. (2002b) Research with children: The same or different from research with adults?. *Childhood* 9 (3), 321–341.

Qvortrup, J. (1994) Childhood matters: An introduction. In J. Qvortrup, M. Bardy, G.B. Sgritta and H. Wintersberger (eds) *Childhood Matters: Social Theory, Practice and Politics* (pp. 1–24). Brookfield, VT: Avebury.

Qvortrup, J. (1997) A voice for children in statistical and social accounting: A plea for children's right to be heard. In A. James and A. Prout (eds) *Constructing and Reconstructing Childhood: Contemporary Issues in the Sociological Study of Childhood* (pp. 85–106). London: Routledge.

Qvortrup, J. (2005) Varieties of childhood. In J. Qvortrup (ed.) *Studies in Modern Childhood: Society, Agency and Culture* (pp. 1–20). New York: Palgrave Macmillan.

Oznobishin, O. and Kurman, J. (2009) Parent-child role reversal and psychological adjustment among immigrant youth in Israel. *Journal of Family Psychology* 23, 405–415.

Rappoport, L. (2003) *How We Eat: Appetite, Culture, and the Psychology of Food.* Toronto: ECW Press.

Richter, D.K. (1988) Cultural brokers and intercultural politics: New York-Iroquois relations, 1664–1701. *The Journal of American History* 75 (1), 40–67.

Rinkoff, B. (1967) *Birthday Parties Around the World.* New York: M. Barrows.

Robins, S. (1996) Cultural brokers and bricoleurs of modern and traditional literacies: Land struggles in Namaqualand's coloured reserves. In M. Prinsloo and M. Breier (eds) *The Social Uses of Literacy* (pp. 123–139). Amsterdam: John Benjamins.

Robinson, A., Crawford, L. and Hall, N. (1990) *Young Children's Explorations in the World of Letters: 'Some day you will no all about me'.* London: Mary Glasgow Publications.

Rogers, R. (2001) Family literacy and the mediation of cultural models. *National Reading Conference Yearbook* 50, 96–114.

Rogoff, B. (1990) *Apprenticeship in Thinking: Cognitive Development in Social Context.* New York, Oxford: Oxford University Press.

Rogoff, B. (1993) Children's guided participation and participatory appropriation in sociocultural activity. In R. Wozniak and K. Fischer (eds) *Development in Context: Acting and Thinking in Specific Environments* (pp. 121–153). Hillsdale, NJ: Lawrence Erlbaum.

Rogoff, B. (1995) Observing sociocultural activity on three planes: Participatory appropriation, guided participation, and apprenticeship. In J.V. Wertsch, P. del Río and A. Alvarez (eds) *Sociocultural Studies of Mind.* Cambridge: Cambridge University Press.

Rogoff, B. (2003) *The Cultural Nature of Human Cognitive Development.* New York, Oxford: Oxford University Press.

Rook, D. (1985) The ritual dimension of consumer behaviour. *Journal of Consumer Research* 14, 189–199.

Rutter, J. and Candappa, M. (1998) *Why Do They Have To Fight? Refugee Children's Stories from Bosnia, Somalia, Sri Lanka and Turkey.* London: Refugee Council.

Sanders, B. (2004) Childhood in different cultures. In T. Maynard and N. Thomas (eds) *An Introduction to Early Childhood Studies* (pp. 53–64). London: Sage.

Sanger, J. (1996) Problems and pitfalls. (Chapter 1) in *The Compleat Observer? A Field Research Guide to Observation.* London: Falmer Press.

Schieffelin, B. and Cochran-Smith, M. (1984) Learning to read culturally: Literacy before schooling. In H. Goelman, A. Oberg and F. Smith (eds) *Awakening to Literacy* (pp. 3–23). London: Heinemann Educational.

Sealey, A. (2000) *Childly Language: Children, Language and the Social World.* Harlow: Longman.

Shamgar-Handelman, L. and Handelman, D. (1991) Celebrations of bureaucracy: Birthday parties in Israeli kindergartens. *Ethnology* 30 (4), 293–312.

Shannon, S. (1990) English in the Barrio: The quality of contact among immigrant children. *Hispanic Journal of Behavioural Sciences* 12 (3), 256–276.

Silverman, D. (2001) *Interpreting Qualitative Data: Methods for Analyzing Talk, Text and Interaction* (3rd edn). London: Sage.

Simmel, G. (1950) *The Sociology of George Simmel. Kurt H. Wolff, Editor.* London: Free Press of Glencoe.

Simons, H. and Usher, R. (2000) Introduction: Ethics in the practice of research. In H. Simons and R. Usher (eds) *Situated Ethics in Educational Research* (pp. 1–11). London: RoutledgeFalmer.

Smith, D. (1989) *Children of China: An Historical Inquiry Into the Relationship Between Chinese Family Life and Academic Achievement.* U.S. Department of Education.

Solberg, A. (1994) *Negotiating Childhood: Empirical Investigations and Textual Representations of Children's Work and Everyday Life.* Dissertation 12 Nordic Institute for Studies in Urban and Regional Planning. Stockholm: NORDPLAN.

Solberg, A. (1997) Negotiating childhood: Changing constructions of age for Norwegian children. In A. James and A. Prout (eds) *Constructing and Reconstructing Childhood: Contemporary Issues in the Sociology of Childhood* (pp. 126–144). London: Falmer Press.

Song, M. (1996) Helping out: Children's labour participation in Chinese take-away businesses in Britain. In J. Brannen and M. O'Brien (eds) *Children in Families: Research and Policy* (pp. 101–113). London: Falmer Press.

Song, M. (1999) *Helping Out: Children's Labour in Ethnic Businesses.* Philadelphia, PA: Temple University Press.

Spencer, L., Richie, J. and O'Connor, W. (2003) Analysis: Practices, principles and processes. In J. Lewis and J. Richie (eds) *Qualitative Research Practice: A Guide for Social Science Students and Researchers* (pp. 200–218). London: Sage.

Spradley, J. (1979) *The Ethnographic Interview.* New York: Holt, Rinehart and Winston.

Spradley, J. (1980) *Participant Observation.* New York: Holt, Rinehart and Winston.

Spungin, P. (2006) See www.raisingkids.co.uk/fi/fi_27.asp (accessed 13 July 2006).

Stenhouse, L. (1988) Case study methods. In J.P. Keeves (ed.) *Educational Research, Methodology, and Measurement: An International Handbook* (pp. 48–53). Oxford and New York: Pergamon Press.

Stephens, S. (1995) *Children and the Politics of Culture: Rights, Risks and Reconstructions.* Princeton, NJ: Princeton University Press.

Stern, E. (1988) *The Very Best From Hallmark: Greeting Cards Through the Years.* New York: Harry Abrams.

Storti, C. (2001) *The Art of Crossing Culture* (2nd edn). London: Nicholas Brealey Publishing.

Suárez-Orozco, C. and Suárez-Orozco, M. (2001) *Children of Immigration.* Cambridge, MA: Harvard University Press.

Sun-Hee Park, L. (2002) Asian immigrant entrepreneurial children. In L.T. Vo and R. Bonus (eds) *Contemporary Asian American Communities: Intersections and Divergences* (pp. 161–174). Philadelphia, PA: Temple University Press.

Sy, S.R. (2006) Family and work influence on the transition to college among Latina adolescents. *Hispanic Journal of Behavioral Sciences* 28, 368–386.

Szasz, M.C. (1994) *Between Indian and White Worlds: The Cultural Broker.* Norman, OK: University of Oklahoma Press.

Taft, R. (1966) *From Stranger to Citizen: A Survey of Studies of Immigrant Assimilation in Western Australia*. London: Tavistock Publications.

Taft, R. (1981) The role and personality of the mediator. In S. Bochner (ed.) *The Mediating Person: Bridges between Cultures* (pp. 53–88). Cambridge: Schenkman Publishing Company.

Taylor, M.J. (1987) *Chinese Pupils in Britain: A Review of Research into the Education of Pupils of Chinese Origin*. Windsor: NFER-NELSON Publishing Company.

Taylor, S. and Bogdan, R. (1998) *Introduction to Qualitative Research Methods*. New York: John Wiley and Sons.

Thomas, N. (2004) Sociology of childhood. In T. Maynard and N. Thomas (eds) *An Introduction to Early Childhood Studies* (pp. 75–87). London: Sage.

Thomas, N. and O'Kane, C. (1998) The ethics of participatory research with children. *Children & Society* 12, 336–348.

Titzmann, P.F. (2012) Growing up too soon? Parentification among immigrant and native adolescents in Germany. *Journal of Youth Adolescence* 41, 880–893. doi: 10.1007/s10964-011-9711-1.

Triandis, H.C. (1988) Collectivism v. individualism: A reconceptualisation of a basic concept in cross-cultural social psychology. In G.K. Verma and C. Bagley (eds) *Cross-Cultural Studies of Personality, Attitudes, and Cognition* (pp. 60–95). New York: St. Martins.

Trimble, J.E. (2003) Introduction: Social change and acculturation. In K.M. Chun, P.B. Organista and G. Marin (eds) *Acculturation: Advances in Theory, Measurement, and Applied Research* (pp. 3–14). Washington, DC: American Psychological Association.

Trompenaars, F. and Hampden-Turner, C. (1997) *Riding the Waves of Culture*. London: Nicholas Brearley.

Tsai, J.L., Chentsova-Dutton, Y. and Wong, Y. (2002) Why and how researchers should study ethnic identity, acculturation, and cultural orientation. In G.C.N. Hall and S. Okazaki (eds) *Asian American Psychology: The Science of Lives in Context* (pp. 41–66). Washington, DC: American Psychological Association.

Tsai, J.L., Ying, Y. and Lee, P. (2000) The meaning of 'being Chinese' and 'being American: Variation among Chinese American Young Youth. *Journal of Cross-Cultural Psychology* 31 (3), 302–332.

Tse, L. (1995) Language brokering among Latino adolescents: Prevalence, attitudes, and school performance. *Hispanic Journal of Behavioural Sciences* 17 (2), 180–193.

Tse, L. (1996a) Language brokering in linguistic minority communities: The case of Chinese- and Vietnamese-American students. *The Bilingual Research Journal, Summer/Fall* 20 (3&4), 485–498.

Tse, L. (1996b) Who decides?: The effects of language brokering on home-school communication. *The Journal of Educational Issues of Language Minority Students, Special Issues* 16, 225–234.

Ulrych, M. (1992) *Translating Texts from Theory to Practice*. Rapallo: Cideb Editore.

Valdés, G. (2003) *Expanding Definitions of Giftedness: The Case of Young Interpreters From Immigrant Communities*. Mahwah, NJ: Lawrence Erlbaum.

Valenzuela, A. Jr (1999) Gender roles and settlement activities among children and their immigrant families. *American Behavioural Scientist* 42 (4), 720–742.

Valtonen, K. (1998) Resettlement of Middle Eastern refugees in Finland: The elusiveness of integration. *Journal of Refugee Studies* 11 (1), 38–60.

Vandenbroeck, M. and Bouverne-De Bie, M. (2006) Children's agency and educational norms: A tensed negotiation. *Childhood* 13 (1), 127–143.

Vasquez, O., Pease-Alvarez, L. and Shannon, S. (1994) *Pushing Boundaries: Language and Culture in a Mexicano Community*. Cambridge and New York: Cambridge University Press.

Villanueva, C.M. and Buriel, R. (2010) Speaking on behalf of others: A qualitative study of the perceptions and feelings of adolescent Latina language brokers. *Journal of Social Issues* 66, 197–210.

Vygotsky, L.S. (1978) *Mind in Society: The Development of Higher Psychological Processes*. London: Harvard University Press.

Vygotsky, L.S. (1986) *Thought and Language* (A Kozulin, revised and edited). Cambridge, MA: MIT Press.

Wadensjo, C. (1998) *Interpreting As Interaction*. London and New York: Longman.

Wagner, D. (1993) *Literacy, Culture and Development: Becoming Literate in Morocco*. Cambridge: Cambridge University Press.

Walichowski, M.F. (2001) Language brokering: Laying the foundation for success and bilingualism. In R. Lara-Alecio (Chair), *Research in Bilingual Education*. Symposium conducted at the Annual Educational Research Exchange, College Station, TX.

Walsh, D. (2004) Doing ethnography. In C. Seale (ed.) *Researching Society and Culture* (2nd edn) (pp. 225–237). London: Sage.

Walsh, S., Shulman, S., Bar-on, Z. and Tsur, A. (2006) The role of parentification and family climate in adaptation among immigrant adolescents in Israel. *Journal of Research on Adolescence* 16 (2), 321–350.

Ward, C. (1996) Acculturation. In D. Lanis and R. Bhagat (eds) *Handbook of Intercultural Training* (2nd edn) (pp. 124–143). London: Sage.

Ward, C. (2001) The ABCs of acculturation. In D. Matsumoto (ed.) *Handbook of Culture and Psychology* (pp. 411–445). New York: Oxford University Press.

Ward, C., Bochner, S. and Furnham, A. (2001) *The Psychology of Cultural Shock*. Hove: Routledge.

Ward, C., Leong, C. and Low, M. (2004) Personality and sojourner adjustment: An exploration of the big five and the cultural fit proposition. *Journal of Cross-Cultural Psychology* 35 (2), 137–151.

Watson, J.L. (2005) China's Big Mac attack. In J. Watson and M. Caldwell (eds) *The Cultural Politics of Food and Eating: A Reader* (pp. 70–79). Oxford: Blackwell Publishing.

Weil, S. (1986) The language and ritual of socialization: Birthday parties in a kindergarten context. *Man* 21, 329–341.

Weinstein-Shr, G. (1995) Learning from uprooted families. In G. Weinstein-Shr and E. Quintero (eds) *Immigrant Learners and Their Families: Literacy to Connect the Generations* (pp. 113–134). McHenry, IL: The Center for Applied Linguistics and Delta Systems.

Weisskirch, R.S. (2005) The relationship of language brokering to ethnic identity for Latino early adolescents. *Hispanic Journal of Behavioral Sciences* 27 (3), 286–299. doi: 10.1177/0739986305277931.

Weisskirch, R.S. (2006) Emotional aspects of language brokering among Mexican American adults. *Journal of Multilingual and Multicultural Development* 27, 332–343. doi: 10.2167/jmmd421.1.

Weisskirch, R.S. (2007) Feelings about language brokering and family relations among Mexican American early adolescents. *Journal of Early Adolescence* 27, 545–561.

Weisskirch, R.S. (2012) Family relationships, self-esteem, and self-efficacy among language brokering Mexican American emerging adults. *Journal of Child Family Studies*. doi: 10.10007/s10826-012-9678-x.

Weisskirch, R.S. and Alva, S.A. (2002) Language brokering and the acculturation of Latino children. *Hispanic Journal of Behavioral Sciences* 24 (3), 369–378.

Weisskirch, R.S., Kim, S., Zamboanga, B.L., Schwartz, S.J., Bersamin, M. and Umana-Taylor, A.J. (2011) Cultural influences for college student language brokers. *Cultural Diversity and Ethnic Minority Psychology* 17, 43–51. doi: 10.1037/a0021665.

Wenger, E. (1998) *Communities of Practice: Learning, Meaning and Identity.* New York: Cambridge University Press.

Wertsch, J.V. (1998) *Mind as Action.* Oxford: Oxford University Press.

Wikipedia, the free encyclopedia (2006) See www.en.wikipedia.org/wiki/British_ Chinese (accessed 15 November 2006).

Wilkins, R. and Gareis, E. (2006) Emotion expression and the locution "I love you": A cross-cultural study. *International Journal of Intercultural Relations* 30 (1), 51–75.

Willett, J. and Bloome, D. (1993) Literacy, language, school, and community: A community-centered view. In A. Carrasquillo and C. Hedley (eds) *Whole Language and the Bilingual Learner* (pp. 35–57). Norwood, NJ: Ablex Publishing Company.

Willian, J. (2004) Research projects in early childhood studies: Students' active explorations of children's worlds. In J. Willian, R. Parker-Rees, R. and J. Savage (eds) *Early Childhood Studies: An Introduction to the Study of Childhood's Worlds and Children's Lives* (pp. 156–171). Exeter: Learning Matters Ltd.

Willis, P. (1979) *Learning to Labour: How Working Class Kids Get Working Class Jobs.* London: Saxon House.

Wilson, A. (2000) Absolutely brill to see you from you: Visuality and prisoner's letters. In D. Barton and N. Hall (eds) *Letter Writing as a Social Practice* (pp. 179–198). Amsterdam: John Benjamins.

Wolcott, H.F. (1994) *Transforming Qualitative Data: Description, Analysis, and Interpretation.* London: Sage.

Woodhead, M. (1996) *In Search of the Rainbow: Pathways to Quality in Large-Scale Programmes for Young Children.* The Hague: Bernard van Leer Foundation.

Wu, N. and Kim, S.Y. (2009) Chinese American adolescents' perceptions of the language brokering experience as a sense of burden and sense of efficacy. *Journal of Youth and Adolescence* 38, 703–718.

Wu, Y. (1996) *British Scenes.* Shanghai: Oriental Publishing Centre.

Wyness, M. (1999) Childhood, agency and education reform. *Childhood* 6 (3), 353–369.

Wyness, M. (2006) *Childhood and Society: An Introduction to the Sociology of Childhood.* Basingstoke: Palgrave Macmillan.

Xiao, H. (1999) Independence and obedience: An analysis of child socialization values in the U.S and China. *Journal of Comparative Family Studies* 30 (4), 641–657.

Xiao, H. (2000) Structure of child-rearing values in urban China. *Sociological Perspectives* 43 (3), 457–471.

Yan, Y. (2005) Of hamburger and social space: Consuming McDonald's in Beijing. In J. Watson and M. Caldwell (eds) *The Cultural Politics of Food and Eating: A Reader* (pp. 80–103). Oxford: Blackwell Publishing.

Ye, Z. (2004) Chinese categorization of interpersonal relationships and the cultural logic of Chinese social interaction: An indigenous perspective. *Intercultural Pragmatics* 1-2, 211–230.

Zane, N. and Mak, W. (2003) Major approaches to the measurement of acculturation among ethnic minority populations: A content analysis and an alternative empirical strategy. In K.M. Chun, P.B. Organista and G. Marin (eds) *Acculturation: Advances in Theory, Measurement, and Applied Research* (pp. 39–60). Washington, DC: American Psychological Association.

Zelizer, V.A. (1994) *Pricing the Priceless Child: The Changing Social Value of Children.* Princeton, NJ and Chichester: Princeton University Press.

Zelizer, V.A. (2005) The priceless child revisited. In J. Qvortrup (ed.) *Studies in Modern Childhood: Society, Agency and Culture* (pp. 184–199). New York: Palgrave Macmillan.

Zhou, M. and Bankston, C.L. III (1998) *Growing Up American: How Vietnamese Children Adapt to Life in the United States.* New York: Russell Sage Foundation.

Zhou, M. and Xiong, Y. (2005) The multifaceted American experiences of the children of Asian immigrants: Lessons for segmented assimilation. *Ethnic and Racial Studies* 28 (6), 1119–1152.

Index